D1555525

# HABITATS FOR CHILDREN:
The Impacts of Density

# CHILD PSYCHOLOGY

A series of books edited by **David S. Palermo**

# HABITATS FOR CHILDREN:
## The Impacts of Density

Edited by
Joachim F. Wohlwill
and
Willem van Vliet--
The Pennsylvania State University

**LEA** LAWRENCE ERLBAUM ASSOCIATES, PUBLISHERS
1985   Hillsdale, New Jersey                    London

Lawrence Erlbaum Associates, Inc., Publishers
365 Broadway
Hillsdale, New Jersey 07642

**Library of Congress Cataloging in Publication Data**

Main entry under title:

Habitats for children.

   (Child psychology)
   Includes bibliographies and indexes.
   1. Crowding stress in children.   2. Dwellings—
Psychological aspects.   3. Child mental health.
4. Social interaction in children.   5. Environment
and children.   I. Wohlwill, Joachim F.   II. van Vliet--,
Willem.
BF353.5.C74H33   1985        155.4        85-10254
ISBN 0-89859-533-9

Printed in the United States of America
10   9   8   7   6   5   4   3   2   1

# Contents

# List of Contributors

**John R. Aiello,** *Department of Psychology, Rutgers — The State University of New Jersey*

**Andrew S. Baum,** *Department of Medical Psychology, Uniformed Services University of Health Sciences*

**Alan Booth,** *Department of Sociology, University of Nebraska — Lincoln*

**Ellen Cromley,** *Department of Geography, University of Kentucky*

**James Garbarino,** *Department of Human Development, The Pennsylvania State University*

**Harry Heft,** *Department of Psychology, Denison University*

**Maxine Schoggen,** *Department of Human Development and Family Studies, Cornell University*

**Philip H. Schoggen,** *Department of Human Development and Family Studies, Cornell University*

**Gary W. Shannon,** *Department of Geography, University of Kentucky*

**Donna E. Thompson,** *Graduate School of Management, Rutgers — The State University of New Jersey*

**Willem van Vliet--,** *Department of Community Studies, The Pennsylvania State University*

**Joachim F. Wohlwill,** *Department of Individual and Family Studies, The Pennsylvania State University*

# Preface

Much has been written from the diverse perspectives of the economist, the sociologist, the designer and planner, and others about the pros and cons of different patterns of housing and settlement for our population. Yet rarely have the implications and consequences of these different residential contexts for the behavior, development, and well-being of the children living in them been systematically considered. This is a signal omission, in view of the considerable amount of time that children, at least through middle childhood, spend in and around their home environment, and given the apparent impact of particular residential patterns on children's behavior, whether acting as facilitators of or constraints on such behavior.

In the spring of 1980 a study group was formed, sponsored by the Society for Research in Child Development, with support from the Foundation for Child Development, to examine a particular aspect of this topic, namely the ways in which and the extent to which different density levels in our residential environment affect the development of children. Apart from being a problem that fits effectively the ecological focus to which the Foundation is committed in its support of activity in the child-development field, this issue is of interest from several different standpoints.

To begin with, this topic clearly relates to the work on effects of crowding that has constituted a major and lively area of research within environmental psychology and, to a lesser extent urban sociology (Fischer, Baldassare, & Ofshe, 1975), and that has included a considerable amount of research on children. Although these studies have shed some light on children's adaptive responses to specific situations of crowding, research on this topic to date appears limited in a number of respects. First, most work has been confined to the study of density effects under relatively contrived conditions, in laboratory, school, and other institutional environments (Loo, 1979). Furthermore, most of these studies have been restricted to assessing short-term effects, and have not taken into account the role of external variables that may aggravate or alleviate particular density effects. Another major limitation of research in this area pertains to its biased focus, singling out for study only possible detrimental effects of high levels of density on children, such as manifested in aggressiveness, delinquency, and ill health, while ignoring potential benefits to children from life in residential areas marked by relatively high concentration of population. Furthermore, in these studies, density is typically considered as a unipolar variable, i.e., implicitly or explicitly high-density conditions are compared with some arbitrarily defined norm representing an assumed normal density condition. This conceptualization fails to recognize that in actual fact we are dealing with a bipolar variable that has the potential of positive as well as negative effects at each pole.

By way of illustration, one might contrast the situation of relative isolation faced by a child living on a farm at some distance from its neighbors to that which a child living in a high-density high-rise complex in a city experiences. In the former setting children may benefit from a secure place in a recognized and clearly defined social network and direct exposure to and acquaintance with the natural environment, but they may suffer from the relative absence of children, as well as from the relative lack of variety in their environmental experience. On the other hand, children living in high-density environments will enjoy access both to other children, and to opportunities for the development of skills, but may be subjected to stresses associated with the higher levels of physical and social stimulation, the greater complexity of structure of the institutional environment, etc. These examples obviously refer to external density (that is, density in the area surrounding the domicile), but the same logic is applicable to internal density.

It is worth pointing out the correspondence of this bipolar conceptualization of density, with isolation and crowding as opposite poles, to Altman's (1975) theoretical interpretation of crowding as an aspect of the individual's regulation of social interaction. In a different vein, this framework also fits in with recent work that has related the development of children's feelings of independence, self-esteem and identity to type and structure of the home and its environment.

In connection with the attention we are proposing to devote to both ends of the density continuum, it is worth calling attention to demographic patterns that suggest that children in the U.S., and in other developed countries, will be increasingly growing up in settings outside of urban areas. The movement from rural areas to cities has in fact run its course, and there are strong indications of a reversal of this migration pattern (though not necessarily of a return to rural life per se). The implications of residence under such conditions appear thus to be particularly deserving of attention.

This bipolar conceptualization of the role of residential density as a factor in child development requires some elaboration, however, so as to allow proper consideration of the ecological context in which the child finds itself. That is to say, the role of density undoubtedly varies according to a variety of other characteristics of the child's ennvironment, social, cultural, physical, economic, and otherwise. Further, it is necessary to consider density separately for different scales at which the environment may be conceived, from the micro- to the macrosystem (cf. Bronfenbrenner, 1977), and to differentiate between the internal (home) environment and the environment external to the dwelling. And, to cite yet another complicating factor, it is apparent that the way in which density effects may express themselves in child behavior are relative to the child's stage of development, and to the particular forms of activity that appear at different age levels. In particular, it seems reasonable to suppose that the relative influence of internal versus external density may well change, and indeed undergo a reversal, as the child's own mobility increases as a function of its development and maturation.

The aforementioned considerations point to a need for work that will complement, as well as transcend current investigations of effects of density on behavior. Such a focus would incorporate recent theoretical formulations in child and developmental psychology that conceptualize the outcomes of child developmental processes as a function of the interplay of situational and organismic factors (e.g., Magnusson & Allen, 1983). It would examine the child's mode of response to given density conditions prevailing in its environment, that is, the manner in which they adjust or adapt to particular conditions. Such coping behaviors have typically been excluded from traditional, short-term research on crowding, nor have they been considered within a developmental perspective.

In short, the problem under consideration appears to call for a broad-based ecological approach, in which the child's development and behavior is conceptualized as being interdependent with a complex set of contextual forces in its environment, both physical and social. In this sense we may view this problem as situated amidst a burgeoning ecological literature in the social sciences generally and in specific disciplines such as urban sociology (Berry & Kasarda, 1977), anthropology (Hardesty, 1977), and psychology (Wicker, 1979), as well as in the field of child development itself (e.g., Bronfenbrenner, 1977; Little & Ryan, 1979). The more recent ecological viewpoints share an orientation towards a holistic interpretation of the relationships between people and their environment, as embedded in more encompassing systems. They recognize the physical environment not only as a necessary context for human activities, but also as a source of direct impacts on human behavior and functioning. This dual characterization of the ecological literature is effectively expressed in a recent issue of the *American Behavioral Scientist* examining issues of ecology and environmental quality from the perspective of diverse social sciences (Dunlap, 1980). It similarly

links the chapters in the present volume, which deal with the effects of residential density on children as mediated by such diverse factors as familial circumstances, building structure, neighborhood and school environment.

We thus see this problem area not only as situated at the intersection between environmental and developmental approaches to the study of behavior
(cf. Wohlwill, 1980), but transcending the confines of any single discipline,
and thus calling for a task force that is interdisciplinary in its scope. Accordingly, our Study Group was formed to include representatives from a broad
array of fields, including anthropology, geography, pediatrics, psychology,
and sociology, providing a diversity of perspectives on the role of the residential environment in child development.[1]

The Study Group included within its purview a broad array of issues on
both the environmental and the behavioral sides. With regard to the former,
we examined such issues as the influence of specific forms of housing (e.g.,
apartment houses vs. single-family houses) in conjunction with size and composition of the family, the effects of conditions of relative isolation as found
in rural areas, and the role of institutional and socio-cultural factors in
modulating density effects. On the behavioral side we gave consideration to
exploratory activity and play; to interpersonal behaviors (including peer-
group interaction and modes of parent–child contact); and to friendship formation, and patterns of social development.

The format within which the group undertook its work involved two meetings, both held at The Pennsylvania State University. The first, held in May
1980, was devoted to the delimitation of topics and problems and identification of relevant theoretical and methodological issues that were to be addressed in the set of papers to be written by the participants. These papers
were prepared over the following 8 months and circulated to the other group
members. At a second meeting, held in March 1981, the contributions were
reviewed, discussed, and criticized. They were then revised, and the final ver-
sions are assembled in the pages of this volume.

A final chapter was prepared by the editors, with successive drafts
submitted to all the Study Group members for comments and suggestions for
revision. It presents an overview of the field covered by the Study Group, organized in terms of a set of specific questions that emerged as salient to members of the Study Group on the basis of the discussion at our two meetings
and the individual papers prepared by each.

The participants in the Study Group comprised the contributors to this
volume listed on p. ix, along with two other persons who were part of the
group initially and took part in the first meeting, but who were, for personal

---

[1]Regrettably, the representatives from two of these disciplines (anthropology and pediatrics)
were forced to resign from the Study Group before its work could be completed (as explained
further on in this Preface).

reasons, forced to resign from the group before they had had an opportunity to prepare papers. They are Robert Aldrich, Professor Emeritus of Preventive Medicine and Pediatrics at the University of Colorado Medical Center, and Marida Hollos, Professor of Anthropology at Brown University. The former (along with contributor Gary Shannon), had been expected to deal with relationships between density and child health, whereas the latter was to have examined the cognitive and language development of children in rural and other relatively isolated settings. Thus, these topics did not receive the coverage in this volume that we would have liked to have seen, although more incidental reference to both is made in certain chapters, and in the concluding one in particular.

In closing, we should like to express our appreciation to the Society for Research in Child Development and to the Foundation for Child Development for their generous support of the work of our Study Group. Also, a veritable phalanx of secretaries undoubtedly labored patiently and effectively to see the individual contributions to this volume through their several phases; we cannot acknowledge them individually, but we are all clearly indebted to them. We would, however, like to give particular thanks to Joy Barger, of the staff of the Department of Individual and Family Studies at Penn State, for the cheerful, efficient, and improbably prompt way in which she helped us move the concluding chapter through its tortuous path to its final shape, as well as for her similarly superb job on the typing of the Preface and Chapter 2, and of the final version of Chapter 1.

## REFERENCES

Alman, I. *The environment and social behavior.* Monterey, Ca.: Brooks/Cole, 1975.

Berry, B. J. L., & Kasarda, J. D. *Contemporary urban ecology.* New York: Macmillan, 1977.

Bronfenbrenner, U. *The ecology of human development.* Cambridge, Mass.: Harvard University Press, 1977.

Dunlap, R. D. (Ed.). Ecology and the social sciences: An emerging paradigm. *American Behavioral Scientist,* 1980, *24,* 3-151.

Fischer, C. S., Baldassare, M., & Ofshe, R. J. Crowding studies and urban life: A critical review. *Journal of the American Institute of Planners,* 1975, *41,* 406-418.

Hardesty, D. L. *Ecological anthropology.* New York: Wiley, 1977.

Little, B. R., & Ryan, T. J. A social ecological model of development. In K. Ishwaran (Ed.), *Childhood and adolescence in Canada.* Toronto: McGraw-Hill, 1979. Pp. 273-301.

Loo, C. M. Consequences of crowding on children. In M. R. Gurkaynak & W. A. Lecompte (Eds.), *Human consequences of crowding.* New York: Plenum Press, 1979. Pp. 99-114.

Magnusson, D., & Allen, V. P. (Eds.). *Human development: An interactional perspective.* New York: Academic Press, 1983.

Wicker, A. W. *An introduction to ecological psychology.* Monterey, Calif.: Brooks-Cole, 1979.

Wohlwill, J. F. The confluence of environmental and developmental psychology: Sign-post to an ecology of development? *Human Development,* 1980, *23,* 254-258.

# 1 Settlement and Density Patterns: Toward the 21st Century

Gary W. Shannon
*Department of Geography*
*University of Kentucky*

Ellen Cromley
*Department of Geography*
*University of Connecticut*

## INTRODUCTION

With apologies to Wolf Schneider (1963), "Is Babylon Everywhere?" Are we now living in or moving inexorably toward a world of cities? Moreover, will this world of cities be a dream or a nightmare? Selected aspects of the latter question as it pertains to the habitat of the child are addressed in subsequent chapters. The present discussion is directed toward the former questions. The purpose of this chapter is to paint, albeit with a rather broad brush, a picture of current settlement patterns and selected future trends in settlement as they reflect changing population density. The disjuncture between the scale of deliberation of this chapter and the detailed and in-depth reviews and analyses of subsequent chapters may seem abrupt. Nevertheless, while examining in detail the many trees of specific associations between children, their development and density, it is important also to keep the forest of general settlement patterns in view.

Patterns and trends in the concentration and distribution of population in urban settlements are presented and assessed on three levels. At one level a description of the current world patterns of urbanization as well as the distribution and growth of large urban agglomerations is presented. At another level, information is presented pertaining to inter-urban or inter-metropolitan variations in population density. Finally, examples of variations in density within cities and metropolitan areas are presented. Emphasis is directed, especially in the latter two instances, toward the United States' experience.

## URBANIZATION: DEFINITIONS

Any discussion pertaining to *urbanization* must necessarily pay attention at the outset to the meaning of the term. When viewed from a geographical perspective, urbanization signifies a settlement pattern characterized by measures of size, density, and spacing of settlements. The sociological definition of urbanization is based on *urbanism* as a way of life characterized by specific kinds of social relations (Wirth, 1938). Of course, the sociological perspective on urbanization interprets the characteristic social relations as consequences of the size, density, and heterogenity of urban settlements. Urbanization as a settlement pattern and urbanism as a "way of life" are therefore related approaches to assessing the form and meaning of human population distributions.

Internal comparisons of urbanization are impeded by the fact that "urban settlements" are diversely defined. In some instances, "urban places" are those settlements with a minimum of 2,000 to 5,000, 7,000, or some other number of inhabitants; in others, places having an urban "character" or "enjoying a political status" as capital of a district may be treated as urban regardless of size (Davis, 1969). In South Africa, urban centers include "well-established towns with specified urban characteristics with fewer than 500 inhabitants but having at least approximately 100 white inhabitants" (U.N. Conference on Human Settlements, 1976). Though the data are not strictly comparable and should not be used to compare individual nations without taking variations of definitions into account, it would be a mistake to exaggerate the degree of incomparability or to reject the data entirely as having no utility (Davis, 1969; U.N., 1976).

Another problem arises in differentiating human settlements into "urban" and "non-urban." Human settlements form a continuum and range in size from isolated farmsteads to massive urban agglomerations such as the original "megalopolis" of the United States' east coast. Yet, we impose a dichotomy between places that are urban and those that are not. There is no definitive answer to the criticism of the use of this dichotomy. All that can be said is that it is useful for some purposes but, due to its deficiencies, not for all.

Other, alternative definitions of urban and urbanization may be especially relevant for children. For example, the presence of institutions such as schools, museums, hospitals, and so forth may be particularly important in considering the habitat of children and needs to be reflected in measures of urbanization (Weber, 1938). Urbanization as a process particularly relevant to children might include the variable distribution of cultural and behavioral patterns, or the "density" of family and/or social networks.

Acknowledging the potential significance of alternative definitions of urban and urbanization, our focus here is on the most universally available measures of urbanization and population density. The variability in the simple arithmetic density of population (the number of people per unit area), aside from its social and behavioral consequences, has created, to use a spatial metaphor, "islands and continents" of humankind on a global scale.

## GROWTH OF URBAN SETTLEMENT

At the beginning of the 19th century the world was estimated to be about 3% urban. By 1900, the concentration of population in cities was considered as representing a remarkable social phenomenon, even though less than 15% of the world's population were then urban. The process of urbanization accelerated and the world is now about 40% urban. It is estimated that by the year 2000 fully 50% of the world's population will be living in cities.

Nevertheless, there are important regional variations in the level of urbanization on a global scale and these patterns are related to the regional level of development. Some 23 world regions have been identified by the United Nations. The urbanized population as a percentage of the total population in each region is depicted in Figure 1.1. Nine regions have been classified as "developed" and fourteen as "developing" or "less developed" by the United Nations based on a number of criteria (Table 1.1) (U.N., 1976).

By examining levels of urbanization in these regions as depicted in Figure 1.1, it is clear that the most highly urbanized areas, with over 60% of their

TABLE 1.1
Regions of the World by Level of Development

| More Developed Regions | Less Developed Regions |
| --- | --- |
| Australia and New Zealand | Tropical South America |
| Temperate South America | Middle America |
| Northern America | East Asia (excluding China and Japan) |
| Japan | |
| Soviet Union | Caribbean |
| Southern Europe | Southern Africa |
| Eastern Europe | Western South Asia |
| Northern Europe | Northern Africa |
| Western Europe | Oceania (Micronesia, Melanesia, and Polynesia) |
| | Middle Africa |
| | China |
| | Eastern South Asia |
| | Middle South Asia |
| | Western Africa |
| | Eastern Africa |

Source: United Nations (1976). *Habitat: U.N. Conference on Human Settlements.*

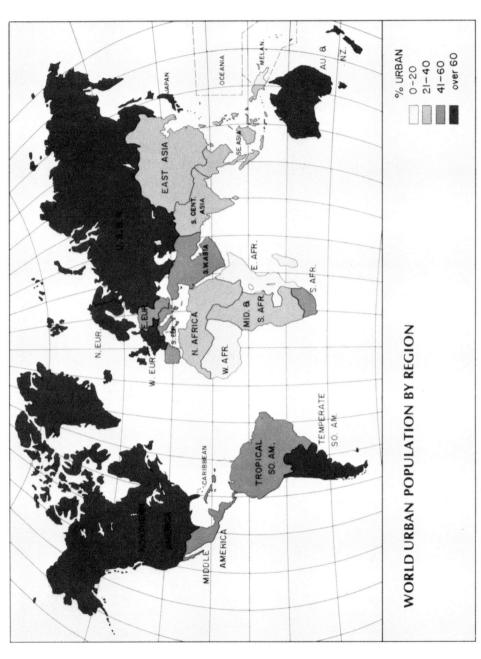

**FIG. 1.1.** Distribution of world urban population by region. Source: United Nations (1976; Table 6).

4

populations living in urban places, are generally the most developed regions including North America, Northern and Western Europe, the Soviet Union, Japan, and temperate South America. From 1970 to 1975, however, the rate of urbanization of the less developed regions was twice that of the more developed regions (70% vs. 30% respectively).

Worldwide, more than 500 million children under the age of 15 reside in urban areas (McHale, McHale, & Streatfield, 1979). The global distribution of children under the age of 15 indicates that 80% reside in less developed regions. Within the more developed regions, 69% of the children under 15 live in urban areas. Within the less developed regions, only 27% live in urban areas. However, this percentage is expected to increase to 41% by the year 2000 as the number of children in urban areas of less developed regions more than doubles.

## POPULATIONS IN LARGE CITIES

The percentage of the world's population living in cities of 100,000 or more by region is illustrated in Figure 1.2. The regions with the largest percentage of their populations living in cities of at least 100,000 are Australia (61%), Northern Europe (60%), Northern America (57%), Japan (56%), and temperate South America (52%). Western Europe also has approximately one-half (46%) of its population in cities of at least 100,000 people.

As a further indication of urban concentration, Figure 1.3 depicts for each region the percentage of urban population in cities of 1 million or more. The highest concentration of people in these "million" cities appears in East Asia (other than China and Japan) where 58% of the people in cities reside in agglomerations of at least 1 million people. Other regions with between 40 and 50% of their urban populations in "million" cities include Northern America (48%), temperate South America (45%), and Northern Europe (41%).

Not only are the more rapid rates of urbanization occurring in the less developed regions of the world, but these regions are also developing greater numbers of cities with populations of at least 100,000 persons. For example, in 1950 there were about 900 cities in the world with populations of at least 100,000 people and 62% of these were in developed regions. By 1980, however, there were about 2,200 cities in the world of this size and only 48% were then in developed regions.

A similar picture emerges when other city-size categories are considered. For cities of at least 500,000 population, the percentage of the world total in developed regions is expected to decline from the 63% (109 of 172) observed in 1950 to 37% of the total (302 of 809) by the year 2000. For cities of at least 1 million population, the percentage in developed regions is expected to de-

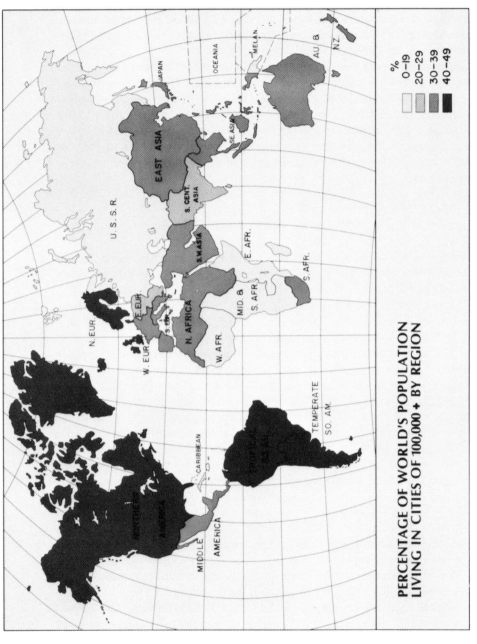

**PERCENTAGE OF WORLD'S POPULATION LIVING IN CITIES OF 100,000 + BY REGION**

%
0–19
20–29
30–39
40–49

FIG. 1.2.    Percentage of world's population living in cities of 100,000 + by region. Source: United Nations (1976; Table 6).

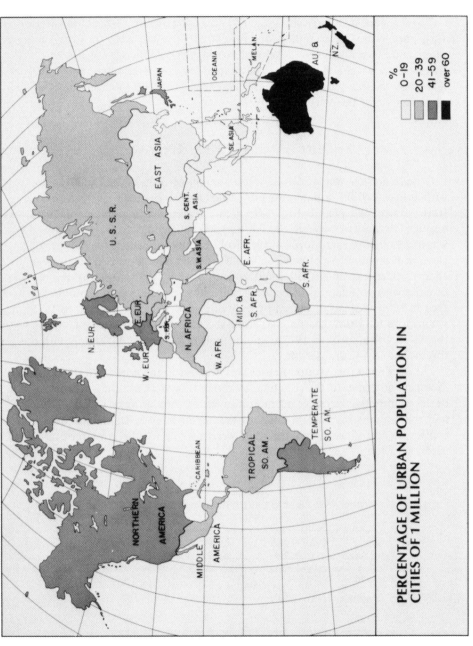

**PERCENTAGE OF URBAN POPULATION IN CITIES OF 1 MILLION**

| % | |
|---|---|
| 0–19 | |
| 20–39 | |
| 41–59 | |
| over 60 | |

**FIG. 1.3.** Percentage of world's population residing in cities of 1 million +, by region. Source: U.N. Population Division (1970) and United Nations (1982).

crease from the current 49% (down from 68% in 1950) to 36% by the turn of this century.

To these classes of large cities we must now add cities or metropolitan areas with populations of 5 million or more. In 1950 there were only six such places, and five were in the developed world. By 1980 there were 26 cities of this size and less than half were in developed regions. And, by the year 2000, it is estimated that only 27% of these giant cities (16 of 59) will be in the developed regions of the world.

## THE UNITED STATES' EXPERIENCE

*Growth and Decline of Cities.* The number of cities in the United States with at least 100,000 inhabitants grew by over 25% between 1960 and 1975, from 129 to 162 (Table 1.2). The greatest increase in number of cities occurred in those of between 100,000 and 500,000 people. In this group there was a 28% increase, from 108 in 1960 to 138 in 1975. Further, the number of cities with populations of between half a million and one million people was 16 in 1960, rose to 20 in 1970, but decreased to 18 by 1975. And, the number of cities with populations of between one and five million people numbered four in 1960 and had increased by only one as of 1975. From 1960 to 1975 seven cities fell below the 100,000 population level and 40 increased beyond this level. From 1970 to 1975 five cities fell below the 100,000 population threshold and 14 surpassed it.

The decline in this group of cities was greatest in the northeastern manufacturing quadrant of the country. Although they were not the only regions of the country to experience net migration gains, the south and the southwest had the greatest increase in cities of this size (Berry & Dahmann, 1980). California and Florida, in particular, were notable for the growth of large cities.

TABLE 1.2
Number of Cities in United States by Size Category,
1960–1975

| Year | 1,000,000–4,999,999 | 500,000–999,999 | 100,000–499,999 |
|---|---|---|---|
| 1960 | 4 | 16 | 108 |
| 1970 | 5 | 20 | 127 |
| 1975 | 5 | 18 | 138 |

Source: U.S. Bureau of the Census (1967; 1972; 1977; Table 4: Cities).

This pattern of growth and decline reflects significant changes occurring in the nation's settlement pattern since 1970. These changes involve not only a redistribution of population over regions, and metroplitan and nonmetropolitan areas; they also affect the age composition of the population. For instance, migrants into the South and West from 1975 to 1978 were younger than would be expected on the basis of the age distribution of the total United States' population (Biggar, 1979). The median age of migrants to both regions was five years below the median for the total population. These migrants have contributed to the rapid growth taking place in the smaller metropolitan areas in the South and West.

As a whole, metropolitan areas have lagged substantially behind nonmetropolitan areas in population growth since 1970, markedly reversing the trend of preceding decades. From 1970 to 1977, for the first time since the turn of the century, population growth was higher in nonmetropolitan areas than in metropolitan areas. Between 1970 and 1975, for example, some 2.3 million more people moved into nonmetropolitan counties than moved out of them. Central city population of all metropolitan areas grew slightly from 1960 to 1970 but have declined at an average annual rate of 0.4% over the last decade (Berry & Dahmann, 1980). These patterns of population redistribution have had an impact on another important measure of urbanization: population density. It is the different manifestations of this urban condition to which we turn our attention now.

*Inter-Metropolitan Density Variations.*    It is important to recognize that gross population size is only one measure of urbanization. Certainly no one would suggest, for example, that New Orleans is comparable in its urban character to Columbus, Ohio, though each has about a half-million population; nor that Jersey City is similar to St. Petersburg, Florida, or Richmond, Virginia, though each of these has a population of about 250,000. From an ecological perspective, population density (defined here as the number of people per square mile) represents a different dimension in terms of which cities may be compared, and which is often indicative of qualitatively differing environments.

In the United States there is considerable geographical variation in the average density of large cities. The average density for cities with at least 100,000 inhabitants by major census division is displayed in Table 1.3. In 1975 the average population density for cities of this size was about 4,800 people per square mile. The highest average population density of large cities occurred in the northeast quadrant of the United States, with cities there averaging over 9,000 people per square mile. The South had the lowest average population per square mile in large cities, about 3,000.

When the average population density of cities is examined by size class, as depicted in Table 1.4, we find that, on the average, the larger the population

TABLE 1.3

Average Density for Cities of at Least 100,000 Population and Percent
Change from 1960 to 1975 by Census Division

| Region | 1960 Density | 1970 Density | 1975 Density | Percent Change 1960–1975 |
|--------|--------------|--------------|--------------|--------------------------|
| Total | 5,781 | 5,140 | 4,826 | |
| Northeast | 10,214 | 9,737 | 9,103 | − 11% |
| Northcentral | 5,863 | 4,812 | 4,375 | − 25% |
| South | 3,989 | 3,262 | 3,071 | − 23% |
| West | 4,826 | 4,708 | 4,597 | − 5% |

Source: U.S Bureau of the Census (1967; 1972; 1977; Table 4: Cities).

TABLE 1.4

Average Density for Cities of at Least 100,000 Population and Percent
Change from 1960 to 1975 by Size Class

| Region | 1960 Density | 1970 Density | 1975 Density | Percent Change 1960–1975 |
|--------|--------------|--------------|--------------|--------------------------|
| 100,000 to 499,999 | 5,133 | 4,649 | 4,383 | − 15% |
| 500,000 to 999,999 | 8,849 | 6,405 | 6,072 | − 31% |
| 1,000,000 to 4,999,999 | 12,267 | 10,018 | 9,253 | − 25% |
| 5,000,000 + | 25,940 | 26,319 | 24,939 | − 4% |

Source: U.S Bureau of the Census (1967; 1972; 1977; Table 4: Cities).

of a city, the more densely settled it is. In cities with populations of between 100,000 and 500,000, the average population density was about 4,400 people per square mile. In cities of between half a million and one million the average population density was about 6,100 people per square mile. The number of people per square mile in cities of between one and four million was about 9,300. And, New York City, the only city in the United States with a population of over five million had far and away the highest average population density, about 25,000 people per square mile.

The overall effect of recent population redistribution trends has been the reduction of urban population densities. Table 1.3 illustrates this phenomenon in cities of at least 100,000 population between 1960 and 1975, regardless of geographic location. Percentage decreases in the average population density of cities with at least 100,000 population ranged from a low of 5% in the

West to 23% and 25% declines in the South and North Central sessions, respectively.

Decline in average population density also characterized cities in each population size category (Table 1.4). The greatest decrease in population density between 1960 and 1975 occurred in cities of between half a million and one million population. The decline in these cities was about 31%. Cities of between one and five million had an average population density decline of 25%. Cities of populations of less than half a million but at least 100,000 people declined in average population density by 15%.

Decline and regional variations in household size provide additional insight into declining densities in metropolitan areas. The factors behind decreasing household size include lower fertility resulting in fewer children per household, reduced mortality increasing the number of older persons living in households after their children have left home, and high divorce rates (Gober, 1981). The results of decreasing household size are less intensive use of existing housing and need for development of additional units to house a constant population.

The smaller household size in Florida's metropolitan areas and in western cities and the decline in household size in the metropolitan areas of the South since 1970 heighten the demand for new housing in these growth areas and contribute to low-density sprawl. In declining central cities, population losses and smaller households may drop neighborhood populations below the threshold levels required to support services like neighborhood schools (Gober, 1981).

Early evidence from the 1980 Census indicates that the emptying of large central cities due to regional shifts, nonmetropolitan growth, and changing household size has continued since 1975. Thus, while the latter part of the 19th and first half of the 20th centuries was characterized by the concentrating of people in large cities, the decades since may be characterized by a "de-population," which has considerably altered the internal spatial organization of America's metropolitan areas.

*Intra-Metropolitan Density Variations.*    Urban densities are, of course, not uniform within each city. We are all familiar with the variation in density as we move from the periphery to the center of cities. Changes in population density may be dramatic in many instances. The study of spatial variation of urban densities is relatively recent. An article published in 1951 commented upon the lack of "adequate quantitative study" received by this subject of urban geography (Clark, 1951). Evidence was presented in the same article that regardless of time or place, the spatial distribution of population densities within cities appeared to conform to a single empirically derived expression:

$$d_x = d_0 e^{-bx};$$

where $d_x$ is the population density $d$ at some distance $x$ from the city center; $d_0$ is the density at the populated center of the city, and $b$ is the density gradient, indicating the rate of diminution of density with distance from the center of the city — a negative exponential decline.

Thirty-six cases were used in the original formulation of the expression, including cities (at different time periods) from the United States, Europe, Great Britain, and Southwest Asia. About 10 years later, almost one hundred cases were presented as evidence supporting the general applicability of this expression (Berry, Simmons, & Tennant, 1963).

It was observed in this study that, through time, in Western cities, the central population density of cities, $d_0$, had increased and subsequently decreased. And, $b$, the rate of population density decrease with increasing distance from the center of the city, had declined due to deconcentration in the central part of the city and "decompaction" or suburbanization generally.

As for the recent decline in population density in the more central parts of large cities, it is most likely the result of two processes. The first of these involves size related to life-cycle changes. Traditional models of urban population density and land-value patterns focused primarily on the number of dwellings per unit land area and the consumption of housing per household unit. In treating households as the basic unit of analysis and assuming uniform average household size, the role of the number of persons per household in influencing population density patterns was neglected. More recently, attention has been directed toward the substantial variations in household size within urban areas in an attempt to deal more effectively and accurately with population density at its smallest scale — the intensity of use of individual dwelling spaces.

Decreases in household size are primarily a function of the aging of the population as older children leave the parental home. In a study of Phoenix, Arizona, household size in 1970 was found to generally increase with increasing distance from the city center. The presence of smaller households in the older inner city areas partially offset the more compact structural density of these areas. Thus, the overall population density in this area was reduced. On the other hand, housing units in the outer areas of the city contained approximately 50% more occupants, thus compensating for larger lots and fewer housing units per acre (Gober, 1980).

The spatial distribution of change in household size in Phoenix from 1970 to 1975 indicates that the smallest declines occurred in the innermost census tracts (occupied by older residents where household size was already low) and in the newly-built periphery (where children were too young to be leaving home). The largest declines were registered in areas between the core and periphery where high proportions of the population in 1970 were from 15 to 19 years of age and (presumably) left home between 1970 and 1975. This phenomenon suggests, or is indicative of, an "age wave" moving from the center of the city to the periphery and influencing household size and, ultimately, density. This change in density is effected without notable change in the density of the built environment.

A second process contributing to the decline in population density in many central urban areas has been labeled "gentrification." Essentially, this process involves the reoccupation of portions of the central city by higher level socioeconomic groups (Hamnett & Williams, 1980). These people are generally younger, professional couples without children, or older people whose children have left home. Row houses and townhouses, once converted into apartment houses for the poor, are now being purchased, renovated, and occupied at a much lower density than previously. The extent, duration, and ubiquity of this movement has yet to be adequately assessed as it might pertain to the changing density patterns of Western cities.

Also contributing to the general decline in the intra-urban variation of population density patterns is the increasing percentage of people living in multi-family complexes near the periphery of cities and in the suburbs. Apartments, condominiums, and other relatively high population density dwellings throughout most cities are contributing to observed homogenization of intra-urban population density patterns.

Population density changes for selected central cities of different size and regional location illustrate basic trends in intra-urban density over the last twenty years. In the population density "profiles" of cities examined in 1960, 1970, and 1980, an urban density "crater" appears in the innermost tracts of the central business district reflecting the overwhelmingly commercial nature of these areas. In most cases, density increases at intermediate distances from the city center and declines in outlying areas.

In older cities like Milwaukee, Louisville, and Hartford, population densities were two to three times higher than densities in newer cities like Tampa and Tucson, and population densities declined fairly consistently from 1960 to 1980. As total density decreased, the density peak shifted toward the periphery of the central city. This suggests dramatic decreases in population density in the census tracts at intermediate distances while the tracts in the innermost and peripheral areas maintained their densities through time.

Large intra-metropolitan density differentials characterizing the density profiles of Milwaukee, Louisville, Hartford, and other cities are not reflected in the intra-urban density profiles of growing cities in the South and West. In these areas, fairly uniform densities are maintained as population growth diffuses over the areally expanding city.

It should be pointed out that these density profiles reflect residential population density patterns over the long term. Other measures of population density would reflect quite different patterns. For example, the population density of any area in the city is temporally variable, especially in the short run. Daily commuting patterns to work, school, shopping, and other destinations redistribute the urban population throughout the city. These short-term variations in density might also be expected to have an impact on the situation of the urban child. Nevertheless, population densities within urban areas in the United States appear to be becoming more homogeneous through time although the character of the built environment in the urban core and sprawling peripheral areas remain quite different, particularly in older metropolitan areas.

## POLICY CONCERNS

The regional variations in international and intranational patterns of urbanization noted in this review have meaningful policy and research implications. Population dispersal in the United States has occurred spontaneously rather than as a result of direct policy (Oosterbaan, 1980). In contrast, other urbanized countries have made direct efforts to influence urban population growth. In the Soviet Union, policy has emphasized limiting the growth of large cities partially through controlling the growth of employment opportunities in urban centers (Parkim, 1973). In Western Europe, particularly in Great Britain and France, efforts have been directed at providing specific settlement alternatives (new towns) to congested metropolitan centers (De Jong, 1975; Oosterbaan, 1980).

A number of arguments have been put forth in the United States for a national policy reinforcing the movement to nonmetropolitan areas. These include the results of locational preference surveys indicating that a majority of the polled respondents expressed a preference for nonmetropolitan places of residence, and the inability of urban planning to overcome problems of metropolitan stagnation (Oosterbaan, 1980). Implementation of a dispersal policy would not necessarily involve the construction of "new towns" – in light of the failure of recent American experiments in the development of new communities – but rather a revitalization of existing small communities and inner city neighborhoods.

Some commentators on the urban scene emphasize space, privacy, reduced crime and pollution, and relaxed lifestyles as positive aspects of smaller – and perhaps less dense – settlements. However, others are concerned that recent population redistribution trends in the United States will result in an expensive and wasteful restructuring of the environment. Current urban policy would need to be shaped to deal with associated changes in energy consumption, employment, transportation, air and water quality, social service utilization, education, and criminal justice (Berry & Silverman, 1980).

Efforts to assess the effects on residents of living in low-density areas are confounded by the different forms low-density settlement might take: for example, sprawling urban bedroom communities versus low-density, or self-contained satellite communities. Further complicating the picture, some supposed benefits of low-density development may be more related to middle-class status of area residents or distance from the central city than low density per se (Popenoe, 1979). Sprawl has particularly characterized urban development in the United States while it is not a prominent feature of the landscape in other highly urbanized countries like Sweden, Switzerland, and West Germany.

Low-density development in the form of sprawl has had major negative consequences in the United States (Popenoe, 1979). Low-density development has intensified racial segregation. The costs of sprawl have been regressively distributed with wealthier residents enjoying the benefits of suburbanization. Sprawl has accelerated the decline of the central city as amenities and services suburbanize. Finally, due to the organization of urban government in the United States, sprawl has been accompanied by creation of fragmented and overlapping governmental units.

## CONCLUSIONS

On the international scene in particular, there is considerable evidence that we are, in fact, moving toward a world of cities. At the same time, it is apparent that these cities do and will represent widely different types of habitats for children. An important organizing principle underlying the whole spectrum of urban forms is residential density. This chapter has described some facets of this basic environmental condition and has indicated some trends currently in evidence. This material serves as a context for the treatments of the relationships between density and the development of the child presented in the following chapters.

## REFERENCES

Berry, B. J. L., & Dahmann, D. C.  Population redistribution in the United States in the 1970s. In B. J. L. Berry & L. P. Silverman (Eds.), *Population redistribution and public policy.* Washington, D.C.: National Academy of Sciences, 1980. Pp. 8–49.

Berry, B. J. L., & Silverman, L. P. (Eds.). *Population redistribution and public policy.* Washington, D.C.: National Academy of Sciences, 1980.

Berry, B. J. L., Simmons, J. W., & Tennant, R. J.  Urban population densities: Structure and change. *Geographical Review,* 1963, *53,* 389–405.

Biggar, J. C.  The sunning of America: Migration to the sunbelt. *Population Bulletin,* 1979, *34.* Washington, D.C.: Population Reference Bureau.

Clark, C. Urban population densities. *Journal of the Royal Statistical Society,* 1951, Ser. A, *114,* 490–496.

Davis, K. *World urbanization, 1950–1970. Vol. I: Basic data for cities.* Berkeley: Institute of International Studies, University of California, 1969.

De Jong, G. F. Population redistribution policies: Alternatives from the Netherlands, Great Britain, and Israel. *Social Science Quarterly,* 1975, *56,* 262–273.

Gober, P. Shrinking household size and its effect on urban population density patterns: A case study of Phoenix, Arizona. *Professional Geographers,* 1980, *32,* 55–62.

Gober, P. Falling household size and its effect on metropolitan population growth and density. *Annals of Regional Science,* 1981, *15,* 1–10.

Hamnett, C., & Williams, P. R. Social change in London: A study of gentrification. *Urban Affairs Quarterly,* 1930, *15,* 469–487.

McHale, M. C., McHale, J., & Streatfield, G. F. *Children in the world.* Washington, D.C.: Population Reference Bureau, 1979.

Oosterbaan, J. *Population dispersal.* Lexington, Massachusetts: Lexington Books, 1980.

Parkim, M. *City planning in Soviet Russia.* Chicago: University of Chicago Press, 1973.

Popenoe, D. Urban sprawl: Some neglected sociological considerations. *Sociology and Social Research,* 1979, *63,* 255–268.

Schneider, V. *Babylon is Everywhere* (W. Schneider, English Translation). Great Britain: Hodder & Stoughton, 1963.

United Nations. *Habitat: U.N. conference on human settlements.* Statistical Annex, 1976.

United Nations. *Demographic Yearbook 1980.* Department of International Economic and Social Affairs, Statistical Office. Table 8: Population of Capital Cities and Cities of 100,000 and Over, 1982.

United Nations Population Division, *Urban and Rural Population: Individual Countries 1950–1985 and Regions and Major Areas 1950–2000,* ESA/P/WP.33/Rev. 1. New York: United Nations, 1970.

United States Bureau of the Census. (Department of Commerce). *County and city data book 1967: A statistical abstract supplement.* Washington D.C.: United States Government Printing Office, 1967.

United States Bureau of the Census. (Department of Commerce). *County and city data book 1972: A statistical abstract supplement.* Washington, D.C.: United States Government Printing Office, 1972.

United States Bureau of the Census. (Department of Commerce). *County and city data book 1977: A statistical abstract supplement.* Washington, D.C.: United States Government Printing Office, 1978.

Weber, M. *The city.* Edited and translated by Don Martindale and Gertrude Neuwirth. New York: Free Press, 1958.

Wirth, L. Urbanism as a way of life. *American Journal of Sociology,* 1938, *44,* 1–24.

# 2 Residential Density as a Variable in Child-Development Research

Joachim F. Wohlwill
*The Pennsylvania State University*

## INTRODUCTION

The variable with which we are concerned in this volume, that of the density of other human beings in the child's environment, is not one that child psychologists have paid much attention to in the past. A number of reasons may be suggested for this neglect. First of all, density, defined as number of individuals per unit of space, is clearly a "distal" variable in Brunswik's (1956) sense, at least for the purposes of a psychologist. Whatever effects it may have as an influence on the development of the child must clearly be mediated by variables correlated with it that impinge on the child. These may be conceptualized as amount of social stimulation, opportunity for interaction with others, over- or under- "manning," or any of a number of alternative ways of looking at the role of density that are considered in general terms in this paper, and in greater depth in those by the other contributors to this volume.

A second, probably more significant point concerning the lack of attention by developmental psychologists to the density variable is that it implies a gross quantitative and almost paradoxically depersonalized conception of the role of people in human behavior, and child behavior in particular. Child psychologists have dealt at great length with such issues as parent-child relationships, effects of siblings on one another, and inter-peer relationships. What has mattered to them, however, is the quality of such interactions between a child and other people, rather than how few or many there are. Thus a formulation of environmental influences on development such as Wachs' (1979), which includes rate of encounter with other unspecified individuals, as well as opportunity for temporary escape from contact with others as major components, remains a rare exception in our approaches to behavioral development, though the results found by Wachs with regard to these factors suggest that they are far from negligible. (See Heft's chapter in this volume.)

To be sure, effects of crowding have frequently been studied in children, and in fact some of the best-known work in this area consists of investigations of children (Aiello, Nicosia, & Thomson, 1979; Hutt & Vaizey, 1966; Loo, 1972). Yet most of this work has been carried out more from an interest in the problem of crowding than in child behavior and its development, and thus it has not been effectively integrated into our conceptions of behavioral development.

Part of the aim of this chapter, and in a larger sense of the volume as a whole, is thus to draw attention to the relevance of density as a variable in developmental research. This presumes, of course, some at least tacit understanding of the meaning of the concept in a behavioral context, and an analysis of relevant components of this dimension that require differentiation. The first part of the chapter is devoted to these aspects of the problem, and more particularly to a consideration of the dimensional status of the isolation-crowding polarity, i.e., to the question whether we are dealing here with a single continuum, or rather with a multidimensional attribute. The paper proceeds to an examination of some environmental correlates of density that may be more directly related to the impact of particular conditions of density on the child. In the concluding section I consider the relevance of this variable in a developmental perspective, i.e., by reference to diverse theoretical views of the developing child, and of the role of environmental conditions in development.

At the outset, the focus on density, rather than on a more psychologically meaningful concept such as crowding may need explanation. There are two very different reasons for preferring the density term.

First, the emphasis in past research and discussions of density has been almost entirely on one end of this dimension, i.e., the high-density or crowding pole. We do find one influential theory of crowding postulating a bi-polar dimension of rate of social interaction, with social isolation placed at the other pole (Altman, 1975). Yet possible effects of low rates of social interaction have rarely been considered, at least in this bi-polar framework, although they have been addressed from a different perspective in studies of effects of isolation (Rasmussen, 1973). Curiously, this situation is just the reverse of what has happened in the field of sensory stimulation, where virtually all of the work has been concentrated at the low-stimulation end (e.g., effects of sensory deprivation), while ignoring, with only sporadic exceptions (Zuckerman et al., 1970), the other end of the continuum. Yet here again much of the theoretical discussion has started from an assumed bi-polar dimension, and an optimal level of stimulation hypothesis (Fiske & Maddi, 1961; Suedfeld, 1969). From a developmental perspective the need to consider both ends of this continuum has been recognized, however, by Wachs (1977; cf. also Wohlwill & Heft, 1977).

One of the major tasks facing us in this regard, then, will be to operationalize the two ends of this continuum of density as they pertain to the development of the child, and to the different kinds of environments in which children live. Just what is meant by high-density conditions, in this context, and what are the different forms that high density may take that need to be differentiated? Similarly, at the other end, what does low density mean, and to what extent is it equivalent to physical and social isolation?

These questions are examined in the following section of this paper. Before turning to them, however, a second point needs to be made concerning the conceptualization of density, and the distinction between density and crowding that, at least since it was addressed by Stokols (1972), has been a major subject of discussion in the literature on effects of crowding. A general theme running through this discussion is the alleged inadequacy of the density concept, since it may bear little direct relationship to the experience of crowding. The latter, it is argued, depends not only on objective density defined in terms of some index such as number of persons per unit of area, but on various factors relating to the context (a person may experience crowding in a subway, but not at a baseball stadium, under equivalent conditions of density), to the behavior being carried out and its functional significance for the person, to personality traits, etc. For this reason, many of those in the field of crowding have urged the avoidance of the use of the density variable altogether in favor of a direct focus on the individual's experience of crowding.

Work with children — especially younger children — should serve as a useful antidote to this tendency, all too common in the environment and behavior field, to define environmental variables in terms of personal experience. For young children are notoriously unreliable sources of information about their own internal state or experience. Their verbalizations may serve to supplement or even validate the investigator's assumption about the effect of different conditions of density, but can hardly replace them, no more than would be the case in animal research. On the other hand, as we shall note, the quite justifiable criticisms of a simplistic reliance on a single index of objective density does not at all preclude the continued use of such indices, albeit in more sophisticated fashion.

## DIFFERENTIABLE COMPONENTS OF THE DENSITY DIMENSION

As noted in the preceding section, the density concept is defined in terms of number of individuals per unit of area. That definition does not, however, indicate the unit of analysis in terms of which density is to be calculated: e.g., an apartment or residence, a neighborhood, a community, a county. As will be seen presently, the density variable takes on very different meanings, depending on the size of the unit of aggregation chosen.

Furthermore, there are a variety of environmental variables that covary with density in an ecological sense. Thus a consideration of the impact of density on the life of the child must include reference to these correlates of density, whether in order to try to partial out their effects or to give recognition to them in their own right.

## Components of Density

There are at least three different sets of distinctions to be made involving differentiations among alternative units of analysis, or alternative environmental contexts. All are based on objective environmental indices that are of direct relevance for behavior.

*Indices of Residential Density.* In their classical demographic study of the correlates of manifestations of social pathology in an urban area, Galle, Gove, and McPherson (1972) distinguished among the following indices of density applying to an individual's living conditions: Number of persons per room; number of rooms per housing unit, number of housing units per structure, number of structures per acre. Obviously, only the first of these qualifies literally as an index of density that describes the distribution of people over a given area;[1] yet all have clear implications for the conditions in which the people residing in these rooms, housing units or structures were living. That point emerges succinctly out of the findings, which show that for three out of four different indices of social pathology (mortality ratio, juvenile delinquency rate, and public assistance rate),[2] number of persons per room contributed most strongly to the prediction of pathology, via a multiple regression equation. The exception was the incidence of admissions to mental hospitals, where number of rooms per household turned out to be the best predictor.

These indices are cited here, not so much because they can be expected to be equally relevant to aspects of the normal development of children, but rather to suggest that by refining and increasing the specificity of objective density indices, their value as predictors of psychological response can be en-

---

[1]It should be noted in this connection that Galle et al. write as sociologists, who are accustomed to deal with social units at higher levels of aggregation than those that a psychologist would favor.

[2]Gove et al. included a further index of social pathology: fertility ratio; mention of it is omitted here, since no justification is presented in their paper for considering high fertility *eo ipso* as a sign of social breakdown.

hanced. Thus it makes sense that number of persons per room, a direct index of crowding inside the home, would relate to variables such as delinquency and mortality, while number of rooms per household would reflect, in a negative sense, the extent of isolation of the dwellers of that household (i.e., one or two rooms generally means a person living alone), and thus predict susceptibility to mental illness.

As far as the development of the child is concerned, there is one measure, apart from general indices of crowding in the home such as number of persons per room, that warrants special mention, because it has been found to be consistently related to the early cognitive growth of the child (Wachs, 1979; Wachs, Uzgiris, & Hunt, 1971). This is the availability, or lack of it, of a room for the child to "escape" to, and be by itself, free from the noise, congestion and general activity in the shared spaces of the home (living room, kitchen, family room, etc.). Essentially what this measure represents is a measure of temporal variation in amount of social stimulation; at the same time it brings out the point that individuals, even as young as the children studied by Wachs (e.g., between the ages of one and three) can to a degree determine the rate of social stimulation that they desire at a particular time, and that certain environments are more responsive to this need than others. This is a particularly pertinent point in regard to Altman's (1975) theory of privacy and crowding, which considers the regulation of amount of social interaction a key process in determining people's response to numbers and densities of others around them.

*Indoor versus Outdoor Density.* A fairly obvious distinction, and one that is of evident relevance to the development of the child, is that between indoors and outdoors density (cf. Zlutnick & Altman, 1972). Crowding means different things, depending on whether we are considering interior space in a home, school, store, etc., or outside space on a playground, park, or sidewalk. The point bears extending to the opposite pole, i.e., that of low-density conditions: Relative isolation of a child inside its home (as in the case of a six-year-old living alone with a single parent in an apartment) is surely a condition different from that of playing in a sparsely frequented playground, woods or beach.

The distinction derives additional importance from the fact that the two types of density are ecologically far from correlated. Thus we find apartment houses with relatively high living densities in fairly small towns, where outdoors environments are for the most part characterized by low densities. Similarly, there are many farm children living in large families, and thus under conditions of relatively high density in the home, who at the same time are fairly isolated from others outside of the home, and for whom prevailing densities on the outside are quite low. Indeed, data from the U.S. Census (U.S. Bureau of the Census, 1979) indicate that the number of persons per housing unit is *higher* in farm than nonfarm areas; results from Canadian housing surveys (e.g., Canada Mortgage and Housing Corporation, 1979) point in the same direction. (An analogous, but even more extreme case though not involving children, is that of the submarine, whose crews live under highly cramped conditions, yet have the vast expanse of the oceans, whether above or under the surface, effectively to themselves.)

Does the reverse condition, a combination of low indoor with high outdoor density exist? It may, if we define indoor density in the most restricted sense, e.g., that characterizing a family's residence, such as an apartment. There are certainly spacious apartments that may contain very few people, such as a couple and a single child, living in a neighborhood of high population density, such as an area of condominiums in a down-town section of a major city.

Indices of outdoor density are of course much more problematical, since they require a determinate unit of area, when such a unit may be difficult to specify — e.g., in the case of a large urban park, or a suburban development, or a fishing hole along a stream. Perhaps some higher-order index that takes into account the gradients of density present in the field in question would prove more revealing than a simple index of number of occupants divided by area. This suggestion appears especially pertinent for environments utilized for unstructured activities, as opposed to a playground, for instance. Further complicating the matter are the important temporal variations in amount of use commonly found in such areas, relating to time of day, weather, and season.

*Density for Primary versus Secondary Environments.* This distinction was introduced by Stokols (1976, 1978), to differentiate between conditions of crowding in environments that are of primary functional significance for the individual (e.g., the home), as compared to others used in more incidental fashion (e.g., a store). The distinction is not too easily operationalized, particularly in the case of children. Is the corner drugstore, for instance, acting as a typical meeting ground for preadolescent kids after school, a primary or a secondary environment? Perhaps, in a crude way, the distinction could be approached in terms of the amount of time spent in a given location, so that an index of functional density might consist of some joint function (probably nonlinear) of time and number of individuals divided by area.

## Isolation versus Crowding: Single Dimension or Composite?

The example of the submarine crew cited above shows that isolation and crowding, far from being polar opposites, may in fact co-exist in one and the same setting. This suggests, on the one hand, that we need a label other than "isolation" to denote the pole opposite to "crowding" on the density dimension — we may have to settle for "lack of crowding," or in its adjectival form "uncrowded" to designate low density. What, then, is the relationship between isolation and lack of crowding?

Isolation, as studied both under laboratory and under field conditions (e.g., Rasmussen, 1973), has generally been used to refer to lack of direct contact between an individual or group and other individuals or groups. This is the case in studies of farm children, for instance, such as those studied by Hollos in Norway and Hungary (Hollos, 1975; Hollos & Cowan, 1973), living under conditions of relative isolation from others. It is true in a slightly different sense in studies of children growing up under conditions of cultural isolation, such as those carried out in Appalachia in the '30s (see Anastasi & Foley, 1958); here the children live in small villages of varying sizes (the "hollows" of rural Appalachia), but each village is more or less isolated from the outside world — or was at the time these studies were conducted.

There are several ways of resolving the problem of how to conceptualize isolation in these studies, and other similar ones of isolation under field conditions. The first would be simply to consider densities in a series of concentric zones, ranging from the home at one end through the community of which it is a part (if any) to other larger social or geographic units that may be of functional importance for a child in particular. Thus a particular farm might be characterized by a series of densities, e.g., as high-density with regard to home, medium density with regard to community; low density with regard to region. Is a child from such a farm isolated? The answer would depend on the functional importance for that child of home vs. community vs. region — a factor that might be difficult to assess objectively [though studies of home range would surely be relevant — cf. Moore & Young (1978)], and that would also be expected to differ according to the age of the child.

But apart from this difficulty, there are more serious problems with this solution. First, individuals are generally not distributed in a homogeneous fashion over an area; rather, habitats are distributed in a fairly haphazard fashion over a community, and even more over a region. Thus the overall density of a county or province, for instance, is of limited relevance for the conditions of life of the children residing in a community located in that area. More fundamentally, however, the question arises whether isolation, in a functional sense, is a matter of number of people living in an area of some predefined unit, or whether it may have to do rather with means of access, communication, etc. These will tend to be correlated with the overall density in that area, but only imperfectly. For instance, children living on a small island some 15 to 20 miles from a major metropolitan area (such as those on Puget Sound in the state of Washington) might well be considered to be more isolated than children in a town such as State College, Pennsylvania, which, though lying in a relatively sparsely populated region of that state, offers ready access to other communities of varying sizes and at varying distances. Thus it is possible that a child growing up in that town will have more opportunity for interaction with persons outside of its community than would a Puget Sound child. (Objective data on this point remain to be collected, to the best of my knowledge.)

The mention of an island existence brings up another question, i.e., the relationship between the community in which the child lives and the outside world, in terms of its size, self-sufficiency, etc. Are children in Honolulu "isolated"? Probably not, because their island, apart from being one of the most densely populated areas in the U.S.A., is large enough to constitute a world onto itself. Thus the fact that a majority of children in this city may never leave their island during their childhood does not make them functional isolates — no more than are many children in Brooklyn, who in principle live in a much more "connected" universe, but who in practice may be as confined to New York City as the Honolulu children are to their home city.

Accordingly, it would seem to make better sense to consider two separate, although perhaps partially correlated dimensions. The first is a dimension of density of the environment in the area of major functional importance to the child, extending from home to school and neighborhood, and for older children to the borders of the populated area in which they live (thus including, for suburban children, the downtown area of a city, if it is frequented by them — e.g., the "urbanized" area as defined by the Census). This dimension would thus run from highly crowded or congested to highly uncrowded or uncongested.

A second, separate dimension concerns the "connectedness" of a child's habitat with the larger world outside, beyond the area considered in the previous dimension, through regular channels of communication, as well as the media; it thus runs from isolation to high interaction. Admittedly this dimension is more difficult to define and measure objectively, because it includes a number of diverse aspects. The primary aspect is of course the access to the outside world available to the child through physical transport. This access is itself a function of a combination of geographic, logistic, economic and social factors, determining the availability, affordability, and opportunity of trips beyond the home area for the child. But to this access by bodily transport must be added the diverse forms of contact that the child is able to achieve with the outside world through various channels of electronic communication, both two-way (telephone) and one-way (the media). While on a purely pragmatic basis a composite index of accessibility could undoubtedly be determined — perhaps in a fashion similar to the calculation of quality-of-life indices — the problem of weighting the diverse components in some rational fashion appears as a formidable one. This problem is complicated still further by the necessity to take into account not merely forms of access and communication potentially available to the child, but those functionally attainable, given the limits on their use set by the child's age, as well as by economic and social barriers.

Lest the preceding be dismissed as an empty formalistic exercise in measurement lacking in functional significance, it is worth pointing to the divergent results found for the intellectual development of children in isolated areas in Appalachia in the '30s, in comparison with those obtained by Haggard (1973) as well as by Hollos (1975) for children living on isolated farms in Norway and Hungary. One may suggest that part of the answer for the discrepancy relates to the very different conditions of connectedness of the world of these two groups of children.

## Some Correlates of Density

As noted previously, density is a "distal" variable, in terms of its relationship to individual behavior. That is, whatever correlations between density and behavior may be found are presumably mediated by other variables covarying with density that are of more direct relevance for individual behavior. What are these correlates of density? Among them, four appear of particular interest: Activity level and level of intensity of environmental stimulation; competition for limited resources; diversity in choice of peers and other associates, and diversity of settings and facilities.[3] Each of these is associated with a particular theoretical framework for which the variable in question becomes relevant, and their role is discussed more specifically in the section to follow, in which alternative theoretical models for the interpretation of effects of density are considered. But it will be helpful to discuss each of them briefly, in order to enlarge our conception of social density.

*A. Activity Level and Level of Intensity of Environmental Stimulation.* Consider Macy's Department Store on a weekday morning, and compare it to the same store on a Saturday afternoon during the Christmas shopping season. Similarly, consider a sports stadium such as a major league baseball park, filled with a crowd of over 60,000 for a World Series game, as compared to that same park on a weekday afternoon early in the season, with a few thousand fans scattered through the stadium. In each of these cases, the two variants represent contrasting environments, in terms of the amount of noise, movement, and sheer intensity of stimulation (visual, auditory, even kinesthetic and olfactory) afforded by the aggregate collection of individuals that form a significant part of the environmental context for the individual visitor. In one case, that of the department store, the crowd may act to impair the individual's enjoyment of the activity (shopping), and create a possible

---

[3]Other variables could of course be cited that would be more relevant for other disciplines outside of psychology, such as geography, sociology, or economics.

background of tension and frustration, while in the other, that of the stadium, the crowd generally will have the effect of heightening enjoyment. In either case, however, the other individuals encountered serve at least in part as stimuli impinging on the individual, essentially in a physical rather than a social sense. As we shall see, there is some evidence that such stimulus correlates of social density exert a strong effect on young children's development, particularly in the home environment.

*B. Competition for Resources.*    Partially correlated with density is the degree to which an individual has to compete for limited resources, both material and immaterial, in a given environment. The correlation is only partial, because material resources are generally allocated on a per capita basis, rather than on the basis of area. When we consider resources available to children, however, this per capita principle is found to be only an approximation at best: the amount of disposable income for a family, and thus of the material resources available to the children, increases in a far from linear fashion with increasing family size; the same is true for amount of space available, and as regards the interpersonal environment, the amount of attention, affection and care received by a given child within the family. Thus family size, and to some extent living space, act to modulate the resources available to children. Note, further, that there are a number of separable aspects of density to be differentiated, each bearing a different relationship to this competition-for-resources factor. The one of most direct relevance is that of family size, but that is far from perfectly related to density even in the residential sense (e.g., number of persons per room), and probably only minimally to density outside of the home (e.g., that of a given locality), except to the extent that large families may tend to be concentrated in congested, inner-city areas.

Community density bears a more equivocal relationship to competition for resources, since such resources, e.g., in the form of services for transportation, education, and the like, are much more strongly determined by population than by density. And even within a given community, changes in population or density, such as a rapidly developing area may experience, are apt to occur without increases in resources keeping pace with them. On the other hand, there may be an essentially spurious negative association between density and community resources, to the extent that per capita expenditures in a relatively dense city are likely to be lower than those in the generally more affluent suburbs.

Some of these issues are more specifically addressed by Shannon in his demographically oriented chapter. Suffice it to point here to the psychological implications of resource competition for child behavior and personality development, which have been rarely studied — except in limited experimental research, where the intent has been specifically to differentiate between the role of social density and of resource competition (e.g., Cole-Ramanujan, 1980; Rohe & Patterson, 1974; Smith & Connolly, 1972). A particularly consistent as well as suggestive finding in such research is that of an increase in aggressiveness with resource scarcity, whether in correlation with or independent of social density.

A variant of the competition-for-resources factor that is more directly related to density is that of the surplus or shortfall of individuals required for a particular job or role performance. It relates to resource competition from the standpoint of the outsider, requiring the services of a person, such as a clerk in a super-market, or a teacher in a classroom. It takes on a very different significance when considered from the vantage point of the service-provider him- or herself, or more generally from the standpoint of role performance. This aspect of the problem is considered below, as it relates specifically to the behavioral ecologist's view of density, in terms of "over- vs. under-manned" settings.

*C. Diversity of Choice of Peers and Associates.* Whereas the two preceding correlates of density suggest that high-density conditions should be viewed as having a predominantly negative impact on the child, the one to be considered now, along with the following one, point to more positive, compensating features of such conditions. While a child in a rural setting is apt to be limited to a very small set of potential peers, and thus may have only a very limited choice in regard to age, sex, compatible interests, etc., a child living in a large development or in a row of townhouses is likely to encounter a larger pool of other children from which to select his or her playmates, companions, and friends (see the chapter by Van Vliet — , this volume).

Furthermore, apart from greater opportunity for choice and selectivity under high-density conditions, the latter provide at least potentially a greater variety of individuals for social interaction of a more casual sort. Thus, a child in a high-density neighborhood is more likely to encounter other children differing in socioeconomic, ethnic, and religious backgrounds than a child in a rural setting. Applied to residential settings, this factor is attenuated by the prevailing tendency to homogenization of the inhabitants of a given neighborhood or development; thus the relatively high density to be found in a modern high-rise apartment house near the center of the city does not guarantee socioeconomic diversity, and in fact generally the opposite would be true, due to the social and economic constraints on choice of living quarters. Nevertheless, even a child from an upper-middle class apartment in the city is more likely to come into contact with others from other backgrounds, on the playground, in school, and on streets, buses, etc., than the average small-town or suburban child.

*D. Diversity of Settings and Facilities.* A further advantage conferred by high density is that the more concentrated the population is, the greater the variety of services, settings, and facilities that it has to offer. Accordingly, considering recreational opportunities for instance, it is apparent that a city child will have a considerably larger and broader choice of such activities than a child in a rural area or a small town. Where the latter may be limited to a single movie, the former may have a choice of half a dozen or more. Where the latter may be limited to one or a very few hobbies and sports, because of the lack of facilities and opportunities for instruction, etc., the city child may have a much broader array to choose from, and to specialize in. Here again the relationship is only a partial one, since high density is no guarantee of diversity, especially in the face of socioeconomic and perhaps cultural factors that may discourage it. Thus the average suburban child is probably in a better position to take part in sports, games, cultural activities, and specialized hobbies or interests than the inner-city child. Yet at the other end it is apparent that the small-town child's opportunities are greatly limited, except to the extent that the media (e.g., TV, hobby magazines and correspondence clubs) as well as travel to other locations may compensate for that limitation.

## DENSITY IN DEVELOPMENTAL PERSPECTIVE

To examine the role of density in the development of the child, let us start out by reviewing the four correlates of density considered in the preceding section. The first — level of intensity of stimulation and activity — refers to density in terms of the qualitative and quantitative aspects of the environmental stimulation impinging on the child, while the remaining three, i.e., resource availability and diversity of peers, settings, and facilities concern the role of density from the standpoint of the physical and social character of the environment, as a setting for particular forms of behavior in an ecological sense.

These two different ways of looking at the role of density, and at environmental influences on behavior in a more general sense, turn out to be differently applicable to children at different stages of their development, the former being of primary importance early in life, while the latter (except perhaps for resource availability) assumes its major role for somewhat older children. The two operate differently in other ways as well; for instance, the nature of adaptation processes, to be discussed further on, appears to be quite different when considered from these two perspectives.

The distinction between these two conceptions of density is related to a model of alternative conceptions of the role of experience in development that I sketched out previously (Wohlwill, 1973). For our present purposes, the essential feature of that model consists of a differentiation between experience considered as stimulation to which the individual is exposed versus experience as behavior supported by or elicited in a given physical or social setting. Thus, at one extreme, the environment may affect the organism simply by virtue of the physical stimulation it provides for it, independently of any specific behavioral response to it. This conception of environmental stimulation derives from the work of Hebb (1949) and his followers and was subsequently adapted for developmental psychologists by Hunt (1961, 1979). In its original form it views the organism as an essentially passive recipient of stimulation, although that passivity is modulated by the ability of an ambulatory individual to respond selectively to environmental stimuli, by seeking out or approaching some, while avoiding others. At the other extreme, the environment may be conceived of as a support for, or inhibitor of certain behaviors, which are not specifically related to the particular character of the environment, but merely demand a certain context, defined within generally quite broad limits, to be exhibited. The latter applies to most motor behaviors, and possibly to the development of a variety of cognitive, verbal and perhaps even social skills as well.

These two opposing conceptions of experience should be considered as ideal types, which in practice will occur in different mixes and take on a variety of intermediate forms. There is, furthermore, a third variety, which in the earlier paper was treated as a variant of the second, in that experience is still considered as behavior, but is sufficiently different from the second to warrant separate consideration. This is behavior that is governed by feedback from the environment (which is not involved in the case of the second type), and in particular feedback from other human beings with whom the individual interacts (see Wohlwill, 1983). It is interesting to point out the correspondence between these differing views of experience and its role in the development of the child, on the one hand, and different theoretical accounts of effects of density on behavior generally.

First, at the level of experience as exposure to stimulation, we find interpretations of density effects in terms of amount and intensity of social stimulation, and the arousal and stress responses that may be evoked by too high levels of such stimulation (cf. Aiello, Epstein, & Karlin, 1975; Evans, 1978). Other similar accounts of crowding phenomena are Milgram's (1970) account of life in urban areas in terms of a postulated overload of social stimuli, and Altman's (1975) interpretation of crowding, based on an individual's need to regulate amount of social interaction. Yet, in spite of the popularity of these essentially negative views of crowding, it should be noted that the assumption that high levels of density necessarily result in high arousal, or stress, is far from generally accepted (cf. Freedman, 1975). The possibility that correlations between high density and stress-like behavior under field conditions may be mediated by other nonsocial factors (e.g., noise; traffic congestion; even lack of greenery) must also be entertained, especially in the light of evidence from survey research on residents of high-density environments (Carson, 1972). On the other hand, arousal has figured prominently in interpretations of the effects of sensory deprivation and isolation (e.g., Suedfeld, 1969; Zuckerman, 1969), suggesting that this concept may provide a link between impacts of both very high and very low levels of density, at least in their effects on adults.

The second conception of experience, as a context and support for the development of behavior, bears some relationship to the behavioral ecologist's conception of the role of environment, in terms of behavior settings, as formulated by Barker (1968) and his co-workers, although it must be noted that that conception places a far greater emphasis on the demand character of a behavioral setting as a deterministically operating influence on behavior. Its application to density-related questions has taken the form of the theory of over- vs. undermanning, introduced by Barker and Gump (1964), and developed by Wicker (1978), which considers numbers of people, not in terms of their distribution over a given area, but rather over a set of roles they are required to perform. Thus a crowded setting is one that, paradoxically, is apt to result in undermanning, that is, a shortage of persons to perform the services or functions required by the people frequenting the setting (cf. Wicker & Kirmeyer, 1976).[4]

The third view of experience, focusing on feedback from the child's behavior, especially as provided by other persons, is probably most relevant to the *proxemics* interpretation of crowding, in terms of spatial interrelationships among individuals, and their spatially determined behaviors (Hall, 1966). The emphasis here tends to be on the concept of personal distance regulating the interaction among persons across space, and on those of territoriality defense, governing the individual's personalized definition and use of space. Seen from this perspective, density is of relevance primarily in affecting interpersonal distance, and mainly in terms of the negative effects of high conditions of density, i.e., crowding. Much of the work that has been based on this perspective has emphasized both the situational and the cultural determination of manifestations of crowding (the other end of the dimension having been virtually ignored, except in Altman's theory). The combined focus on situational and cultural factors has been less favorable to the integration of this work with the field of developmental psychology.

Let us return to the three conceptions of experience, and consider how they can help elucidate the different ways in which density may affect the devel-

---

[4]Undermanning, as used by Wicker and Kirmeyer, might seem to be related to Milgram's concept of social overload, in the sense that both are dealing with an overtaxing of an individual's ability to process information resulting from high rates of contact with other persons (particularly strangers). Yet the framework of the two conceptions is quite different, since Wicker and Kirmeyer, as behavioral ecologists, are mainly concerned with role performance, such as that of a park ranger attempting to perform his or her duties in a crowded park, while Milgram is more concerned with incidental social interactions among individuals responding, or failing to respond to one another as persons.

oping child at different points of its development. First, from an early age on, the conditions of residential density in the child's environment can be expected to have a considerable effect on the amount, level and variety of incoming environmental stimulation. Of these aspects, variety is perhaps the most important, especially at the deprivation end. (An *absolute* absence of stimulation is virtually unknown outside of the laboratory, and even there research on sensory deprivation has conclusively shown that it is lack of diversity, or of patterned stimulation, rather than of stimulation per se, that is the critical variable — cf. Zubek, 1969). At the opposite end of the continuum, on the other hand, it is probably not a surfeit of amount or diversity of stimulation that constitutes the major problem; we should generally be concerned rather about either too high levels of intensity of focal stimuli, or about too high amounts of background stimulation, potentially interfering with the child's ability to attend to focal information-laden stimuli (Heft, 1979). Viewed from this perspective, very low-density environments, such as that of an isolated farm, probably exert effects mainly through the relative absence of stimulus variation, while high-density environments, such as that of an inner-city tenement, may create problems for a child through an excess of background stimulation, emanating both from other near-by human beings, and from such sources as television, street noise, etc.

There is considerable evidence, discussed in more detail by Heft, that these qualities of stimulation correlated with density are of particular importance in early life, and indeed during the period of infancy — much of this evidence coming from the work of Wachs that has been repeatedly referred to above. Note that during this early period it is the home environment that is the most important, if only because so much of the infant's life is spent indoors; thus we would expect fewer differences between rural and urban settings in this respect, since as already noted, crowding, and the associated stimulus variables such as noise, may be almost equally prevalent in both settings.

As the child develops and comes to penetrate, in the behavioral ecologists' sense, an increasing diversity of behavior settings in its community (Wright, 1956; cf. also Moore & Young, 1978), the second sense of experience, i.e., as providing opportunities for or constraints on behavior, assumes increasing importance. Here the positive function of high-density environments, that of increasing the diversity of settings available to the child, comes to the fore, although it is apparent that what matters now is density at the level of neighborhood and community, rather than that of residential areas. Similarly it is this aspect of experience that is most directly implicated in the role played by the *connectedness* of the child's environment with the outside world, as discussed earlier in this chapter.

Finally, as regards the third variety of experience, that of providing feedback to the individual's own responses, this is probably of greatest importance in the realm of language development and of skills dependent on language, as well as in the area of social development, and the formulation of a sense of self (cf. Mead, 1934). It can be expected to operate at any point of the child's development, but increasingly so following infancy and early childhood, as language comes to control behavior.[5] But it is plausible to suppose that a principle of diminishing returns sets in as regards the role of density in increasing such feedback. That is, conditions of relatively severe isolation may act to retard language and social development (see Hollos, 1975; Hollos & Cowan, 1973), but a small town or suburb is probably as effective as an urban environment for providing social experience. Indeed, according to Milgram's (1970) account of the impact of urban environments on people, at conditions of very high density the individual adopts a variety of strategies to keep the amount of social contact with others within manageable bounds, and thus the amount of social-stimulation feedback may not increase apace.

*Adaptation to Conditions of Density Through Development.*    The study of functional relationships between environmental conditions such as those associated with particular levels of density and behavior is complicated by the pervasive tendency of the individual to adapt (within certain limits of tolerance) to any condition maintained for a sufficient period of time. Thus it is quite uncertain whether one should expect to find consistent differences in behavioral functioning between long-term residents of areas of contrasting levels of density. The actual evidence on adaptation to conditions of density is scant, and what little there is is not too consistent (cf. Sundstrom, 1978, pp. 51–54); above all, there are virtually no comparisons among groups that have been exposed for several years or more to different degrees of density. The very fact, furthermore, that effects of residential crowding are so difficult to establish in adults (cf. Booth, 1975), tends to point in the direction of adaptation overriding possible short-term effects. Here, as elsewhere, it appears that long-term environmental experience serves to establish an adaptation level that acts to neutralize the individual's affective response to his or her environmental conditions (see Wohlwill, 1974; Wohwill & Kohn, 1976).

At the same time the limited evidence that we have leaves one with the impression that young children may be more susceptible to effects of crowding, and possibly to negative effects of isolation as well, presumably just because for them adaptation has not had an opportunity to occur. This may be particularly so for direct stimulation effects associated with density, such as congestion and activity-level, and noise; again, the results found by Wachs in infancy relating to these dimensions are suggestive. Clearly this is an issue that is at once of major theoretical and practical importance.

---

[5]It is surely significant that studies of the impact of cultural isolation, such as those carried out in Appalachia (Anastasi & Foley, 1958), have almost invariably found a cumulative deficit phenomenon, with the youngest children (up to the time they enter school) being relatively unaffected.

In the preceding discussion we have implicitly treated adaptation as an essentially passive process of "becoming used to" some environmental condition, or to be more precise, as a gradual attenuation of the organism's response to a stimulus as a function of prolonged exposure to it. This conception of adaptation is most relevant to the first of the three models of experience differentiated above, i.e., its stimulation function.

There is another, more active way for an organism to adapt to a situation, namely, by altering its behavior or acquiring new forms of behavior that are maximally congruent with the nature and demands of the situation. Nor is this exclusively a matter of making behavior conform to the situation; frequently the individual may have an opportunity to alter the situation to foster such congruence, and especially to select out situations calculated to optimize it, or even to escape from it, if it is unpleasant or stressful (cf. Rohe, 1979). In some previous discussions of environmental adaptation (Sonnenfeld, 1966; Wohlwill, 1974), such environment-altering behavior has in fact been termed *adjustment,* to differentiate it from adaptation, considered as response attenuation or behavioral change.

Terminology aside, however, it is apparent that behaviors of both types may be adaptive in a larger, functional sense, i.e., of lessening stress and promoting survival and well-being. Adaptation in this broader sense may be demonstrated with respect to the second and third modes of experience discussed above. Thus, a high-density environment may well provide greater opportunities for diverse behaviors (and conversely, according to the behavioral ecologists, fewer opportunities for deep penetration into a given behavior setting, due to over-manning). Yet the main effect may be that, as children grow older, they will come to terms with and become attuned to both the opportunities and the limitations of their environment, and develop a behavior repertoire consonant with their particular "niche" and its ecological demands and potentialities. Much of the work of the human ecologists comparing behavior patterns in different cultures appears to suggest such a notion of adaptation, leading one to view behavioral differences related to density more in terms of qualitative differences than in terms of superiority or inferiority.

The same appears to apply to the third variety of experiential effects associated with density, related to the feedback factor, and specifically to density of interaction with others, as this affects verbal and social development. Here again the work of Haggard (1973), Hollos (1975) and others suggests that children may develop in different directions, according to the demands as well as limitations of their particular environment, which will favor some skills and abilities while inhibiting others. This conception too is closer to the notion of selective adaptation to a particular "niche" than to that of pervasive, across-the-board effects of environmental conditions. More specifically, from a developmental standpoint, it suggests that density may determine the direction of a given child's development, i.e., along some individual-difference dimension, more than its status on some developmental scale of level of attainment.

Here we find processes of adaptation shading over into the broader realm of the coping mechanisms through which children come to terms with the various forms of stress, or the "presses" in Murray's (1938) sense, that confront them in their everyday experience. Psychologists have concerned themselves with problems of coping primarily in the context of individual interpersonal relationships, and mostly at the adult level. Yet in such work as Baumrind and Black's (1967) on the development of competence, and of Block and Block (1980) on ego-resiliency, we find frameworks for analyzing the ways in which children cope with sources of stress or challenge in their environment. None of this work, however, has concerned itself with conditions of isolation or crowding, or indeed with any particular environmental circumstances. It remains to be seen how relevant this work will prove to understanding children's adaptation to conditions of a paucity of other persons (isolation), or of a surfeit of them (crowding)—conditions which involve only in part, if at all, processes of interpersonal functioning.

Let us note one particular aspect of this question that is deserving of attention. This is the tendency of individuals to seek out environments conducive to their well-being, to their goals, needs and perferences. Such behavior may, on the other hand, constitute a means of temporary escape from conditions of density, whether at the isolation or the crowding end, that are experienced as aversive. On the other hand, such behavior may also bring about such conditions, i.e., an individual may select an environment that will satisfy certain aims, but at the expense of subjecting him or her to crowding or isolation. This point brings out both the importance of studying children's environmental exploration, as the Schoggens analyze it in their chapter in this volume, and doing so in a developmental framework, so as to take account of the increasing ability of the developing child to engage in such behavior, and to progressively enlarge its territorial range (see Moore & Young, 1978).

It should be reiterated, in conclusion, that systematic work with children on the effects of different conditions of density, at either end of that dimension, is quite limited, and that much research needs to be done, not only to obtain a clearer picture of the major facts in this area, but to choose among alternative models for viewing its differential expression at different developmental levels. Once such work becomes available, it should clarify further the operation of adaptation processes at different ages, and the different forms that such processes may take. The interest of this question for developmental theory hardly needs belaboring. Since it is of at least equal interest in terms of its practical import—as is brought out in some of the other chapters, and more directly in the concluding one—one may hope that the pace of research on this problem will show a significant increase in the years ahead.

# REFERENCES

Aiello, J. R., Epstein, Y. M., & Karlin, R. A. Effects of crowding on electrodermal activity. *Sociological Symposium,* 1975, *14,* 43-57.

Aiello, J. R., Nicosia, G., & Thompson, D. E. Physiological, social and behavioral consequences of crowding on children and adolescents. *Child Development,* 1979, *50,* 195-202.

Altman, I. *The environment and social behavior.* Monterey, Calif.: Brooks Cole, 1975.

Anastasi, A., & Foley, J. P. Jr. *Differential psychology: Individual and group differences in behavior.* 3rd ed. New York: Macmillan, 1958.

Barker, R. G. *Ecological psychology.* Stanford, Calif.: Stanford University Press, 1968.

Barker, R., & Gump, P. V. *Big school, small school.* Stanford, Calif.: Stanford University Press, 1964.

Baumrind, D., & Black, A. E. Socialization practices associated with dimensions of competence in preschool boys and girls. *Child Development,* 1967, *38,* 291-327.

Block, J. H., & Block, J. The role of ego-control and ego-resiliency in the organization of behavior. In W. A. Collins (Ed.), *Minnesota symposia on child psychology,* Vol. 13. Hillsdale, N.J.: Lawrence Erlbaum Associates, 1980, 39-102.

Booth, A. *Urban crowding and its consequences.* New York: Holt, Rinehart & Winston, 1976.

Brunswik, E. *Perception and the experimental design of psychological experiments.* Berkeley, Calif.: University of California Press, 1956.

Canada Mortgage and Housing Corporation. *Housing Canada's children: A data base.* Ottawa: 1979.

Carson, D. H. Residential descriptions and urban threats. In J. F. Wohlwill & D. H. Carson (Eds.), *Environment and the social sciences: Perspectives and applications.* Washington, D.C.: American Psychological Association, 1972. Pp. 154-168.

Cole-Ramanujam, T. C. *The effects of density and resource availability on children's behavior.* Unpublished M. S. Thesis, The Pennsylvania State University, 1980.

Evans, G. W. Human spatial behavior: The arousal model. In A. Baum & Y. M. Epstein (Eds.), *Human response to crowding.* Hillsdale, N.J.: Lawrence Erlbaum Associates, 1978. Pp. 283-302.

Fiske, D. W., & Maddi, S. R. A conceptual framework. In D. W. Fiske & S. R. Maddi (Eds.), *Functions of varied experience.* Homewood, Ill.: Dorsey, 1961. Pp. 11-56.

Freedman, J. L. *Crowding and behavior.* San Francisco: Freeman, 1975.

Galle, O. R., Gove, W. R., & McPherson, J. W. Population density and pathology: What are the relationships for man? *Science,* 1972, *176,* 23-30.

Haggard, E. A. Some effects of geographic and social isolation in natural settings. In J. E. Rasmussen (Ed.), *Man in isolation and confinement.* Chicago: Aldine, 1973. Pp. 99-144.

Hall, E. T. *The hidden dimension.* Garden City, N.Y.: Doubleday, 1966.

Hebb, D. O. *The organization of behavior.* New York: Wiley, 1949.

Heft, H. Background and focal environmental conditions of the home and attention in young children. *Journal of Applied Social Psychology,* 1979, *9,* 47-69.

Hollos, M., & Cowan, F. A. Social isolation and cognitive development: Logical operations and role-taking abilities in three Norwegian social settings. *Child Development,* 1973, *44,* 630-641.

Hollos, M. Logical operations and role-taking abilities in two cultures: Norway and Hungary. *Child Development,* 1975, *46,* 638-649.

Hunt, J. McV. *Intelligence and experience.* New York: Ronald, 1961.

Hunt, J. McV. Psychological development: Early experience. *Annual Review of Psychology,* 1979, *30,* 103-144.

Hutt, C., & Vaizey, M. J.   Differential effects of group density on social behavior. *Nature,* 1966, *209,* 1371–1372.

Loo, C. M.   The effects of spatial density on the social behavior of children. *Journal of Applied Social Psychology,* 1972, *2,* 372–381.

Mead, G. H.   *Mind, self and society.* Chicago: University of Chicago Press, 1934.

Milgram, S.   The experience of living in cities. *Science,* 1970, *167,* 1461–1468.

Moore, R., & Young, D.   Childhood outdoors: Towards a social ecology of the landscape. In I. Altman & J. F. Wohlwill (Eds.), *Human behavior and environment:* Vol. 3: *Children and the environment.* New York: Plenum, 1978. Pp. 83–130.

Murray, H. A.   *Explorations in personality.* New York: Oxford University Press, 1938.

Rasmussen, J. (Ed.).   *Man in isolation and confinement.* Chicago: Aldine, 1973.

Rohe, W.   *Attitudinal, behavioral, and health correlates of residential density and housing type.* Unpublished Ph.D. Dissertation, The Pennsylvania State University, 1979.

Rohe, W., & Patterson, A. H.   The effects of varied levels of resources and density on behavior in a day care center. In D. H. Carson (Ed.), *EDRA 5: Man-environment interactions.* Vol. 12: *Childhood city* (R. Moore, ed.). Washington, D.C.: Environmental Design Research Association, 1974. Pp. 161–171.

Smith, P. K., & Connolly, K. J.   Patterns of play and social interaction in preschool children. In N. B. Jones (Ed.), *Ethological studies of child behavior.* Cambridge, England: Cambridge University Press, 1972.

Sonnenfeld, J.   Variable values in space landscape: An inquiry into the nature of environmental necessity. *Journal of Social Issues,* 1966, *22* (4), 71–82.

Stokols, D.   On the distinction between density and crowding. *Psychological Review,* 1972, *79,* 275–277.

Stokols, D.   The experience of crowding in primary and secondary environments. *Environment and Behavior,* 1976, *8,* 49–86.

Stokols, D.   A typology of crowding experiences. In A. Baum & Y. M. Epstein (Eds.), *Human response to crowding.* Hillsdale, N.J.: Lawrence Erlbaum Associates, 1978. Pp. 219–255.

Suedfeld, P.   Theoretical formulations, II. In J. P. Zubek (Ed.), *Sensory deprivation: Fifteen years of research.* New York: Appleton-Century Crofts, 1969. Pp. 433–448.

Suedfeld, P.   *Restricted environmental stimulation: Research and clinical applications.* New York: Wiley, 1980.

Sundstrom, E.   Crowding as a sequential process: Review of research on the effects of population density on humans. In A. Baum & Y. M. Epstein (Eds.), *Human response to crowding.* Hillsdale, N.J.: Lawrence Erlbaum Associates, 1979. Pp. 31–116.

U.S. Bureau of the Census.   *Statistical abstract of the United States, 1979.* Washington, D.C.: U.S. Government Printing Office, 1979.

Wachs, T. D.   The optimal stimulation hypothesis and early development: Anybody got a match? In I. C. Uzgiris & F. Weizmann (Eds.), *The structuring of experience.* New York: Plenum, 1977. Pp. 153–178.

Wachs, T. D.   Proximal experience and early cognitive-intellectual development: The physical environment. *Merrill-Palmer Quarterly,* 1979, *25,* 3–41.

Wachs, T. D., Uzgiris, I. C., & Hunt, J. McV.   Cognitive development in infants of different age levels and from different environmental backgrounds: An exploratory investigation. *Merrill-Palmer Quarterly,* 1971, *17,* 283–317.

Wicker, A. W.   *An introduction to ecological psychology.* Monterey, Calif.: Brooks-Cole, 1978.

Wicker, A. W., & Kirmeyer, S.   From church to laboratory to national park: A program of research on excess and insufficient populations in behavior settings. In Wapner, S., Cohen, S. B., & Kaplan, B. (Eds.), *Experiencing the environment.* New York: Plenum, 1976. Pp. 157–186.

Wohlwill, J. F. The concept of experience: S or R? *Human Development,* 1973, *16,* 90–107.

Wohlwill, J. F. Human adaptation to levels of environmental stimulation. *Human Ecology,* 1974, *2,* 127–147.

Wohlwill, J. F. Physical and social environment as factors in development. In D. Magnusson & V. L. Allen (Eds.), *Human development: An interactional perspective.* New York: Academic Press, 1983. Pp. 111–129.

Wohlwill, J. F., & Heft, H. Environments fit for the developing child. In H. McGurk (Ed.), *Ecological factors in human development.* Amsterdam: North-Holland, 1977. Pp. 125–137.

Wohlwill, J. F., & Kohn, I. Dimensionalizing the environmental manifold. In S. Wapner, S. B. Cohen, & B. Kaplan (Eds.), *Experiencing the environment.* New York: Plenum, 1976. Pp. 19–54.

Wright, H. F. Psychological development in Midwwest. *Child Development,* 1956, *27,* 265–286.

Zlutnick, S., & Altman, I. Crowding and human behavior. In J. F. Wohlwill & D. H. Carson (Eds.), *Environmental and the social sciences: Perspectives and applications.* Washington, D.C.: 1972. Pp. 44–60.

Zubek, J. P. (Ed.), *Sensory deprivation: Fifteen years of research.* New York: Appleton-Century Crofts, 1969.

Zuckerman, M. Theoretical foundations, I. In J. P. Zubek (Ed.), *Sensory deprivation: Fifteen years of research.* New York: Appleton-Century Crofts, 1969. Pp. 407–432.

Zuckerman, M., Persky, H., Miller, L., & Levin, B. Sensory deprivation versus sensory variation. *Journal of Abnormal Psychology,* 1970, *76,* 76–82.

# 3

# High Residential Density and Perceptual-Cognitive Development: An Examination of the Effects of Crowding and Noise in the Home

Harry Heft
*Denison University*

## INTRODUCTION

In spite of the long-standing interest of psychologists in the relationship between environment and development, it has only been in recent years that investigations have been undertaken to examine the home environment as a context for developmental processes. This recent focus on human development as it is actuated in the home reflects, to some extent, a more general trend in psychology toward research in natural settings. As a result of these analyses, a complex picture is beginning to emerge of the interrelationships among numerous aspects of the home environment and development.

This chapter is a review of some of this research with an emphasis on environmental conditions related to residential density in the home and their impact on perceptual and cognitive development.[1] Although the concept of person density refers to a continuum ranging from low to high levels of this variable, our focus is limited primarily to the effects of high residential density, and in particular, to two of its experiential correlates, crowding and noise. The research examined was selected largely because of its concern with perceptual-cognitive development. However, although psychological variables were used as one criterion for delimiting the scope of this chapter, the purpose of the presentation is to provide an analysis of the home environment, especially with respect to density-related conditions.

Before examining data pertinent to these issues, it will be helpful to provide a *framework* for such an analysis. For this purpose, the initial portion of the

---

[1]The effects of density on social development is examined in the chapters by Aiello and Baum and by van Vliet-- in this volume.

chapter is a discussion of salient dimensions of the home environment. These dimensions have been suggested by a number of field investigations. Drawing on this discussion I then examine the relationship between high residential density and perceptual-cognitive development. A consideration of environmental measurement follows, and in that section a functional approach to environmental description is sketched. The chapter concludes with a brief examination of some issues that require attention in future research.

## DIMENSIONS OF THE HOME ENVIRONMENT: FINDINGS FROM FIELD INVESTIGATIONS

A difficult problem for the psychologist concerned with environment-behavior issues is to devise a framework for conceptualizing the environment. For the developmentalist, this problem translates into a need for an approach permitting an environmental analysis pertinent to developmental concerns. An examination of the extant studies of the home environment, with a focus on environmental variables rather than on outcome measures, reveals a number of dimensions that may identify several classes of environmental factors significant for perceptual-cognitive development. These dimensions prove to be useful in our subsequent analysis of the effects of residential density. The dimensions considered are object versus social features of the environment, focal versus background stimulus information, order versus disorder in the events of the home, and free versus limited opportunities for exploration. We examine each of these in turn.

### Object versus Social Features of the Environment

The most obvious dimension of the environment that might be predicted a priori is the distinction between object versus social features of the environment. Among the former are included toys, furnishings, decorations, books, and pictorial displays such as paintings and posters, as well as sounds from nonsocial sources. Features of the object environment are typically inanimate, although certain types move mechanically. Aspects of the object environment may initially capture the child's attention; however, sustained interaction with object features must be maintained by the child.

Through perceptual exploration, the properties of object features are revealed. For example, by visually inspecting an object while turning it about in the hands, its invariant shape is detected; and by squeezing and mouthing an object, its solidity and taste are perceived. At the same time that children discover object properties through these perceptual activities, children also learn that they themselves can be the *source* of change in the environment. New sights and sounds can be produced, and reproduced, by their actions on the environment. Perceptual activities which create change in the environment *simultaneously* provide children with information about object properties and about their own efficacies (J. J. Gibson, 1979). For instance, by dropping or banging an object on a surface, children discover both the sound-producing potential of the object and their ability to create that sound. Information about one's ability to control or to effect change in the environment fosters further development of such skills, and this aspect of psychological functioning is often called competence, after White (1959). Certain objects give rise to especially interesting and unexpected changes contingent on some action by the child, and consequently, these objects may facilitate the development of competence. Examples of such objects are rattles, jack-in-the boxes, and busy boxes. Objects with this characteristic are typically referred to as being response-contingent or feedback toys, although most manipulatable objects have this property to some degree.

The social environment includes parents, siblings, and others present in the home. In contrast to most objects, people often initiate interaction with children, and people are always animate. Through interaction with people, children learn the distinctive properties of social features of the environment and also discover the degree to which they can control the actions of others. Thus, here, as through interaction with objects, perceptual activities reveal information to children about social features and about their efficacy in interacting with others. In addition, persons, in contrast to objects, afford children the possibility of a continuous, interactive "dialogue." The interactive possibilities with objects are always limited, that is, the "dialogue" has a small, closed-loop. Further, in the case of persons, children may receive incalculable varieties, as well as intensities, of sensory feedback. Finally, people often act as mediators in children's interaction with object features of the environment.[2]

There is some empirical support for drawing the distinction between object and social features of the environment.[3] Yarrow, Rubenstein, and Pederson (1975) assessed the developmental status of 5-month-olds in relation to a wide range of environmental variables. They found that object and social

---

[2]An additional and highly significant aspect of social interaction is the transference of social rules, language, and sociocultural knowledge. The omission of this critical feature of social experience reflects the focus of the paper and not the importance accorded these phenomena.

[3]Some aspects of the home environment do not appear to fit easily into either of these classes. One case of this sort is television. On the one hand, the most prominent characteristic of most television programs is social interaction, but on the other hand, the medium (at this time) is not responsive to the actions of the child. For this latter reason, it is properly considered a feature of the object environment. A more difficult instance of this problem is the computer-based interactive games. Considering the currently heated debate in philosophical circles about the status of artificial intelligence (e.g., Dreyfus, 1979), and also the fact that these games are best suited for older children and adults, we avoid further comment on them at this time.

features of the home were unrelated for the most part, and further that each class of variables was associated with different aspects of development. Similarly, in a factor analytic examination of the Purdue Home Stimulation Inventory—an instrument designed to assess early developmental environments—object features and social features loaded on different factors (Wachs, Francis, & McQuiston, 1979). Finally, if we consider the child's behavior with respect to the environment, differential amounts of time are spent engaged in interaction with objects and people. For example, based on home observations, White, Kaban, Shapiro, and Attanucci (1977) report that children between the ages of 12 and 33 months spend more time involved in activities such as gross and fine motor behavior, and looking about and listening, than they do in clearly social acts, e.g., trying to gain attention, maintaining social contact. These data provide grounds for conceptual distinction between object and social features, and they indicate that these two classes are differentiated by the young child.

Object and social variables have been found to be correlated with a number of indices of child development. An examination of these relationships will provide a more detailed account of the critical stimulus attributes of each class. In a series of studies, Wachs and his colleagues (Wachs, Uzgiris, & Hunt, 1971; Wachs, 1976; Wachs, 1979) examined infant cognitive development, as assessed by Piagetian-derived measures (Uzgiris & Hunt, 1975), in relation to home environment conditions, as reflected on successive editions of the Purdue Home Stimulation Inventory. The object feature variables that were positively correlated with the development measures included variation in decorations, furnishings, and colors in the home generally (Wachs et al., 1971); decorations in the child's room (Wachs, 1976, 1979); access to magazines and books (Wachs et al., 1971; Wachs, 1976); a mobile over the crib (Wachs, 1976, 1979); availability of small, manipulatable objects (Wachs et al., 1971; Wachs, 1976); presence of feedback toys (Wachs et al., 1971, Wachs, 1976, 1979); change in home decorations (Wachs, 1976, 1979); and new toys for the child (Wachs, 1976, 1979).

Several points need to be made with regard to these studies. First, most of these object feature variables were associated with particular developmental measures rather than being globally related to development. This finding has led Wachs (1979) to argue for "environmental specificity" in the analysis of the relationship between the environment and cognitive development. At the same time, however, some object variables were related to a broad range of developmental measures. The most clear-cut case of these was the variable, feedback toys, which was correlated with numerous aspects of development in all three studies. This suggests that some object features have more far-reaching effects than others. Finally, the developmental effects of experience with certain object features may be evidenced for some period of time. In a longitudinal study of cognitive development between 12 and 24 months,

Wachs (1979) found that certain object features assessed at one age were positively correlated with cognitive measures at a later time. To take but one example, the presence of feedback toys in the home during the period 12-14 months was positively associated with foresight tested at 18 and 21 months of age. Similarly, Wachs (1978) found that availability of feedback toys between 12-14, 15-17, 18-20 and 21-23 months, and decorations in the child's room assessed at 12-14, 15-17, and 21-23 months, were all positively correlated with intelligence (Binet scores) measured at 2½ years (31 months).

The possible long-range effects of experience with object features of the home environment is further substantiated in the research of Caldwell and her colleagues, utilizing the environmental inventory Home Observation for Measurement of the Environment (HOME; Caldwell, Heider, & Kaplan, 1966). Opportunities for varied perceptual stimulation and the availability of play materials both assessed at 6 months were positively related to intelligence, as measured by the Binet (Elardo, Bradley, & Caldwell, 1975), and language development (Illinois Test of Psycholinguistic Abilities) at 3 years of age (Elardo, Bradley, & Caldwell, 1977).

Additional evidence for the relationship between the character of object features and perceptual-cognitive development comes from the observational research of Yarrow et al. (1975). With regard to this aspect of the environment, these investigators focused on the play materials available to a sample of 5-month-olds. They found that *variety* of toys was correlated with measures of infant mental and motor development (Bayley scales), cognitive-motivational indices (e.g., visually directed reaching and grasping, secondary circular reactions), exploratory behavior, and preference for novelty. Similarly, *complexity* of available toys was related to cognitive-motivational development and novelty preference, and *contingent responsiveness* of play materials was associated with mental/motor infant development, cognitive-motivational development, exploration, and novelty preference. In general, Yarrow, et al., indicated that play objects appear to make their strongest contribution to the development of exploration and the related function of preference for novel objects.

Collectively, these observational studies point to several aspects of the object environment which appear to play a significant role in the development of the child. Two of these environmental variables are variation in visual stimulus information and availability of manipulatable objects, particularly objects that provide action-contingent feedback. The former, variety in environmental information, provides the child with opportunities to visually inspect and thereby extract those features which differentiate objects. As E. J. Gibson (1969) put it: "Objects . . . are distinguished by their bundle of features. The set of distinctive features that make any object or class of objects unique must be discovered in the course of exposure to other objects" (pp. 341–342). This finding of a relationship between variation in stimulus information of the home environment and perceptual-cognitive development is consistent with controlled rearing experiments using animals and with analyses of institutionalized populations (cf. Hunt, 1961; Thompson & Grusec, 1970).

In the case of the second variable, manipulatable objects, we saw before that opportunities to interact with these types of features facilitate the discovery of object properties and awareness of one's capacity to effect changes in the environment, i.e., competence. Empirical support for the relationship between responsive objects and the development of competence can be gleaned from a number of sources. Yarrow et al. (1975) report a positive correlation between their index of toy responsivity and the cognitive measure secondary circular reactions, which assesses "the infant's repeated efforts to elicit feedback from objects" (p. 98). Watson and Ramey (1972) exposed 3-month-old infants either to a mobile which rotated a few degrees following a certain head movement, a mobile which rotated periodically independent of the child's actions, or a stationary mobile. Following two weeks, ten minutes each day, of these conditions, all infants were placed in a situation where rotation of the mobile could be controlled. Only those infants whose previous actions were efficacious controlled the mobile in this test condition. Those who did not previously receive response-contingent feedback from the mobiles were passive. Finally, Jennings, Harmon, Morgan, Gaiter, and Yarrow (1979) examined the relationship between environmental measures, including responsiveness of toys, and several measures of play. They found that the presence of responsive toys in the home when the child was 6 months old was positively correlated with the tendency of the child at one year to produce visual and auditory effects, e.g., banging noises, during play, and to engage in sustained and continuous play with a toy.

Social aspects of the child's early environment have generally received more attention than have object features. Indeed, it would seem that for many investigators the environment and the caretaking figures are synonymous. This situation is less true today than it once was, and the studies discussed above have contributed to redressing this imbalance. Here we examine just a few aspects of the social environment of the home which appear to have some bearing on perceptual-cognitive development.

In their observational study of the home environments of a sample of five month old infants, Yarrow et al. (1975) examined four categories of caretaker behavior: provision of sensory stimulation, responsiveness to the actions of the child, expression of affect, and mediation of the child's interaction with objects. They found that tactile and kinesthetic stimulation by the mother was often associated with measures of cognitive-motivational development, and more distal sensory stimulation, eye contact and vocalization, was positively related to social responsiveness on the part of the infant. Contingent responses of the mother, especially to the infant's distress cries, were positively correlated with measures of motor and cognitive development, as were expressions of positive affect, smiling, and play with the infant. Social mediation of object interaction was related to goal-directedness and exploratory behavior. In addition, these investigators examined the infant's development in relation to two global measures of maternal behavior. *Level* of social stimulation—the frequency and intensity of the mother's actions toward the child—and *variety* of social stimulation were both positively correlated with indices of cognitive development and social responsiveness.

In addition to sheer sensory stimulation provided to the child, the caretaker's responsiveness, that is, her participation in a pattern of interaction built on the reciprocal exchange of stimulus information, seems to be a significant variable emerging from these data. This latter characteristic of the social environment appears as a predictor of cognitive development in other studies as well. Elardo et al. (1975) report a positive relation between maternal involvement as well as emotional-verbal responsivity measured at 6, 13, and 24 months with Binet scores at three years. Similarly, these social variables at 6 and 24 months were correlated with language development at age three (Elardo et al., 1977). Clarke-Stewart (1973) found contingent maternal responsiveness at 12 months to be associated with infant cognitive development at 18 months. However, Jennings et al. (1979) report that maternal play with the infant and contingent responding to the infant's vocalization were inversely correlated with production of effects during free play. They interpret these relationships as indicating that high levels of feedback during social play may result in fewer attempts to obtain response-contingent feedback from the object environment, especially when the mother is nearby.

The investigations considered above indicate a positive relationship between the presence of numerous object and social features of the home and perceptual-cognitive development. In a later section of the chapter, we examine the impact of residential density in the home on exploration and interaction with these environmental resources.

## Focal versus Background Stimulus Information

One legacy of Gestalt psychology is a recognition of the significance of relational stimulus information. Perception of qualities such as figure-ground distinctions, achromatic and chromatic color constancy, and object size constancy depend to a great extent on the relation between a stimulus configuration and its surround (cf. Hochberg, 1978). In general, this view points to the significance of context or background for the perception of qualities of a focal feature. The perspective suggests that focal features are never perceived in isolation, but always in relation to a background; the individual perceives both the focal feature and its background. The focal-background distinction is a slippery one, however, because for the most part, it is determined by the attentional focus of the perceiver. What is a focal feature, and its attendant background at one time, may not be at another — in fact this relationship may reverse — as the perceiver focuses on this and then that aspect of the environment.

This dual character of perception, that is, the perception of both focal and background conditions, has been discussed in a functional-neuroanatomical analysis of vision by Trevarthen (1978). He argues that:

> vision of space at large, detected by the whole retina, is mediated through subhemispheric mechanisms; but foveal vision of detail, essential to full conscious perception of the substances of surroundings and of the identities of objects, is mediated by a hemispheric or cerebral cortical mechanism. (p. 114).

Such a view suggests that perception of a focal object and of the broader context occurs simultaneously, and certainly this makes good sense from a functional standpoint. The perceiver is able to monitor the environment for potentially significant conditions while focusing on a particular aspect of it. E. J. Gibson and Rader (1979) offer the following illustration of this process:

> The sidewalk may slip in and out of awareness of a window-shopper; usually attention is drawn toward it only where there is some danger. An icy spot or a curb ahead may claim full consciousness, and so attention is turned away from the newest fashions in the store window to the problem of footing. It seems as though unconscious knowledge signals the conscious self to "look out." In fact, despite shifts in awareness, information specifying the spatial layout is constantly monitored by the perceptual-cognitive system. . . . The shopper is unaware of and yet responding to information necessary for walking. It seems that as long as the perceptual-motor act can continue at an automatic level it will. For this to occur the motor function must be well practiced and the perceptual information very regular. (p. 10).

As this passage indicates, although background may be continually monitored, it will not affect focal exploration unless there is a suggestion of potentially critical information. Functionally significant conditions in the background may be specified by unexpected sights in the peripheral field of vision or unanticipated sounds, as well as by sights and sounds of particular salience such as movement or hearing one's name. Additionally, background conditions may affect inspection of focal features if those conditions are particularly obtrusive. For example, loud background sounds may mask focally attended speech sounds. Therefore, although background may *facilitate* the perception of certain qualities of focal features, as in the case of perceptual constancies, background conditions may also *impede* the perception of focal features.

Because background conditions have the potential to draw the child's perceptual activities away from detailed inspection and exploration of a focal feature, or intrude on the focal aspect of attention, consideration of the ambient background is important for environment-development analyses. As noted earlier, interaction with object and social features of the environment contribute to development. Disruption of this process of exploration and play may affect development in an adverse manner.

Background conditions of the home include sounds originating from within the home as well as from the exterior, and from activity levels in the home. These variables may be related, in part, to the level of residential density in the home, and we consider evidence pertinent to this point in a later section. Some empirical support for the distinction between background and focal conditions can be found in Heft (1979). In an analysis of the home environment, *background* conditions were assessed in terms of a composite score including noise level, summed across four sources of noise; activity level, comprised of the items of general activity in the home and frequency of interruptions in the child's play; and assessments of the degree of overlapping sound and unexpected sounds in the home. Focal conditions were broken down into two types: *variation,* assessed in terms of sheer amount of furniture, decorations, and colors; and *patterning,* which included two estimates of the organization of interior furnishings. A factor analysis of the evaluation of 94 homes utilizing this inventory revealed that background conditions on the one hand, and variation and patterning of focal conditions on the other, loaded on orthogonally distinct factors. Consistent with this finding, a factor analytic study of the items comprising the Purdue Home Stimulation Inventory indicated that variables directed at background noise were independent of those assessing potential focal features, such as toys and books (Wachs et al., 1979).

In summary, theoretical considerations and findings from two field investigations suggest a second dimension that may be utilized in conceptualizing the home environment — the focal-background stimulus information dimension.

## Order versus Disorder in Events of the Home

An often neglected aspect of the environment is its temporal dimension. The environment not only consists of objects and persons, but also *events* which span varying lengths of time (cf. J. J. Gibson, 1979, Chapter 6). In the phenomenal world of the young child the scale of events might range from the fall of a dropped toy to a passing of a day. To understand the structure of an event, it is necessary to perceive the event as it unfolds over time. This is because, as E. J. Gibson (1969) states, "to perceive an event some unity has to be detected over a temporal sequence of stimulation, and only extraction of some invariant rule or relation can give this." (p. 16) Therefore, learning to comprehend events in the environment depends on opportunities to perceive these events over time. At least two factors could disrupt this process: inter-ruptions in the child's following of an event and lack of sufficient structure in the event itself. The former could be attributed to background conditions in the home, which was discussed in the previous section. The latter, relative disorder in the event, is tied to conditions which control the passage of the event. Children can influence, to a degree, events which result from their in-teraction with objects. Other events in the home lay in the control of others, especially caretakers. The likelihood of interruption in perceptually follow-ing an event, and the degree of apparent structure of an event, both may be influenced by the level of residential density in the home. We return to this point later.

To date, the passage of a day has been the only type of event examined in the literature, and order or regularity in daily occurrences has been found to be related to measures of development. Specifically, Wachs (1976) found that the routine of both regular naptimes and regular mealtimes was posi-tively correlated with several cognitive development indices based on Pia-getian concepts. Further, regularity of naptimes at 12–14 and 16–17 months was correlated with Binet scores of 2½ years (Wachs, 1978). Regular meal-times also appears as a significant correlate of development, as does the vari-able number of strangers in the home at the time of assessment – an item which might reflect lack of order (Wachs, 1979). Finally, in their observa-tions of the homes of economically disadvantaged children whose academic performance was below average, Gray and Klaus (1968) remark that these en-vironments were often characterized by a lack of order in daily activities.[4]

Clearly, the evidence for the developmental significance of this environ-mental dimension is meager at the present time. The event structure of the home environment is a variable that demands consideration in future in-vestigations.

## Free versus Restricted Exploration

A fourth dimension of the home differs from the preceding ones in that it is attributable largely to the effects of social mediation rather than the direct characteristics of the environment. This final dimension that we consider is free versus restricted exploration. In order for children to acquire knowledge about the features and events of the environment, as well as about their competencies in interacting with those features and events, there must be am-

---

[4]Elardo et al., (1975), report positive correlations between their home environment variable, organization of physical and temporal environment, measured at 6, 12, and 24 months and as-sessments of mental development at 6, 12 (Bayley), and 36 months (Binet). However, most of the six items comprising this variable do not relate to order as it is discussed here.

ple opportunity to explore the environment. On their own, children spend much of the day inspecting and exploring the world about them. Their investment in these types of activities is clear in White et al.'s (1977) observations of children between 12 and 33 months of age. On the average during this period, 44% of the children's waking hours were spent in seeking visual and auditory information, exploring the properties of their surroundings, and engaging in motor-mastery activities. With this high motivation to explore, a critical factor for development may be whether these activities are facilitated or impeded.

To a large extent, freedom and restriction in exploration is dependent on the manner in which the caretaker intervenes in this process. One way in which exploration can be limited is through the use of physical restraints and barriers, e.g., cribs, playpens, etc. In this regard, the absence of such restraints has been found to be positively correlated with indices of cognitive development (Wachs, 1976, 1979), as has an interior arrangement which permits looking outdoors (Wachs, 1978, 1979). In contrast to these findings, however, Jennings et al. (1979) report use of barriers in the home to be associated with greater exploration in a laboratory setting.

Exploration can also be restricted through the caretaker's verbal admonitions and behavior interventions. "Avoidance of restriction and punishment," a factor on the HOME inventory which is primarily directed at the caretaker's interpersonal style towards children and their play, was positively correlated with intellectual development at three years (Elardo et al., 1975). Similarly, Jennings et al. (1979) found a negative correlation between maternal prohibitions in the home and the child's production of effects during play at one year of age.

## Summary

A consideration of the recent literature concerning the home environment as a context for development suggests four dimensions on which the home can be examined. One dimension refers to the types of features, object versus social, which are available to the child, and a second points to a distinction between ambient or background conditions and focal features. The character of the background may affect interaction with object and social features. Events in the home, which are inherently temporal in nature, may be relatively structured or unstructured, and this quality of the home constitutes a third environmental dimension. The fourth dimension, free versus restricted exploration, refers primarily to the intervention of the caretaker on the child's activities. This dimensional analysis serves as the backdrop for the central focus of the chapter — an examination of the effects of residential density and its correlates on perceptual-cognitive development.

## THE IMPACT OF HIGH RESIDENTIAL DENSITY
## IN THE HOME ENVIRONMENT

Person density is an index referring to the number of people situated within some spatial unit. Accordingly, measures of density can differ in terms of their grain of analysis; that is, density can be assessed, e.g., in terms of number of people per acre, number of people per housing unit, or number of people per room. In aggregate studies of person density, the most reliable predictor of indices of social pathology appears to be persons per room – an index of density within a single dwelling (Galle, Gove, & McPherson, 1972). However, density measures are not always reliable predictors of behavior and health, and in those instances when density and psychological-biological variables co-vary, it is difficult to determine the basis for these relationships (cf. Epstein & Baum, 1978).

One reason for the ambiguity of positive findings of density-behavior/ health relationships is that density is a *psychologically-neutral* concept. It does not carry any meaning about the impact of density on the individual. Comparable levels of density can be associated with drastically different conditions, and as a result, very different consequences. For example, density at an athletic event or in a bus at rush hour may be numerically similar; experientially these situations are quite different, and so may be their psychological consequences. Therefore, whereas density provides a global index of persons per unit of space, it does not specify the impact of person density on the psychological *processes* which take place in a particular setting.

In order to understand the effects of high person density on psychological processes, it will be necessary to consider the *experiential* correlates of density. First, a given level of density may be experienced, e.g., in terms of a certain number of people in the field of view (Desor, 1972), a certain rate of social interaction (Milgram, 1970), or a certain number of persons relative to the role demands of a setting, i.e., manning (Barker, 1968). These attributes may be viewed as *visual correlates* of high density. They can result in the experience of situational *crowding*, which may affect the individual in various ways, such as generating high levels of arousal (Evans, 1978), feelings of lack of control over desired levels of social interaction (Altman, 1975), reduction in motor activity and play (Loo, 1972, 1979), and frustration over the blocking of goals (Stokols, 1976). Second, associated with varying levels of person density are often, but not invariably, corresponding intensities and complexities of sound. Although a variety of situational and personalistic factors mitigate against a perfect correlation between density and noise, it is probably accurate to say that increasingly high levels of noise accompany higher levels of person density. Thus, density also has an *auditory correlate* in experience, namely, *noise*. Noise conditions may affect the perceiver, e.g., by generating high levels of arousal (Broadbent, 1971), masking speech sounds (Deutsch, 1964), and distracting the individual from other tasks (Turnure, 1970).

We see then that two experiential correlates of density are crowding and noise.[5] It should be recognized, however, that neither is strictly correlated with density. Just as one might feel crowded in the presence of one other person (cf. Altman, 1975), so too one person can generate a high level of noise. Further, unlike crowding, which has density as its only source, noise can originate from circumstances unrelated to density.

Noise that emanates from high density conditions can be measured through the use of physical indices such as decibels and frequency analysis. Like the relation between density measures and crowding effects, physical measures of noise are not always good predictors of the way sonic conditions are experienced (Weinstein, 1976). For this reason, just as density as a mathematical index should be distinguished from the situational experiences referred to by the term crowding, so too physical measures of noise should be distinguished from associated auditory experiences. It may be of value to reinforce this point with a consistent use of terminology. Parallel with the density-crowding distinction, the term *sound* is used to refer to physical measures of sonic conditions, and *noise* is used to refer generically to various aspects of auditory experience, such as loudness, pitch, complexity, and predictability of onset.

When examining the effects of *residential* density in particular, it is important to distinguish between density conditions *inside* the home, and density conditions in the area surrounding or *outside* the home (Zlutnick & Altman, 1972). In the following discussion we address crowding within the residence and noise originating from sources inside the home, as well as noise from exterior sources. The effects of crowding in areas adjacent to the home on, e.g., exploration and play, are treated by Schoggen and Schoggen, this volume.

In this section I examine studies that report a relationship between measures of density and indices of perceptual-cognitive development. By drawing on evidence gathered in a number of settings, including schools, I then offer several hypotheses concerning the processes by which density, as manifested by crowding, may affect perceptual-cognitive development in the home. Similarly, a review of studies demonstrating a relationship between noise and development is presented, followed by a consideration of the manner in which noise may affect development. For the most part, the ensuing discussion is structured with respect to the earlier dimensional analysis of the home environment.

---

[5]A third experiential correlate of high density is *warmth* from the presence of others. The potential effects of this variable in conjunction with crowding has been examined by Griffit and Veitch (1970).

## Residential Density and Perceptual-Cognitive Development

In several studies, comparatively high levels of density within the home — typically assessed by the index persons per room — have been found to be inversely related to perceptual-cognitive development. Wachs (1976) reports that higher levels of residential density were associated with poorer performance on a variety of Piagetian-derived measures of infant development, including object permanence, development of schemes, and verbal imitation. More recently, Wachs (1978, 1979) found density to be inversely related to cognitive development, and it is noteworthy that in many instances, home density measures at one age were negatively correlated with performance at later ages. For example, high levels of density at 12-14 months were inversely related to Binet scores at 31 months (Wachs, 1978) and performance on tests of foresight and schema development administered at 24 months (Wachs, 1979). These findings suggest that high person density in the home may have relatively long-term effects.

The level of person density in the home has also been found to relate to the attentional skills of kindergarten age children (mean age – 5 years 8 months; Heft, 1979). In this study, higher levels of density were negatively correlated with performance on a visual search task, and at the same time, those children from homes with higher densities were less susceptible to auditory distraction. Further, in a recent study Saegert (1980) examined the reading achievement performance of elementary school children (second through sixth grade) who lived in public housing. She found that those children residing in high density apartments had lower vocabulary scores on the reading test when performance was examined in relation to both average scores for grade level and average scores for the child's own class.[6]

Finally, density in the home has been linked to the development of feelings of efficacy or control over environmental conditions. In the first of two experiments, Rodin (1976) found the children (6 to 9 years old) from high density homes were less likely to control reward outcomes in an operant learning paradigm, than were their counterparts from homes with lower densities. In the second study, the effects of working on an insolvable or solvable task were examined in relation to subsequent task performance for a group of junior high school age children. Presumably, experience with an insolvable task could lead to feelings of inability to control environmental events, which would be reflected in later performance. It was found that prior exposure to the insolvable problem resulted in lower scores on the subsequent task, and this effect was especially apparent for children who lived in high density residences.

---

[6]A more complete description of this investigation can be found in Aiello and Baum, this volume.

In combination, these studies point to a number of possible developmental *outcomes* of high residential density. In order to understand the *process* by which density affects perceptual-cognitive development, it is necessary to consider the impact of psychological correlates of density, notably crowding and noise, on development in the home environment. Unfortunately, there is little evidence available from home investigations which speaks to the issue of the direct effects of high person density on perceptual-cognitive development. As a result, in the following discussion we hypothesize likely consequences based on our earlier dimensional analysis, and extrapolate from investigations conducted in e.g., school settings, as means of supplementing the existing data from home studies.

## Effects of Crowding on Early Home Experiences: Process Considerations

First, a caveat. Discussions of crowding are complicated by the fact that contrasting levels of density can be a result of either differing amounts of available space given a fixed number of individuals, or differing numbers of persons given a fixed amount of space. These two types of relative density have been called spatial and social density, respectively (McGrew, 1970). Since the effects of high spatial versus social density have been found to differ somewhat (Baum & Koman, 1976; Loo & Kennelly, 1979; McGrew, 1970), it would seem to be important to keep this distinction in mind in analyses of crowding. While factors such as room size and group size are relatively simple to control in laboratory investigations, when we turn to field studies of crowding in residences, the problem of separating spatial and social densities becomes difficult indeed. Not only do homes vary in size of rooms, number of rooms, overall layout — to name just a few potentially important environmental factors — families vary in size, composition, age distribution of children, all of which may well contribute to exacerbating or mitigating crowding effects. One attempt to recognize some of these complexities is the concept of family density (Parke & Sawin, 1979), which refers to *family size* relative to size, i.e., square footage, of the home. Clearly, we need more detailed examination of these variables to better understand crowding in home environments. Bearing in mind these complicating factors, let us proceed with a consideration of crowding in the home and perceptual-cognitive development.

*Exploration and Play with Object Features.* As we have seen, exploration and play with object features of the environment assume a critical role in perceptual-cognitive development. Conditions in the home associated with crowding may affect these activities in several ways. First, the number and variety of objects that the child interacts with may be lessened in a crowded residence to the extent that the available objects in the home are shared by a large number of siblings. While there is no direct evidence for a relationship between relative scarcity of object features as a function of family size and development, Wachs (1976) found that the number of siblings in a household was negatively correlated with measures of cognitive development at two years. This finding is, at best, very indirect evidence for this relationship. It should be noted, however, that there is some indication that scarcity of resources due to high density is related to aggressive acts of children directed at objects and persons (Aiello & Baum, this volume; Rohe & Patterson, 1974).

Second, the child's exploration of object features is more likely to be disrupted in crowded conditions. The discovery of object properties, as well as learning about one's competencies in interaction with objects, often requires sustained periods of examination and play. However, activities of others can interrupt these goal-directed actions, and in crowded conditions such occurrences may not be uncommon, as Loo (1972) observed in a study of play under varying conditions of density. Indirect support for the relationship between residential crowding and disruption of activities is provided by the finding that children living in high density conditions often report "being bothered by others" in the home (Saegert, 1980).

Third, the amount of exploration may be suppressed in a crowded residence. Such a possibility is suggested by the findings that crowding among groups of young children is associated with lower levels of motor activity (Loo, 1972; Smith & Connolly, 1972). A reduction in motoric play in crowded conditions may account for Shapiro's (1974) report of a negative correlation between residential density and development of motor skills among boys. Similarly, degree of involvement in toy play may be a function of level of crowding. Children in crowded settings have been found to engage in less active toy play and to interact with fewer number of toys (Loo, 1979; Loo & Smetana, 1978).

The amount of exploration can also be affected by restrictions imposed on children. As the level of density in a home increases, young children are more likely to intrude on the activities of family members, and for this reason their explorations may be curtailed by others. Limitations may be imposed through verbal and behavioral disciplining. The reports of greater use of punitive measures in crowded circumstances may reflect, to some extent, attempts by parents to regulate the exploration of their children (Newson & Newson, 1963; Roy, 1950). Further, the activities of children may be restricted through use of physical barriers such as closed doors. Parke and Sawin (1979) indicate that bathroom doors are closed more often in crowded homes, and it is possible that this trend toward more stringent boundary regulation in crowded conditions is applicable to other areas of the home as well.

In sum, exploration and play with object features of the home environment may be influenced by crowded conditions in the following ways: the availability of objects may be affected by the number of persons sharing play resources; sustained exploration and play may be interrupted more frequently; and the amount of exploration may be reduced as a result of suppression of motor activity and restrictions imposed on the child. Since many of these factors are derived from developmental research carried out in settings other than the home, more direct evidence needs to be gathered for their support.

*Interaction with Social Features.*    The child's social experiences in the home contribute to the development of a wide range of perceptual and cognitive skills. We have briefly considered a few of these characteristics earlier in this chapter. The quantity and quality of these interactions may be adversely affected by conditions of crowding in the home. Consider, for instance, the frequency and intensity of caretaker-infant interaction as a function of family size. The greater number of family members who require close attention, the less amount of time can be spent with an individual child. Further, caretaking demands from many individuals probably means less involvement in any single episode of social interaction. It may be recalled that the number of siblings in the home was inversely related to several developmental indices (Wachs, 1976). Also, the factor of a high child-to-caretaker ratio has previously been pointed to as a significant characteristic of institutions whose infants lagged behind their peers (cf. Thompson & Grusec, 1970). While it might be supposed that this problem could be mitigated by distributing caretaking responsibilities among adults and older children in the home, Wachs (1976) has found a negative correlation between number of caretakers in the home and several measures of infant cognitive development.

In addition, the amount of social interaction by the child is apparently reduced in crowded circumstances. Investigators who have observed young children in crowded play situations have frequently reported a drop in social interaction and an increase in solitary play (Hutt & Vaizey, 1966; Loo, 1972; McGrew, 1970; Preiser, 1972). However, these investigations were conducted among groups of unrelated children. Whether these same findings would obtain in a crowded familial setting needs to be determined.

*Order in Event Structure and Level of Activity.*    In our dimensional analysis of the home, it was suggested that two factors could impede the perception of events in the home: first, lack of structure in the event itself, and second, interruptions or distractions in following the course of an event. Conditions of high person density can lead to both of these complications. In the case of the former, structure of the large scale event, the passage of a day, can be determined by the regularity or predictability of salient occurrences in the home, such as mealtimes, and this latter characteristic of the event structure may be directly affected by family size. The larger the family, the more difficult it may be for the caretaker to maintain a regular schedule of activities. With regard to developmental concerns, we noted above that irregular scheduling of mealtimes and naptimes has been found to be inversely related to measures of infant cognitive development (Wachs, 1976, 1978, 1979).

Perceived order and predictability in events of the home may also play a role in the development of feelings of control vis à vis the environment. In the area of environmental stressor research, prior experience in being unable to anticipate the onset of a stressor is seen to result in the behavioral disposition of helplessness (Glass & Singer, 1972). It has been suggested that crowding generates feelings of passivity in the face of environmental events (Baron & Rodin, 1978; Baum, Aiello, & Calesnick, 1979), and in this regard, children from high density homes have been found to exert less control in a laboratory setting (Rodin, 1976). These learned helplessness effects may be attributable, at least in part, to disorder and unpredictability in the event structure of the home as a consequence of crowding.

In addition, the relative difficulty of perceiving a particular event over time may be a function of the co-presence of other potentially distracting events in the field of view. In crowded conditions, the spatial proximity of temporally overlapping activities of family members may make the extraction of a single event, e.g., interaction between the parents, very difficult for children. Here they would be confronted with the challenge of following a dynamic event in the context of other dynamic events. This consideration points to the role of activities in the home as a visual *background* for focal exploration and play, and the kinetic quality of this background may pose special problems for children. Movements in the environment are very salient for a perceiver, and this may be especially true for young children. Unexpected motion in the periphery of the visual field typically results in orienting responses and, consequently, distraction from focal tasks. Because sustained examination of environmental features and events is a significant developmental activity, frequent distraction from focal investigations during early childhood may well have adverse effects on cognitive growth. Unfortunately, there is no *direct* evidence for the effects of complexity in event structure and of activity level as impediments to focal perceptual exploration. However, these environmental variables may account for the finding that high levels of activity in the home are negatively associated with indices of cognitive development in infants (Wachs, 1976, 1979; Wachs et al., 1971).

## Residential Noise and Perceptual-Cognitive Development

*Evidence from Field Studies.*    The ambient sound level in a residence is a product of sources located both within and external to the home. Interior sources of noise include sounds from social activity, appliances, noise-generating toys, television, radio, and phonograph. While it is clear that any of these sources can generate high levels of noise independent of person density, high levels of density are likely to exacerbate these conditions. Sources of noise external to the home include social activity, automobiles, trains, airplanes, and industry. Obviously, depending on the location of the home, high sound levels from any of several of these exterior sources will be more or less likely. Homes situated in an area of high residential density may well be exposed to intense sound from sources such as these. At the same time, however, residents of sparsely populated areas are not immune to such experiences; nearby rail, air, and automobile traffic can result in high sound levels even in isolated locales.

Field investigations over the past several years have begun to reveal some potentially adverse effects of high sound levels on perceptual-cognitive development. Cohen, Glass, and Singer (1973) selected as the site of their research, high-rise apartment buildings located directly over an urban expressway. These investigators reasoned that since sound levels from traffic would gradually diminish with building height, any associated effect from noise exposure should correspond to the floor location of the apartment. Specifically, they examined the auditory discrimination and reading abilities of children (grades 2–5) residing in the buildings and found an inverse relationship between floor level and performance on both measures. That is, those children living on the lower floors of the building, and exposed to higher levels of traffic sounds, were relatively deficient in auditory discrimination skills and, to a lesser degree, reading ability, as compared to their counterparts on the upper floors. Two additional points are worth noting. First, the correlation between floor level and reading performance was reduced considerably after scores on the auditory discrimination test were partialled out. This suggests that the lower reading performance of the children in the noisier apartments is attributable, to some extent, to the mediating role played by audition in learning to read. Second, the magnitude of the correlations between floor level and both performance measures increased with the length of time the child had lived in the apartment. This finding points to a progressive deficit from exposure to noise over time.

In their studies of the home as a context for cognitive development, Wachs and his colleagues found a number of noise-related variables to be negatively correlated with their performance measures. These environmental variables are noise from the neighborhood (Wachs et al., 1971); house is noisy and small (Wachs et al., 1971); television is on most of the time (Wachs et al., 1971; Wachs, 1976, 1979); and noise confusion in the home (Wachs et al., 1971; Wachs, 1976, 1978, 1979). This latter variable assessed both level and complexity of noise through a subjective rating made by the home observer. An additional item that was related to several measures of cognitive development referred to whether children had a place in the home to which they could go to be alone (Wachs et al., 1971; Wachs, 1976, 1978, 1979). The investigators described this area as a potential shelter from high levels of noise and activity, and the availability of such a place would allow children to control or modulate, to some extent, their exposure to intensive sensory stimulation. The potentially strong and adverse impact of noise on early cognitive development is suggested by three aspects of these data. First, there is considerable inter-study consistency for most of these variables. Second, in most cases, each of these environmental measures was negatively correlated with several developmental indices. Third, a number of noise ratings obtained at one age were significantly related to development up to one year later. For example, noise confusion ratings betweeen 12 and 14 months were negatively correlated with measures of object permanence at 24 months (Wachs, 1979). Such findings indicate that noise effects may be of more than a transitory nature, and this possibility of long-term effects of noise exposure is consistent with a conclusion of Cohen et al., (1973).[7]

The results of an examination of the relationship between noise in the home and the attentional skills of young children is reported by Heft (1979). The sample consisted of kindergarten age children (average age = 5 years, 8 months) whose homes were located in a number of areas varying in exterior residential density. All children in the sample had lived in their current residences for at least three years. Noise level in the home was assessed by combining ratings obtained through parent interviews concerning four sources of noise: family activities; television, radio, phonograph; appliances; and exterior sources. Noise ratings were found to be correlated with performance on two measures of attention. First, high noise levels were associated with slower response times on a visual search task that required the child to pick out or extract individual items, i.e., black/white drawings, from a stimulus array. At the same time, noise level was inversely related to incidental learning on the same task. In other words, children from noisier homes were less able to extract features selectively from the visual field, and further, were less sensitive to information peripheral to task demands. Their counterparts from relatively quieter homes, with greater facility in extracting information and simultaneously more sensitivity to incidental information, demonstrated a higher level of perceptual skill. Second, analysis of performance on a visual match-to-standard task in quiet and in the presence of an auditory distractor revealed that children from the noisier homes were less affected by the background noise. This attenuated effect of the auditory distractor on the children from noisy homes may indicate adaptation to the

---

[7]Wachs (1978, 1979) also found that males were more adversely affected by noise in the home than females. Similarly, Wachs (1979) reports that measures of home density were correlated primarily with the development of male infants. The reasons for this apparent differential impact of potential stressors across gender is not immediately clear, and a discussion of possible explanations is beyond the purview of this chapter. The reader is referred to Wachs (1979) and the recent book by Wachs and Gruen (1982) for an examination of this issue.

prevailing high noise level conditions in the early environment. However, this adaptation would appear to be only partial in light of the findings from the visual search task. Thus, high noise levels in the home may have an adverse effect on the development of efficient perceptual skills in spite of adaptation to the distracting character of these conditions. This view of adaptation as a selective process is consistent with findings of Glass and Singer (1972, also cf. the discussion by Wohlwill, 1974).

In sum, the studies of Cohen et al., (1973), Wachs et al., (1971), Wachs (1976, 1978, 1979), and Heft (1979) point to potentially adverse effects of high noise levels in the home on perceptual-cognitive development. Specifically, noise has been seen to have an impact on the development of visual and auditory perceptual skills, and on the development of cognitive processes. Further, in combination, these studies suggest that *prolonged* exposure to noise in the home may have long-term effects in spite of partial adaptation to these conditions.

Recent field investigations have assessed the effects of noise on children whose schools are located near airport air corridors or adjacent to train tracks. Because homes are also exposed to high sound levels from such sources, a consideration of these studies is warranted. Cohen, Evans, Krantz, and Stokols (1980) administered a series of cognitive measures to third and fourth graders whose classrooms were subjected to intense sound levels from aircraft. The number of flights over these schools average one every 2½ minutes. Their performance was contrasted with children from schools not exposed to such extreme sonic conditions. The samples were matched for grade level, racial and ethnic composition, occupational and educational level of the parents, and economic status (i.e., percentage of families receiving economic assistance). In general, those children from the schools with the higher sound levels were more apt to fail on a puzzle-solving task. Among all children who failed this task, those from the noisy school tended to give up in their solution attempts more often than their quiet school counterparts. Further, among those who solved the puzzle, those children who had attended the noisier schools for more than two years had longer response latencies than the children situated in the quiet schools for a comparable length of time. In contrast, there was no *overall* difference between the two groups on a test of auditory distractibility. However, the children from the schools with the higher sound levels were *less* distractible than their counterparts if they had attended the school for only a couple of years, but *more* affected by the distractor after two years in the setting. This finding suggests that adaptation to noise exposure may not only be selective, but transitory as well. Finally, differences were found between these groups with respect to math, reading, and auditory discrimination skills.

In a follow-up study one year later, Cohen, Evans, Krantz, Stokols, and Kelly (1981) report findings that are consistent with the prior investigation, with a few exceptions. The tendency for children from the schools with the higher sound levels to give up on the puzzle task did not reappear, and distractibility of this group after a long exposure to the setting was found to be comparable to that of the control group in the present study. Unfortunately, it is difficult to determine whether these differences in the results for the two studies are attributable to psychological processes occurring during the course of the year, or whether they are due to sample attrition. However, the apparent stability of most of the findings lend additional support to the view that children do not adapt in a global manner to prolonged exposure to noise.

Finally, Bronzaft and McCarthy (1975) examined the reading achievement scores of second to fourth grade children whose classrooms were adjacent to elevated train tracks, in relation to those of comparable grades on the opposite side of the building. Trains passed the school every 4½ minutes, on the average. The investigators found that children whose classrooms were closest to the tracks had significantly lower reading scores than their counterparts located further away from the noise source.

*Measures of Noise.*    In the studies just described, noise is assessed in two different ways. In some cases, noise is measured in terms of a physical parameter — decibels (Bronzaft & McCarthy, 1975; Cohen et al., 1973, 1980). In other investigations the character of sonic conditions in the home is estimated through the use of more qualitative rating scales. On the Purdue Home Stimulation Inventory (Wachs, 1976, 1978, 1979), two estimates of noise in the home based on time sampling observations are derived. One item refers to whether a television, radio, or phonograph was on during a rating period; and the second, the noise confusion score, is directed at both the intensity and complexity of sounds from all sources during a rating period. In Heft (1979), interview questions were directed at the caretaker concerning the intensity and frequency of occurrence of noise from four sources, as well as the proximity of the source to primary play areas. The home observer translated the caretaker's comments into a single scale value, and noise level was estimated in terms of the combined score across the four noise sources (i.e., family activities; television, radio, phonograph; appliances; exterior).

The use of decibel values may be seen as being preferred over qualitative ratings because the former provides a measure which is consistent across observers and across studies. For this reason, findings from studies employing decibel measures may be more generalizable than those derived from observation or interview (Cohen & Weinstein, 1982). However, the fact that physical measures of sound intensity, as well as other characteristics of sound, are poor predictors of experiential ratings (Weinstein, 1976), raises some serious problems for the use of decibel values. As we saw with indices of density, a physical index of sound intensity carries little meaning about the impact of these conditions on psychological processes. We know anecdotally that comparable intensities of sound are sometimes experienced negatively, at other times positively, depending on the source of the sound, e.g., machinery versus a piano, and the setting, e.g., one's bedroom at 3 a.m. versus a concert hall. Thus, while physical parameters of noise have the value of objectivity, i.e., inter-observer consistency, and while they may correlate with physiological measures (Cohen et al., 1980), they are not very informative about the *psychological impact* of sonic conditions.

One measure of sound that appears to be consistently associated with adverse behavioral effects is the schedule of sound onset. Unpredictable presentations of sound have been found to result in performance deficits and lower frustration tolerance after noise exposure (Glass & Singer, 1972; for a review, cf. Cohen, 1980). However, predictability is not a *physical* parameter, as is intensity, frequency, and wave complexity. It refers to *both* environmental and psychological factors. A predictable pattern of sound is one where sound onset can be anticipated by the perceiver; it reflects the perception of structure in the temporal spacing of sound. Consequently, short of artificially generated sounds, predictability of a sound pattern cannot be readily determined a priori. These characteristics of the predictability variable, while raising difficulties for measurement, also point to a potentially valuable approach to environmental assessment. This issue is examined in a later section of this chapter.

At the present time, let us re-examine the relationship between noise and development in terms of the potential impact of these conditions on psychological processes. Here, as in the previous consideration of crowding effects, our discussion must consist primarily of hypotheses derived from available data pertinent to this issue.

## Effects of Noise on Early Home Experiences: Process Considerations

*Exploration and Play with Object Features.* High noise levels in the home may impede exploration of object features of the environment. Background noise serving as a context for perceptual activities can act as a distractor. Unexpected sounds typically elicit orientation toward their source and thereby disrupt ongoing focal activities. As argued above, frequent interruption of *sustained* exploration and play with object features may adversely affect perceptual learning and cognitive development. Although *direct* evidence of long-term effects of distraction is not available, there is some indication that brief exposure to background noise in a testing setting affects performance of children on visual tasks (Heft, 1979; Turnure, 1970). While continued exposure to high levels of noise in the home may result in lessened distractibility (Heft, 1979), Cohen et al. (1980, 1981) suggest that with prolonged exposure to noise, resistance to distraction disappears and susceptibility to distraction reappears.

In addition, some have argued that exposure to high sound levels results in elevated arousal, which in turn, affects performance (e.g., Broadbent, 1971). High levels of arousal are hypothesized to lead to a decreased sensitivity to peripheral aspects of a task or situation (Cohen, 1978). In the earlier discussion of background and focal stimulus information it was suggested that an awareness or a monitoring of background conditions in the course of focal activities was highly adaptive in that the perceiver could be prepared to react to significant, peripheral information. To the extent that high arousal, engendered by the ambient noise conditions, affects sensitivity to nonfocal features, and that chronic stressor conditions result in a high modal level of arousal (cf. Denenberg, 1964), prolonged exposure to noise in the home could result in limited perceptual skills. The inverse relationship between noise level and incidental learning in Heft (1979) points to this possibility.

In sum, high levels of noise in the home may affect perceptual-cognitive development by disrupting the focal activities of exploration and play with object features. Furthermore, sensitivity to significant nonfocal information in general may be affected by noise through the mediation of elevated arousal.

*Interaction with Social Features.*    Children's interaction with persons in the home may be affected in the same manner as their object interactions. They may be distracted from ongoing social exchange by unexpected sounds, and high sound levels may lead to a lowered responsivity to subtle, peripheral social nuances. Some evidence that noise may affect the perception of social information comes from Siegel and Steele (1979), who report that adults who were exposed to unpredictable, loud noise had comparatively greater difficulty in discerning differing levels of performance when observing a competitive game. Also, subjects were less discriminating between personal and situational factors in making attributions of responsibility. If high noise levels impede perceptual learning of social information, the development of cognitive-social skills may be adversely affected. One measure of cognitive-social development in infancy is the *imitation of gestures,* and performance on a measure directed at this aspect of development has been found to be negatively correlated with several indices of noise in the home (Wachs, 1976, 1979; Wachs et al., 1971).

In addition, because high levels of sound can mask human speech, home conditions such as these may adversely affect perceptual learning of speech sounds and, more generally, language skills. Auditory discrimination of both normal and learning-disabled children has been found to be impaired in the presence of background noise (Nober & Nober, 1975), and residual effects of noise exposure on auditory discrimination (Cohen et al., 1973) and on reading ability (Bronzaft & McCarthy, 1975; Cohen et al., 1973) have been reported. Further, Wachs (1976, 1979) found inverse relationships between the environmental variables, television on most of the time and noise confusion in the home, and verbal imitation among infants in his samples. Since verbal imitation is an index of language learning in infancy, it would appear that noise in the home had an adverse effect on this aspect of perceptual-cognitive development. Finally, Saegert's (1980) finding of lower vocabulary-reading scores for children living in high density homes may be attributable in part to high sound levels in the home, which serve to mask speech.

*Noise and Control.*    Children have little control over stimulus conditions of the home environment, and this relative lack of control is especially true with respect to noise. Unlike visual stimulation, noise cannot be avoided by turning away from the direction of its source. At best, the child can escape from noise by moving some distance from its source, but in the case of particularly intense noise, this may be difficult within the confines of the home.

A child who is unable to control or escape from noise in the home may develop behavioral manifestations of passivity or helplessness when exposed to environmental conditions. There is evidence that adults who are unable to escape from noise exposure, regardless of whether its intensity is low or high, subsequently have difficulty in learning to escape when that opportunity is available to them (Krantz, Glass, & Snyder, 1974). Further, it will be recalled that children exposed to intense sound from aircraft were more likely to give up on a puzzle-solving task (Cohen et al., 1980).

One way that a child may control exposure to noise is to retreat to a place in the home which provides shelter from this, as well as other potential stressors. In this regard, the availability of such a place has been found to be positively correlated with measures of early cognitive development (Wachs, 1976, 1978, 1979; Wachs et al., 1971).

In sum, lack of control over noise conditions in the home may result in the behavioral disposition of helplessness. Perhaps Rodin's (1976) findings that children from high density homes made less of an effort to control environmental outcomes, than did those from low density homes, is attributable in part to long-term exposure to noise in their residences.[8]

## Summary

Residential density, a quantitative index of persons per unit of area, has been seen to have two experiential correlates: crowding and noise. In recent field studies the relationship has been examined between, on the one hand,

---

[8]A more detailed analysis of the relationship between environmental stressors and feelings of control over environmental events is presented in Aiello and Baum, this volume.

density in the home and noise from sources located within and outside of the residence, and on the other hand, perceptual-cognitive development.[9] Both environmental variables have been found to be negatively correlated with a number of aspects of development, including visual and auditory discrimination; object permanence, development of schemes, and other characteristics of early cognitive development; language skills such as verbal imitation and reading; and development of the behavioral disposition to control environmental conditions. Furthermore, there is an indication that high density and noise conditions have relatively lasting effects, although some evidence suggests at least partial adaptation to prolonged noise exposure.

While these studies point to significant relationships between the environment and development, they do not indicate the process by which crowding and noise directly affect behavior and development. Empirical and theoretical considerations suggest the following possibilities. Crowding may effect interaction with object features by reducing availability of resources, creating disruptions in play and exploration, and through a general reduction of motor activity and exploration. Crowding may also reduce the frequency and intensity of social encounters, and lead to relative disorder or unpredictability in the event or activity structure of the home. Further, high activity levels associated with crowding may give rise to a background for focal perceptual activities which has many potential visual distractors. Similarly, noise can distract the child from exploration and play, and perhaps decrease sensitivity to peripheral information. Noise can also mask human speech, and thereby interfere with language learning, as well as a result in feelings of helplessness to the extent that it is unpredictable and unavoidable.

## THE PROBLEM OF ENVIRONMENTAL MEASUREMENT: TOWARDS A FUNCTIONAL APPROACH TO ENVIRONMENTAL DESCRIPTION

Hopefully, this discussion has demonstrated that considerable gains have been made over the past decade in documenting the relationship between environmental conditions and perceptual-cognitive development. However, in spite of this progress, our knowledge of environment-development relations is still quite limited. While a consistent pattern of *relationships* between certain environmental variables and development is emerging from the literature, we have little certainty about the manner in which various environmen-

---

[9]The employment of "noise" in this sentence may appear to violate the parallel usage of density-sound versus crowding-noise suggested earlier. Inasmuch as many of the studies reviewed here utilized nonobjective measures of sonic conditions, this choice in the present context is appropriate.

tal conditions directly affect psychological processes. In part, this problem stems from the fact that the data are mostly correlational in nature; consequently, unequivocal, casual inferences cannot be readily drawn.[10] But at the same time, our lack of understanding concerning the impact of the environment on developmental processes is attributable, to some extent, to the approach to environmental measurement reflected in many of the investigations.

A number of the environmental measures employed in the studies reviewed earlier involved either obtaining direct physical measures of certain conditions (e.g., density, sound) or estimates of some level of a variable (e.g., sound and availability of decorations, toys, and furnishings). The result of this approach is often a quantitative value which fails to reflect significant qualitative differences among environmental conditions, and as a result, it is a measure which has little psychological content. As we have seen in the case of density indices and decibel readings, each measure can cover a wide range of conditions, and comparable levels of a particular variable in two different instances can be associated with very different experiences and behavioral outcomes. Similarly, a measure of the number of objects of a particular type which are available in a setting obscures potentially significant qualitative differences among objects in a given category. For example, a frequency count of the number of toys which are available per se might fail to indicate the presence of feedback toys. We have seen that this type of toy has distinctive, developmentally significant qualities. In short, apart from the level of nonspecific arousal generated by overall environmental stimulation and reflected by these indices, such measures do not convey much meaning about the impact of environmental conditions on the psychological functioning of the child. Measures are needed which highlight the *functional significance* of environmental conditions.

In order to understand what this latter type of approach would be like, let us briefly reconsider the nature of those indices which assess physical characteristics or levels of environmental variables. To specify an aspect of the environment in terms of its physical characteristics (i.e., employing the concepts of the physical sciences), is to provide a description in terms which are largely *independent* of how the environment is experienced. For example, a human face as a feature of the visual field, can be described in terms of the characteristics of the light which reflects from its surface. While this physical description may have certain primitive experiential correlates, such as brightness and hue, it does not convey the ecological distinctiveness and significance of

---

[10]Cross-lagged correlational analysis provides some grounds for claims about causal inferences and the direction of effects. Bradley, Caldwell, and Elardo (1979) have employed this approach in examining the relationship between the activities of the mother and measures of infant development.

this aspect of the environment. In the same vein, a numerical estimate of the number of objects in a room is a value which is independent of the *psychological significance* of those features.

Alternatively, a measure that conveys the psychological significance of environmental conditions would be one delineating features and events which have functional implications for an individual. This approach accounts for some of the most important work in ethology. In attempting to describe the stimulus information which is associated with important species' functions — e.g., feeding, mating, flight, imprinting — ethologists have specified this information in relation to the activities of the animal in question. For example, the stimulus information that conveys a predator to ducks and geese was determined by manipulating form models of predators, and then by observing the incidence of escape reactions (Tinbergen, 1951). The critical information in this case is an objectively specifiable feature of the environment which is delimited in terms of its behavioral consequences. This type of analysis for a particular species would result in an inventory of the functionally significant features of the environment; in other words, it would provide a description of the species' ecological niche.

An environmental feature that is identified as being functionally significant for an animal is a *relational* feature (Heft, 1980; Turvey & Shaw, 1979). Unlike a physical correlate of environmental conditions that is independent of functional considerations, such a feature is distinctive precisely because of its relevance for an animal. Thus, an environmental feature with functional significance refers to both the environment and an animal. To return to the example offered above, the informational parameters that specify a predator point to a feature of the environment, but one which is significant for an animal. It is a predator for a particular species, and as such it is *identified in relation to an animal*. Further, the predator is an *ecological reality* that is critical in an animal's *experience* of the environment, and in this respect it can be seen that this functional approach cuts across the objective-subjective distinction. Traditionally, psychologists have considered only two options in environmental description: objective analysis, typically employing physical measures, and subjective accounts, often relying on verbal, introspective reports. Each option is seen to be advantageous for different reasons; the former because it results in objectively specified indices, and the latter because it permits inclusion of meaning into the environmental analysis. The functional approach outlined here offers a third alternative. By identifying relational environmental variables in terms of their functional significance, an objective *and* biologically meaningful taxonomy of the environment is possible. Features of the environment are to be specified in an objective manner, but the criteria for determining the relevant physical or geometrical parameters in the description reside in the animal's actions. As a result, the environment is described in objective terms, but at the same time this description is functionally meaningful.

The conceptual foundations for this functional approach have been articulated by J. J. Gibson (1966, 1979). Gibson has attempted to describe the ecological properties of the terrestrial environment to which species, and in particular species' perceptual systems, have adapted. Taken with respect to an animal's functional characteristics, the environment can be described in terms of what it affords an animal, that is, in terms of its *affordances*. Consider the following example of an affordance:

> If a terrestrial surface is horizontal (instead of slanted), nearly flat (instead of convex or concave), sufficiently extended (relative to the size of the animal), and if its substance is rigid (relative to the weight of the animal), then the surface affords support. . . . It is stand-on-able, permitting an upright position for quadrapeds and bipeds. It is, therefore, walk-on-able and run-over-able. (Gibson, 1979, p. 127)

Other affordances are a brink (affords falling-off), a looming object (affords collision), a stick (affords grasping), a hut (affords shelter), and another animal (affords nurturance, social interaction, etc.). Because affordances are identified with reference to molar activities of an animal, they convey the psychological significance of the environmental feature in question. Furthermore, because affordances are potentially specifiable in terms of a geometrical analysis of information available to the perceiver (cf. Gibson, 1979, Chapter 8), this concept offers the possibility for an objectively rigorous description of functionally significant environmental features. While Gibson's work has generated considerable interest in the area of perception and in philosophical circles, it has received comparatively little attention among environmentally oriented psychologists. However, his functional approach may prove to be of value in future environment-behavior investigations (Heft, 1981).

In our previous review of research, several of the environmental variables that proved to be the most consistently related to developmental measures reflect the relational and functional character of affordances. Three of these variables are response-contingent or feedback toys, a shelter from excessive sensory stimulation, and predictability of noise. The distinctive attribute of a feedback toy is the latent properties that are manifested through the child's interaction with that object. In essence, to describe a feedback toy necessitates a consideration of what the toy affords the child; that is, it is defined in relation to an individual. It is an object that reveals new properties as a result of specific actions by a child. Thus, a feedback toy is a feature of the environment that is identified because of its functional significance, and its structural characteristics can be specified objectively. This same point of view is applicable to the variable, a shelter from high levels of sensory stimulation. To designate a room in the home as a stimulus shelter is to indicate what that room affords a person who enters it. The room is functionally significant because it serves as a buffer between the individual and the ambient stimulus conditions of the environment beyond it. The room is a location in the home that is identified because of its psychological significance, and the potential for a room to serve as a stimulus shelter can be objectively determined. Finally, let us reconsider the variable, predictability of noise. One functionally significant feature of a noise pattern is its potential to act as a distractor. While the temporal structure of sound is objectively specifiable, as noted earlier its predictability depends on characteristics of a perceiver. Thus, predictability of noise, like feedback toys and a room as a stimulus shelter, is a relational description referring to both characteristics of the environment and of the individual; the critical property, i.e., predictability, feedback, shelter, is manifested in relation to an individual. The perception of pattern in sound differs from the other two variables in that it is more dependent on the perceiver's prior experience, and for this reason it is more difficult to specify in advance. However, this is a difference in degree only. All three environmental variables are relational, objectively specifiable, and functionally significant.

The relatively high degree of consistency of these variables as predictors of development and performance provides some empirical support for the potential value of this functional approach to environmental description. In the case of possible environmental stressors, such as crowding and noise, it may be important to examine the way in which perceptual activities in relation to functionally significant aspects of the environment are impeded or disrupted (Heft, 1981). In retrospect, our preceding discussion of the potential impact of crowding and noise on perceptual-cognitive development can be viewed largely as this type of functional analysis.

In general, the approach advocated here directs the investigator's attention to functionally significant aspects of the environment. The critical environmental variables for perceptual-cognitive development may not be immediately apparent, but continued research and observation of children in natural settings is bound to lead to an objectively specifiable and psychologically meaningful taxonomy of the home environment.


## CONSIDERATIONS FOR FUTURE RESEARCH

Finally, let us briefly examine three issues that will require attention in the course of future investigations of the relationship between the home environment and perceptual-cognitive development. The issues to be considered are adaptation and the long-term consequences of exposure to stressors, the value of theory-directed research, and the complex interrelations among environmental variables.

## Adaptation and Long-Term Consequences of Exposure to Crowding and Noise

Adaptation is a ubiquitous characteristic of psychological functioning. The term refers to the fact that organisms modify their functional frame of reference concerning the normative level of stimulation (Helson, 1964), or the structure and organization of stimulus information (Kohler, 1964), as a result of continued exposure to the prevailing conditions of the environment (cf. Wohlwill, 1974). Because of the adaptive quality of the organism's relation to the environment, some investigators have argued in the past that the effects of potential stressors are largely mitigated. For example, after a review of investigations addressing the effects of noise on performance, Kryter (1970) concluded that "Man should be able . . . to adapt physiologically to his noise environment with only transitory interference effects of physiological and mental and motor behavioral activities during this period of adaptation" (p. 587). However, research since Kryter's review has cast doubt on this general conclusion with respect to noise, as well as other stressors including crowding. Recent laboratory investigations of the *aftereffects* of exposure to stressors, and field studies focusing on children chronically exposed to high levels of noise, have revealed possible long-term consequences of exposure to environmental stressors *in spite of* adaptation (cf. Cohen, 1980). As we have seen, some research findings suggest that adaptation to a potential stressor, such as noise, may be functionally selective (Glass & Singer, 1972; Heft, 1979) and perhaps only temporary at that (Cohen et al., 1980). These investigations serve to emphasize the highly significant question of the residual effects of stressors in the home on the development of the child.

Additional detailed analysis of the impact of prolonged exposure to environmental stressors on children are needed in order to substantiate and to extend these findings. In particular, longitudinal studies which assess *both* psychological and environmental variables will be invaluable in that they will permit an examination of development in relation to environmental conditions over time. This type of investigation will help to clarify the nature of adaptation, as well as the adaptive potential of children at different ages. The long-term consequences of exposure to environmental stressors on development needs to be assessed in light of the effectiveness, the limitations, and the costs of adaptation (cf. Wohlwill, this volume).

## Environment-Development Specificity and the Need
## for Theory-Guided Research

In his analysis of the relationship between the home environment and infant cognitive development, Wachs (1979) found that some environmental conditions appear to affect rather specific areas of development, whereas others seem to have more generalized or global consequences for development. These findings are significant for two reasons. First, from a theoretical standpoint, they reveal the complex relations between environmental variables and developmental processes. Second, in an applied vein, they provide guidance concerning the specific impact of particular environmental conditions, and by extension, particular environmental modifications, at various ages during infancy.

The fairly coherent picture of environment-development relations that is beginning to emerge from Wachs' research is somewhat of a contrast to many of the other investigations of crowding and noise on children. In comparison, the latter provide instead a somewhat disconnected set of findings that do not easily lead to conceptual integration and, most important, to definitive applied guidelines. To be specific, while the research literature permits general claims about the adverse effects of crowding and noise on children, more precise statements about the exact nature of these effects and when in the course of development these effects are likely to occur, cannot be made. It is detailed information of this sort that most readily lends itself to application.

What sets Wachs' research program apart from most other investigations in the area, and consequently permits a more precise analysis of environment-development relations, is that it is derived from a well-articulated theoretical framework (cf. Wachs & Gruen, 1982). Most of the other research is problem-guided and largely atheoretical, and this is characteristic of much work in environmental psychology generally. While practical problems should direct our research questions, the latter need to be fashioned in terms of a framework that provides coherence to the resulting findings. This theoretical organization will serve as a stepping-stone to application, as the promise of Wachs' research suggests. To repeat the oft-cited statement of Kurt Lewin, "There is nothing so practical as a good theory."

## Complex Interrelations among Environmental Systems:
## The Ecological Network

Most of the investigations examined in this chapter have assessed psychological processes in relation to a single environmental variable in isolation. However, any characteristic of the home environment typically occurs in concert with many others, and in combination with these conditions, the effects of individual variables may be strengthened or reduced. For this reason, it is most important that future investigations consider the interaction among environmental variables within the home. Both Yarrow et al. (1975), and Wachs (1979) have employed multivariate techniques to some extent in their studies of the home environment, and further work along these lines is needed.

In addition, it must be recognized that characteristics of the home environment interact with variables associated with settings and institutions beyond the home. As Garbarino (this volume) points out, the child's environment is not monolithic, but consists of nested systems that include the home, the school, the neighborhood, media, and political institutions. These "layers" of the environment have reciprocal influences; each interacts with the others. Consequently, positive or negative effects stemming from one system in isolation can be magnified or offset by influences from other parts of this ecological network. Collectively, these various facets of the environment comprise the ecological resources for the child. An analysis of development that is truly in the spirit of an ecological perspective will need to recognize the complex network of nested systems that is the child's environment.

## ACKNOWLEDGMENTS

The author would like to acknowledge the assistance of Cynthia G. Kreger and Michael Minutilli in the preparation of this chapter. The project was supported in part by the Denison University Research Foundation. The author's address is: Department of Psychology, Denison University, Granville, Ohio 43023.

## REFERENCES

Altman, I. *The environment and social behavior.* Monterey, Calif.: Brooks/Cole, 1975.

Barker, R. G. *Ecological psychology.* Stanford, Calif.: Stanford University Press, 1968.

Baron, R. M., & Rodin, A. Personal control as a mediator of crowding. In S. Baum, J. E. Singer, S. Valins (Eds.), *Advances in environmental psychology: Vol. 1 The urban environment.* Hillsdale, N.J.: Lawrence Erlbaum Associates, 1978. Pp. 145–190.

Baum, A., Aiello, J. R., & Calesnick, L. E. Crowding and personal control: Social density and the development of learned helplessness. In J. R. Aiello & A. Baum (Eds.), *Residential crowding and design.* New York: Plenum Press, 1979. Pp. 141–159.

Baum, A., & Koman, S. Differential responses to anticipated crowding: Psychological effects of social and spatial density. *Journal of Personality and Social Psychology,* 1976, *34,* 526–536.

Bradley, R. H., Caldwell, B. M., & Elardo, R. Home environment and cognitive-development in the first 2 years: A cross-lagged panel analysis. *Developmental Psychology,* 1979, *15,* 246–250.

Broadbent, D. E. *Decision and stress.* New York: Academic Press, 1971.

Bronzaft, A. L., & McCarthy, D. P. The effect of elevated train noise on reading ability. *Environment and Behavior,* 1975, *7,* 517–527.

Caldwell, B., Heider, J., & Kaplan, B. *Home observation for measurement of the environment.* Paper presented at the meetings of the American Psychological Association, New York, September 1966.

Clarke-Stewart, K. A. Interactions between mothers and their young children: Characteristics and consequences. *Monographs of the Society for Research in Child Development,* 1973, *38,* Serial No. 153.

Cohen, S. Environmental load and the allocation of attention. In A. Baum, J. E. Singer, & S. Valins (Eds.), *Advances in environmental psychology: Vol. 1, The urban environment.* Hillsdale, N.J.: Lawrence Erlbaum Associates, 1978. Pp. 1-30.

Cohen, S. The aftereffects of stress on human performance and social behavior: A review of research and theory. *Psychological Bulletin,* 1980, *88,* 82-108.

Cohen, S., Evans, G. W., Krantz, D. S., & Stokols, D. Physiological, motivational, and cognitive effects of aircraft noise on children: Moving from the laboratory to the field. *American Psychologist,* 1980, *35,* 231-243.

Cohen, S., Evans, G. W., Krantz, D. S., Stokols, D., & Kelly, S. Aircraft noise and children: Longitudinal and cross-sectional evidence on adaptation to noise and the effectiveness of noise abatement. *Journal of Personality and Social Psychology,* 1981.

Cohen, S., Glass, D. C., & Singer, J. E. Apartment noise, auditory discrimination, and reading ability in children. *Journal of Experimental Child Psychology,* 1973, *9,* 407-422.

Cohen, S., & Weinstein, N. Nonauditory effects of noise. In G. W. Evans (Ed.), *Environmental Stress.* New York: Cambridge University Press, 1982. Pp. 45-74.

Denenberg, V. H. Critical periods, stimulus input, and emotional reactivity: A theory of infantile stimulation. *Psychological Review,* 1964, *71,* 335-351.

Desor, J. A. Toward a psychological theory of crowding. *Journal of Personality and Social Psychology,* 1972, *21,* 79-83.

Deutsch, C. P. Auditory discrimination and the learning process: Social factors. *Merrill-Palmer Quarterly,* 1964, *10,* 277-296.

Dreyfus, H. L. *What computers can't do: The limits of artificial intelligence.* New York: Harper Colophon, 1979.

Elardo, R., Bradley, R. H., & Caldwell, B. M. The relation of infants' home environments to mental test performance from six to thirty-six months: A longitudinal analysis. *Child Development,* 1975, *46,* 71-76.

Elardo, R., Bradley, R. H., & Caldwell, B. M. A longitudinal study of relation of infants' home environment to language development at age three. *Child Development,* 1977, *48,* 595-603.

Epstein, Y. M., & Baum, A. Crowding: Methods of study. In A. Baum & Y. M. Epstein (Eds.), *Human response to crowding.* Hillsdale, N.J.: Lawrence Erlbaum Associates, 1978. Pp. 141-164.

Evans, G. W. Crowding and the developmental process. In A. Baum & Y. M. Epstein (Eds.), *Human response to crowding.* Hillsdale, N.J.: Lawrence Erlbaum Associates, 1978. Pp. 117-139.

Galle, O., Gove, W., & McPherson, J. Population density and pathology: What are the relationships for man? *Science,* 1972, *176,* 23-30.

Gibson, E. J. *Principles of perceptual learning and development.* New York: Appleton-Century-Crofts, 1969.

Gibson, E. J., & Rader, N. Attention: The perceiver as performer. In G. A. Hale & M. Lewis (Eds.), *Attention and cognitive development.* New York: Plenum Press, 1979. Pp.1-22.

Gibson, J. J. *The senses considered as perceptual systems.* Boston: Houghton Mifflin, 1966.

Gibson, J. J. *The ecological approach to visual perception.* Boston: Houghton Mifflin, 1979.

Glass, D. C., & Singer, J. E. *Urban stress: Experiments on noise and social stressors.* New York: Academic Press, 1972.

Gray, S. W., & Klaus, R. A. The early training project and its general rationale. In R. D. Hess &

R. M. Bear (Eds.), *Early education: Current theory, research, and action.* Chicago: Aldine Publishing Company, 1968. Pp. 63–70.

Griffit, W., & Veitch, R. Hot and crowded. *Journal of Personality and Social Psychology,* 1971, *17*, 92–98.

Heft, H. Background and focal environmental conditions of the home and attention in young children. *Journal of Applied Social Psychology,* 1979, *9*, 47–69.

Heft, H. What Heil is missing in Gibson: A reply. *Journal for the Theory of Social Behavior,* 1980, *10*, 187–194.

Heft, H. An examination of constructivist and Gibsonian approaches to environmental psychology. *Population and Environment: Behavioral and Social Issues,* 1981, *4*, 227–245.

Helson, H. *Adaptation-level theory: An experimental and systematic approach to behavior.* New York: Harper, 1964.

Hochberg, J. E. *Perception* (2nd ed.). Englewood Cliffs, N.J.: Prentice-Hall, 1978.

Hunt, J. McV. *Intelligence and experience.* New York: Ronald Press, 1961.

Hutt, C., & Vaizey, S. J. Differential effects of group density on social behavior. *Nature,* 1966, *209*, 136–146.

Jennings, K. D., Harmon, R. J., Morgan, G. A., Gaiter, J. L., & Yarrow, L. J. Exploratory play as an index of mastery motivation. Relationships to persistence, cognitive functioning, and environmental measures. *Developmental Psychology,* 1979, *15*, 386–394.

Kohler, I. The formation and transformation of the perceptual world. *Psychological Issues,* Vol. III, No. 4, 1964.

Krantz, D. S., Glass, D. C., & Snyder, M. L. Helplessness, stress level, and the coronary-prone behavior pattern. *Journal of Experimental Social Psychology,* 1974, *10*, 284–300.

Kryter, K. D. *The effects of noise on man.* New York: Academic Press, 1970.

Loo, C. M. The effects of spatial density on the social behavior of children. *Journal of Applied Social Psychology,* 1972, *2*, 372–381.

Loo, C. M. A factor analytic approach to the study of spatial density effects on preschoolers. *Journal of Population: Behavioral, Social, and Environmental Issues,* 1979, *2*, 47–68.

Loo, C. M., & Kennelly, D. Social density: Its effects on behaviors and perceptions of preschoolers. *Environmental Psychology and Nonverbal Behavior,* 1979, *3*, 131–146.

Loo, C. M., & Smetana, J. The effects of crowding on the behavior and perception of 10 year-old boys. *Environmental Psychology and Nonverbal Behavior,* 1978, *2*, 226–249.

McGrew, P. L. Social and spatial density effects on spacing behavior in preschool children. *Journal of Child Psychology and Psychiatry,* 1970, *11*, 197–205.

Milgram, S. The experience of living in cities. *Science,* 1970, *167*, 1461–1468.

Newson, J., & Newson, E. *Infant care in an urban community.* London: Allen & Unwin, 1963. [Cited in Parke, R. D., Children's home environments: Social and cognitive effects. In I. Altman & J. F. Wohlwill (Eds.), *Human behavior and environment. Vol. 3, Children and the environment.* New York: Plenum Press, 1978, p. 71.]

Nober, L. W., & Nober, E. H. Auditory discrimination of learning disabled children in quiet and classroom noise. *Journal of Learning Disabilities,* 1975, *10*, 656–659.

Parke, R. D., & Sawin, D. B. Children's privacy in the home: Developmental, ecological, and child-rearing determinants. *Environment and Behavior,* 1979, *11*, 87–104.

Preiser, W. Behavior of nursery school children under different spatial densities. *Man-Environment Systems,* 1972, *2*, 24.

Rodin, J. Density, perceived choice, and response to controllable and uncontrollable outcomes. *Journal of Experimental Social Psychology,* 1976, *12*, 564–578.

Rohe, W., & Patterson, A. H. *The effects of varied levels of resources and density on behavior in a day-care center.* Paper presented at Environmental Design Research Association, Milwaukee, Wisconsin, 1974.

Roy, K. Parents' attitudes toward their children. *Journal of Home Economics,* 1950, *42*,

652–653. [Cited in Parke, R. D. Children's home environments: Social and cognitive effects. In I. Altman & J. F. Wohlwill (Eds.), *Human behavior and environment,* Vol. 3, *Children and the environment.* New York: Plenum Press, 1978, p. 71.]

Saegert, S. *The effect of residential density on low income children.* Paper presented at the meetings of the American Psychological Association, Montreal, September 1980.

Shapiro, A. H. Effects of family density and mothers' education on preschoolers motor skills. *Perceptual and Motor Skills,* 1974, *38,* 79–86.

Siegel, J. M., & Steele, C. M. Noise level and social discrimination. *Personality and Social Psychology Bulletin,* 1979, *5,* 95–99.

Smith, P. K., & Connolly, K. Patterns of play and social interaction in pre-school children. In N. Blurton Jones (Ed.), *Ethological studies of child behavior.* Cambridge: Cambridge University Press, 1972.

Stokols, D. The experience of crowding in primary and secondary environments. *Environment and Behavior,* 1976, *8,* 49–86.

Thompson, W. R., & Grusec, J. Studies of early experience. In P. H. Mussen (Ed.), *Carmichael's manual of child development* (3rd ed.), Vol. 1. New York: Wiley, 1970. Pp. 565–654.

Tinbergen, N. *The study of instinct.* Oxford: Clarendon Press, 1951.

Trevarthen, C. Modes of perceiving and modes of action. In H. L. Pick, Jr. & E. Saltzman (Eds.), *Modes of perceiving and processing information.* Hillsdale, N.J.: Lawrence Erlbaum Associates, 1978.

Turnure, J. E. Children's reactions to distractors in a learning situation. *Developmental Psychology,* 1970, *2,* 115–122.

Turvey, M. T., & Shaw, R. The primacy of perceiving: An ecological reformulation of perception for understanding memory. In L. Nilsson (Ed.), *Perspectives on memory research.* Hillsdale, N.J.: Lawrence Erlbaum Associates, 1979. Pp. 167–222.

Uzgiris, I. C., & Hunt, J. McV. *Assessment in infancy: Ordinal scales of psychological development.* Urbana: University of Illinois Press, 1975.

Wachs, T. D. Utilization of a Piagetian approach in the investigation of early experience effects: A research strategy and some illustrative data. *Merrill-Palmer Quarterly,* 1976, *22,* 11–30.

Wachs, T. D. The relationship of infants' physical environment to their Binet performance at 2½ years. *International Journal of Behavioral Development,* 1978, *1,* 51–65.

Wachs, T. D. Proximal experience and early cognitive-intellectual development: The physical environment. *Merrill-Palmer Quarterly,* 1979, *25,* 3–41.

Wachs, T. D., Francis, J., & McQuiston, S. Psychological dimensions of the infant's physical environment. *Infant Behavior and Development,* 1979, *2,* 155–161.

Wachs, T. D., & Gruen, G. E. *Early experience and human development.* New York: Plenum Press, 1982.

Wachs, T. D., Uzgiris, I. C., & Hunt, J. McV. Cognitive development in infants of different age levels and from different environmental backgrounds: An explanatory investigation. *Merrill-Palmer Quarterly,* 1971, *17,* 283–317.

Watson, J. S., & Ramey, C. Reactions to response-contingent stimulation in early infancy. *Merrill-Palmer Quarterly,* 1972, *18,* 219–227.

Weinstein, N. D. Human evaluations of environmental noise. In K. H. Craik & E. H. Zube (Eds.), *Perceiving environmental quality.* New York: Plenum Press, 1976. Pp. 229–252.

White, B. L., Kaban, B., Shapiro, B., & Attanucci, J. Competence and experience. In I. C. Uzgiris & F. Weizmann (Eds.), *The structuring of experience.* New York: Plenum Press, 1977. Pp. 115–152.

White, R. H. Motivation reconsidered: The concept of competence. *Psychological Review,* 1959, *66,* 297–333.

Wohlwill, J. F. Human response to levels of environmental stimulation. *Human Ecology,* 1974, *2,* 127–247.

Yarrow, L. J., Rubinstein, J. L., & Pederson, F. A. *Infant and environment: Early cognitive and motivational development.* New York: Halsted Press, 1975.

Zlutnick, S., & Altman, I. Crowding and human behavior. In J. F. Wohlwill & D. H. Carson (Eds.), *Environment and the social sciences: Perspectives and applications.* Washington, D.C.: American Psychological Association, 1972. Pp. 44–60.

# 4 Play, Exploration, and Density

Phil Schoggen
Maxine Schoggen
*Cornell University*

## INTRODUCTION

In recent years, exploratory behavior and play have received prominent attention in both the theoretical and the empirical literature of child development (e.g., Berlyne, 1960; Hughes, 1978; Hutt, 1970; Minuchin, 1971; Piaget, 1962; Vandenberg, 1978; Weisler & McCall, 1976). In planning the present volume, it seemed important to identify possible links between such behavior and population density of residence, institution, and community. We begin with the importance of play and exploration to individual development. The complexity of continuing interaction of organism and environment suggests no simple one-to-one correlation of play or exploration with density. Rather, there appear to be continuing opportunities for the process of organism-environment interaction to contribute to the developmental process throughout the life course. These opportunities are not limited to direct interaction but may include distal events at a variety of levels that together mediate the relationship between population density and play.

## PLAY AND EXPLORATION

### The Definition of Play and Exploration

Although exploration, play, and curiosity are interrelated (Bradbard & Endsley, 1980; Hutt, 1970; Hutt & Hutt, 1970; Maw & Maw, 1970; Minuchin, 1971), there have been attempts to differentiate between play and exploration. Exploration has been described as a fixed sequence of behavior with relatively stereotyped patterns across situations and species, the purpose of which is to reduce uncertainty about an unfamiliar object and answer the question, "What does this object do?" (Berlyne, 1960; Henderson & Moore, 1979; Hutt, 1966, 1970; Schiller, 1957; Weisler & McCall, 1976). Exploration has also been used to characterize the range of space used by people (Coie, 1974; Hart, 1979), the "home range" (Anderson & Tinsdall, 1972), or the behavior settings (community parts) used by a person or a category of persons (Barker & Schoggen, 1973; Barker & Wright, 1955; Gump & Adelberg, 1978; Wright, 1969, 1971).

Exploration is seen as preceding play; once the object becomes familiar, play may occur (Hughes, 1978). Play has been described as behavior that is less consistent than exploration across situations and species (Dolhinow & Bishop, 1970; Hutt, 1970; Loizos, 1967; Piaget, 1962); is characterized by assimilation without accommodation (Piaget, 1962); has a pleasurable component (Beach, 1945; Dolhinow & Bishop, 1970; Hutt, 1970) and is dominated by the organism's dedication to the question, "What can *I* do with this object?" (Hutt, 1970). Play leads to mastery (Arnaud, 1974; Groos, 1978; Scott, 1968).

Although play usually is distinguished from exploration, several conceptualizations of curiosity, exploration, and play do not seek such clear differentiation. Curiosity is defined in terms of exploration behavior with novel objects (Bradbard & Endsley, 1980). The definition of curiosity is close to that of exploration, i.e., both involve predictable sequences and information seeking, and both come before play. The effects of curiosity are described as similar to those of play, e.g., mastery and adaptation. Dember and Earl (1957) argue that both exploration and curiosity are facets of attentional behavior, which brings the organism into contact with one part of the environment rather than another. They relate the dynamics of attention to the ability of the stimuli to increase the psychological complexity of the organism. McMahon (1966) suggests that children's exploration and curiosity in new situations increased consistently with increases in measures of complexity of their environmental experience.

Miller (1973) argues that exploration, make-believe or fantasy play, and organized, rule-bound games display certain patterns or *motifs* which unify these apparently diverse kinds of activity. All involve "galumphing," which he defines as "patterned, voluntary elaboration or complication of process, where the pattern is not under the dominant control of goals" (p. 92). The child who, in walking to school on the sidewalk, carefully avoids stepping on a crack is galumphing—setting silly obstacles in his own path. So is the chess player who accepts the rules of the game which are, in fact, obstacles to putting the pieces to the desired locations. "Play is not means without the end; it is a crooked line to the end; it circumnavigates obstacles *put there by the player, or voluntarily acceded to* by him" (p. 93, emphasis added). Perhaps this conceptualization is a good response to Bruner, Jolly, and Sylva's (1976) query, "How . . . can one encompass so motley a set of capers as childish punning, cowboys-and-Indians and the construction of a tower of bricks into a simple or even a sober dictionary entry?" (p. 13).

## Evolutionary and Developmental Significance of Exploration and Play

Both play and exploration have somewhat similar evolutionary and developmental significance. Although exploration is often described as being constrained by evolutionary pressures and play is characterized by heterogeneity and innovation (Hughes, 1978; Hutt, 1970), both are thought to be necessary to assure the competence of the young of the species (Bruner & Connolly, 1974). Despite the heterogeneity of play, it is seen to reflect the culture (Bruner, Jolly, & Sylva, 1976; Vandenberg, 1978). Across phylogenetic levels, the more social the animal the more necessary play appears to be (Bruner, Jolly, & Sylva, 1976; Vandenberg, 1978). Play has been observed across a wide range of species (Hutt, 1970).

Some of the significant factors of play in maintaining the species are also involved in the development of the individual. Play is seen as an energizer leading to mastery and adaptation as well as innovation (Arnaud, 1974); such a mechanism would also protect the species. Other effects of play also protect the species: the control of the body through locomotion, pursuit, fighting, and hiding (Groos, 1978; Scott, 1968); control of the environment through fantasy; control of danger and the learning of new skills (Csikszentmihalyi, 1975; Vandenberg, 1978); the incorporation of observed behavior (Dolhinow & Bishop, 1970); the development of adult-like behavior (Scott, 1968); and the loosening of the bond between adult and infant (Rheingold & Eckerman, 1973).

Nunnally and Lemond (1973) conceive of exploratory behavior as a temporal scheme rather than a developmental one, i.e., the sequence is followed for new experiences generally. Langer (1980) suggests that the rudiments of cognition may be built into play, a possibility that Langer believes is not sufficiently recognized by researchers and teachers.

The important point is that exploration and play are relevant to the development of the individual and the survival of the species in somewhat similar ways. There is a great deal at stake in play. In reviewing this literature we were struck with similarities involved in hypotheses and in data about play with objects, exploration of objects and space, and the use of the environment by children.

## Similarities Between Object Exploration and Exploration of Space and Events

In ontogenetic development, object exploration and the exploration of space display similar sequential patterns. Object exploration begins with attention (including visual regard) followed by increasing interaction with the object, i.e., reaching, grasping, inspection and manipulation (Hutt & Hutt, 1970; Sherrod, Vietze, & Friedman, 1978). Space exploration necessarily awaits the development of locomotor mobility and very young children on their own initiative stay within sound and sight of their mothers as they enter and explore new situations, and new objects (Anderson, 1972). Increased locomotion and separation occur for toddlers in the service of increased exploration of new spaces, new situations and new objects (Goldberg & Lewis, 1969; Hartup & Lempers, 1973).

Rheingold and Eckerman (1973) suggest that what is called the "fear of strangers" response is better conceptualized as response to an unfamiliar object and argue for a better description of how the unfamiliar person behaves and how the infants respond. The child may need the equivalent of an exploration sequence to relate to the unfamiliar person (new object) (Eckerman & Rheingold, 1974). A balance between change and continuity is important for children interacting with objects (Murphy & Moriarity, 1976); perhaps this is true for people and situations as well.

The similarity of the responses of children to objects on the one hand and space on the other has been specifically demonstrated in research on the mental mapping of space. Transformations that are involved in mapping space appear to be an extension of basic operations involved in interaction with objects. Blaut, McCleary, and Blaut (1970), in empirical studies, tested the hypothesis that scale and projection would emerge at an early age because these consistencies are relatively primitive (Bruner, Olver, & Greenfield, 1966; Piaget, 1969). Blaut et al. (1970) showed that six-year-old children can interpret an aerial photograph, abstract from such a photograph, use map-like signs, and use reduced rotation abstraction to solve a simple navigational problem, as well as engage in a primitive form of map reading, map making, and map use.

In addition to the developmental characteristics related to exploring space and objects, the few sex differences that do appear are similar for object and space/event/behavior setting exploration. At thirteen months of age girls were more reluctant to leave their mothers' sides than were boys (Goldberg & Lewis, 1969). In the early school years, boys explored more objects when no specific permission was given (Coie, 1974); more space was traversed by boys compared to girls when no specific permission was involved (Coates & Bussard, 1974; Hart, 1979; Moore & Young, 1978). Anderson & Tindall (1972) report that boys' home range, i.e., nonredundant path length, was substantially greater than that for girls. On the other hand, breadth of schemata of space is not seen as radically different for boys compared with girls (Moore & Young, 1978), and similarly the territorial range, i.e., the number of different community areas entered and participated in was not different for boys and girls (Barker & Wright, 1955; Gump & Adelberg, 1978; Wright, 1969, 1971).

Older children use more sophisticated techniques when playing with objects than do younger children (Coie, 1974; Rabinowitz, Moely, Finkel, & McClinton, 1975). Older children also traverse more space (Anderson & Tindall, 1972; Hart, 1979; Moore & Young, 1978); gradually enter more behavior settings (community parts) and take responsible positions in more of these parts than do younger children (Adelberg, 1977; Barker & Schoggen, 1973; Barker & Wright, 1955; Gump & Adelberg, 1978; Wright, 1969, 1971). These developmental changes are strikingly similar and mutually productive, i.e., increased locomotion serves to increase the number of objects encountered and objects entice the child into locomoting further and further from the caregiver until full interaction with the community is achieved independently.

This brief review, although not comprehensive, encompasses some of the essentials of the exploration-play-curiosity concepts. It suggests that such behavior is important at a variety of levels, i.e., objects, including people; objects in space; space itself; and community parts or behavior settings. Effects of density will have to be examined carefully. Different definitions of density, e.g., number of people — per room, per square foot, per acre, per country cannot be applied equally to all levels of behavior. Logically, the level of density closest to the behavior in question would be expected to show the greatest effect, e.g., number of people per room should affect the interaction of the toddler with objects more than the number of people per acre. However, indirect effects are clearly possible, e.g., high levels of people per acre may be associated with deprivation of food and objects with subsequent reduction in play and exploration.

## STUDIES OF DENSITY EFFECTS IN HOMES AND FAMILIES

Home studies are rare. Several studies shed light on potential relationships, even though they may be indirect. Wohlwill and Heft (1977) found agreement in the literature that intermediate amounts of diversity and intensity of stimulation are most conducive to optimal development (Endsley, 1979; Torrance, 1970b; Yarrow, Rubenstein, & Pedersen, 1975). This may be the kind of relationship that would be similar across levels of density. The importance of visual perusal and pursuit for early infant development has been documented (Chatelanat & Schoggen, 1980; Yarrow, et al. 1975). High room density conditions may interfere with the process both by providing noise against which auditory stimuli are not discriminable (Wachs, 1976) and/or by people getting in the way of the visual exploration, tracking and contact so important to the developing organism. For the somewhat older baby it was shown that if mothers interrupted their babies' play there was no subsequent effect upon social initiation from the baby to the mother, responsivity to the mother, or exploratory play of the infant (Gray, Tracey, & Lindberg, 1979). At toddler age, high room density may, however, interfere with the toddler using the mother as a "safe" base; toddlers return to the mother either physically or visually for assurance when exploring new situations (Anderson, 1972; Goldberg & Lewis, 1969; Rheingold & Eckerman, 1970).

Both family size and socioeconomic conditions, i.e., parental education and income of family are confounding factors. Family size data are rarely accompanied by density data either in terms of people per square foot, per room, or per acre. There is further complication from family size introduced through the effects of sibling spacing (MacDonald, 1969). Firstborns receive more attention from and interact more extensively with parents than later borns (Jacobs & Moss, 1976). Birth order, family size, spacing of siblings, age of parents, and education of parents are all important to the development process and all are confounded by and related to socioeconomic level.

Personal space needs are also involved in considering the effects of density on development. They are discussed elsewhere in this volume. It is clear that density is not simply measured nor are the effects simple to extract. Two mediating factors are implicated by some studies, stress on one hand and resources on the other.

## STRESS, RESOURCES, AND DENSITY

### Density and Stress

Stress beyond a minimum level may also be found in high density situations. The stress may arise through a variety of mechanisms. Interfering with the need for privacy is one suggested source (Altman, 1975; Wolfe, 1978). There is general agreement that it is a person's lack of control over an event that leads to stress rather than the event itself, e.g., lack of control over experiencing loud sounds (Cohen, Glass, & Singer, 1973) and lack of control generally (Baum, Aiello, & Calesnick, 1978; Lazarus & Cohen, 1977; Wortman & Brehm, 1975). Stress that generates anxiety can be a factor in disturbing the development of exploratory behavior (McReynolds, Acker, & Pietila, 1961; Mendel, 1965). Given that the quality of play (continuity, maturity) has been used as an indicator of mastery motivation (Jennings, Harmon, Morgan,

Gaiter, & Yarrow, 1979), these studies about the effects of anxiety on exploration behavior and play highlight the importance of understanding these relationships.

Stress may also be related to interference with the exploration and play sequence. Interference can result from too many people "in the way," e.g., the child cannot return to the caregiver either visually or physically or the child must share the caregiver and other resources with too many other people. Interference in crowded situations was seen as one mechanism for producing stress (Schopler & Stockdale, 1977), and with college students, high social density was seen as interfering with performance (Glassman, Burkhart, Grant, & Vallery, 1978).

## Programs and Resources

One difficulty that intrudes is that with increased numbers of people, program changes are usually also found in schools, hospitals, and other institutions. Generally speaking, as a school or a classroom increases in population size, programs become more structured with less time and room for "exploration and play" (Fagot, 1977; Huston-Stein, Friedrich-Cofer, & Susman, 1977; Prescott & Jones, 1967). Kleiber and Barnet (1980) found that children in highly structured situations were more attentive and neater than children in classes with less structure, but that the latter were more imaginative, prosocial, and less likely to become discouraged when difficulties were encountered.

The importance of rich environmental resources is stressed in an intriguing theoretical paper by Nicholson (1971). His "Theory of Loose Parts" holds that inventiveness and creativity in children are a function of the number and kinds of variables available in any given environment. For Nicholson, variables include materials, shapes, smells, magnetism, gases, liquids, sounds, people, animals, etc., which he takes to be intrinsically interesting to children. No empirical tests of the theory of loose parts have come to our attention.

When resources, e.g., blocks, sandbox, and space were systematically arranged for the same children, Rohe and Patterson (1974) found a complex interaction between space and resources for different aspects of behavior. For example, aggression was lower in the high resource situation for both high and low density conditions, but was an infrequent event generally; cooperation was high in the high resource situation generally, but was highest in the high density, high resource condition. Ramsey (1975) found further that children selected a resource site that was already occupied even if an unoccupied site with the same resource was available. When Smith and Connolly (1977) controlled both square footage and resources, they found that aggression was related to greater density only at the extreme values. Schopler and Stockdale (1977) relate these issues to crowding by suggesting that feeling crowded may result from interference with resources.

It is possible to consider other people as one kind of resource. Classroom size effects are similar to family size effects in showing less interaction time between individual children and the adults in the class or family as the number of children increases. Question asking by children in a classroom decreases per child as the ratio of children to teacher increases from two; two children to one adult yields the highest number of *total* questions (Endsley & Gupta, 1978; Torrance, 1970a), but one-to-one yields the highest number of questions per child (Stallings, 1975). Child-adult ratios with only one or two children are surely infrequent in classroom situations but these studies may provide clues to differences between only children or first born children and later born children in families.

To the extent that question asking relates to exploration — finding out what this "object" does — the effect of a high ratio of children to adults is similar to the effect of reduced nonsocial resources resulting in decreased individual interaction with the resources (Prescott & Jones, 1967).

We have seen similarity between play and exploratory behavior of children with regard to objects, to space, and to people. Spatial and social density create different effects which are related to resources, interference, stress and other factors of the environment. We turn now to some effects of community size more generally on the play and exploration of its young.

## SIZE OF INSTITUTION OR COMMUNITY, DENSITY, AND EXPLORATION

There appears to be a widely held assumption that, as size of institution or community increases, people spend more time in situations marked by high density and crowding. This is what Hauser (1965) identified as "the size-density model" which has been discussed by many writers, most notably perhaps by sociologists Durkheim and Wirth. Milgram's influential paper (1970) follows in this tradition. There is little empirical evidence relevant to the size-density model (Baldassare & Fischer, 1977) and the position has its critics (e.g., Gans, 1968). The difficulties encountered in relating classroom or family density patterns to play are compounded at the level of institution or community.

When discussing the development of the individual in relation to density, we must recognize that density may be different for the same individual from home to school to neighborhood and community. Schmidt, Goldman, and Feimer (1979) report a weak but significant correlation between self-reported perceived "crowdedness" between residence and neighborhood ($r = .18$), and residence and city ($r = .13$) and a stronger ($r = .33$) relationship between neighborhood and city. However, it is possible for a child to live in a high-density family environment, a low-density neighborhood within a high-density city, measured objectively.

## Research on Low Density Settings

Extremely low-density conditions within homes and neighborhoods have rarely been investigated. Haggard (1973) in a study of Norwegian small communities found that children from a middle-density range of population size were subjected to inescapable pressures from society and family. They seemed more inhibited and more dependent than either isolated children or the children in urban communities. Wright (1971) suggested a similar possibility. Hollos and Cowan (1973) and Hollos (1975) showed that extreme isolation interfered more with performance on role taking than on cognitive tasks in a study of small farm communities in Norway and Rumania. All communities were quite small; the largest had a population of about 6,000.

## Behavior Settings as a Measure of Environmental Structure

If cities and institutions do exert influence on the behavior of people, it does not occur in some mystical or amorphous fashion but through the characteristics of and the relationship among the parts of the city or institution. The concept of the ecological environment (Barker, 1963, 1968) as an organized system of structured parts applies equally to institutions, towns, and cities (Garbarino, this volume). In this section we consider research on behavior settings, a basic unit for the study of the ecological environment and the relation of the ecological environment to behavior.

The Behavior Setting Survey (Barker, 1960, 1963, 1968; Barker & Gump, 1964; Barker & Schoggen, 1973; Barker & Wright, 1955) provides one method of measuring the structure of the environment and its impact on behavior. In this approach, the institution or community is seen as consisting of a finite number of parts — behavior settings — each of which is a system, itself bounded by time and space with both human and nonhuman components, all of which are synchronized toward some specific purpose or set of purposes. The rules for discovering and defining these parts are sufficiently systematic that each behavior setting is interdependent with all other units at about the same level. In discussing a small town in Kansas as an environment for behavior and development, Barker & Wright (1955) reported that it was possible to identify the behavior settings available for the town's 119 children and that these behavior settings included a wide range of situations and patterns of behavior. More importantly, the behavior settings were "not neutral areas, but demanded different degrees of participation" (Barker & Wright, 1955, p.

459). The number of performances required for the settings to function was high in relation to the number of people available to fill them; there was, therefore, pressure from the community for each person to participate in a responsible way.

Exploration for these children involved increased entrance into and increased participation within the public parts of the town. It was no mere "child's play" but involvement in the real life of the town. In Berg and Medrich's (1980) terms the town was safe because it was known and the people were seen repeatedly in different settings. In Haggard's (1973) terms the children were "unable to escape" family and societal pressures. In the terms used by both Schank and Abelson (1977) and Bower, Black, and Turner (1979) the children were learning the scripts of the town's settings. Rather than "learning about" the town's culture the children were *living* it.

Culture is often posited as residing within the individual: "a collective organization of ideas concerning what is and ought to be; that is, a set of shared beliefs and values approximating the coherence of an ideological system" (Read, 1980, p. 32). The study of the "acquisition of culture will require a conception of culture as something that becomes part of the behavioral and mental repertoire of the individual" (Read, 1980, p. 32). The behavior settings of a town, however, are an outward manifestation of some aspects of the culture; people have structured the behavior settings and structure their own lives with respect to them (Barker, 1968).

Whether the community is a particular school, hospital, town or city, that community can be described for some purposes in terms of its behavior settings. Each behavior setting has its own set of characteristics: of group behavior, i.e., a standing pattern of behavior of people en masse; of objects; of time and space. This constellation keeps providing information and feedback to the inhabitants (Barker, 1960; Barker & Wright, 1955). The continuing interaction of the person with the setting and the information this interaction provides helps keep the behavior of individuals within the "mores" of the setting. What an individual is "used to" and the expectations of the individual arise, in part, from past experience with specific behavior settings and, in part, from experience of behavior variation from one behavior setting to another. Behavior settings are, then, the props, guides, signposts, demanders-of-behavior-on-the-spot; there is no need for *all* of the required behavior repertoire of a culture to be funnelled into the individual.

## Undermanning Theory, Participation, and Exploration

Data from public (nonhome) behavior settings in two small towns in different cultures, England and the United States (Kansas), were used to compare the towns as environments for behavior and development (Barker & Schoggen, 1973). These data showed that children in the Kansas town entered more of the public behavior settings and more often took positions of leadership and responsibility in the operation of these settings than did their counterparts in the English town. Although the towns differed markedly in overall population density—the English town having more people per unit of space —this is not seen as the "cause" of the differences in the children's participation in behavior settings. Rather, the investigators argue that the Kansas children took a more active part in operating the town's behavior settings because the town was short-handed, i.e., there were, relative to the English town, fewer people to carry out the much larger numbers of tasks called for by the greater number of behavior settings in the Kansas town. These and other data led Barker to develop the theory of undermanning (Barker, 1960; Barker & Gump, 1964; Barker & Schoggen, 1973), which has received support from a number of studies of the behavior settings of towns, schools and churches. Perhaps the best known research on undermanning was the study of school size reported by Barker and Gump (1964). Studying primarily nonclass, extra-curricular activities in high schools ranging in size from less than 100 to more than 2000 students, they found more participation and more frequent involvement in leadership positions in such settings by students in small schools. Baird's (1969) report of 21,000 ACT applicants for college showed that high school size was negatively related to participation. Pence and Taylor (1978) reported that dropout rate was correlated + .58 with school population size; percent of seniors planning to go to college correlated − .40 with pupil-teacher ratio. Morgan and Alwin (1980) classified kinds of settings in large and small high schools. They found, in general, that the number of slots to be filled was strongly related to school size but not proportionate to the increase in number of students.

Student involvement in specified kinds of school activities was found to be lower in the large versus small schools by Kleinert (1969) in a sample of 63 high schools in southern Michigan. And, in another study (Wicker, 1968), juniors from large and small schools reported on involvement in six different kinds of extracurricular activities, e.g., basketball games, dances. Within and between large and small school comparisons revealed that the experience of being needed, challenged, having an important job to do, and developing self-confidence are all associated with undermanned activities. Most of the variation was attributed to holding responsible positions within activities (Wicker, 1968).

These studies show that forces toward participation from the environment act as powerful determinants of behavior and experience (Barker, 1960). Participation relates closely to the "need" to explore before play can occur. There may be a similar process in the need to explore potential activities first hand in order to choose. Time magazine (May 24, 1976) reports in an article entitled "Why Small Town Boys Make Good" that "with the exception of J. F. Kennedy, every American president since Taft was born or reared in a small community." The writer suggested it was easier for children in a small community to get a grasp on real life. Although alternative explanations should be explored, it is noteworthy that the data from the undermanning studies also suggest that basic developmental processes may be influenced by growing up in a small town or attending a small school.

The assumption that wide opportunities are provided by urban living or large schools is explored by Barker and Gump (1964). Inside forces of small schools induce students to make more active and responsible contributions than students from large schools (Willems, 1964). Though the large school provided its 794 juniors with 189 settings compared to 48 settings for 23 small school juniors, the small school students held more positions of importance and responsibility in the settings they entered and entered more different kinds of settings. The number of settings entered varied more for students of the large school (Gump & Friesen, 1964).

Experiences reported by the juniors from larger schools related to satisfactions stemming from vicarious pleasure, affiliation with a large organization, learning about school affairs and their inhabitants as well as getting points for participation. Small school juniors reported more satisfaction from developing competence, being challenged, engaging in important activities, being involved with a group in an activity and real achievement of moral and cultural values (Gump & Friesen, 1964).

Manning theory suggests that undermanned settings are less selective than overmanned or optimally manned settings; when the supply of persons to operate the setting is small, the setting cannot afford to be highly selective. This expectation was strongly supported in interview data collected by Willems (1964) on the experience of both regular and "marginal" high schools juniors in small and large schools, marginal here referring to students who, because of aptitude and background factors, were at high risk for dropping out of school. When asked about their reasons for taking part in elective, extracurricular activities, juniors in small schools reported experiencing significantly more forces toward participation than did juniors in the large schools. Regular and marginal students in small schools did not differ appreciably in the number of forces toward participation but in the large school, marginal students reported markedly fewer such forces than did regular students. "It appears that the small school environments, made up of relatively underpopulated behavior settings, produced less discrimination between the two kinds of students . . . than the large school environment, made up of relatively overpopulated settings" (p. 123).

Cognitive complexity, measured by a modified role construct repertory test for 40 juniors, showed a negative relationship to school size; females scored higher on cognitive complexity in both kinds of schools (Wicker, 1969). Wicker's (1969) hypothesis that cognitive complexity is a function of frequency and intensity of interaction with parts of the domain was confirmed. Relative to large schools with their overmanned settings, small schools benfit individual development by inducing children to learn by doing through participation.

Large communities did not provide the needed experience: "The data provide no evidence that the urban environments of the large schools compensated by means of their greater resources and facilities for the relatively meager functional importance of the students within their large schools" (Barker & Gump, 1964, p. 198). Students transported to central district schools from small communities showed somewhat lower rates of participation than students in small schools in small communities.

Wright (1971) reported that children in a large town (33,000) entered more settings of more different kinds, but were active participants in fewer settings than small town (786) children. The large town was 40 times larger than the small town in terms of population, but there were only ten times as many behavior settings and only three times as many different kinds of settings. With increased community size, the number of settings, kinds of settings, opportunities for involvement and number of settings per kind did increase but not in proportion to the size of the population increase. Furthermore, the children in the small town knew more about the settings of the town, the people, and even the pets than the large town children. Exploration for these children was more than geographic distance from the home; it was entrance into town life via the behavior settings and was the forerunner to adolescent and adult participation. In a sense they were asking "What does this behavior *setting* do?" (exploration) so that at the later stages they could use the setting for their own purposes, "What can *I* do with this setting?" This is corroborated by a study of seventeen nursery school children in six behavior settings of the school. In comparing data across settings, Schuster, Murrell, and Cook (1980) found that the interpersonal variation was less than intersituational variation. Younger children were less setting-dominated than older children, although old-timers in the school showed more personal consistency than newcomers, i.e., were freer to use the setting for their own needs.

Experimental studies have confirmed aspects of the theory of undermanning. Wicker, Kirmeyer, Hanson, and Alexander (1976) report an experiment using slot car racing as the task. Greater degree of manning produced weaker and more variable feelings of involvement with the group and its task. Petty and Wicker (1974) tested another undermanning effect, i.e., the acceptance of less qualified persons in undermanned settings and confirmed this in a similar slot car racing experiment. Also using a similar set up, Arnold and Greenberg (1980) showed that undermanned and adequately manned groups ignored their dislike of confederates-as-deviates and perceived themselves as using more energy while overmanned groups rejected the confederates-as-deviates and perceived themselves as expending less effort. Persons in the overmanned groups also perceived themselves to be less important than people in the undermanned groups.

An interesting set of studies discovered and expanded upon by Ingham, Levinger, Graves, and Peckham (1974) and Latané, Williams, and Harkins (1979) depict the other side of the coin, namely: when people perform in a group they exert less effort per person than when they perform singly, even when coordination inefficiencies are taken into account. This is congruent with Latané's Law of Social Impact stating that the nth person has less effect than the (n-1)th (Latané, 1973). Bechtel (1974) uses a different approach and quotes education expenditure statistics showing that less money was spent per capita in small versus large communities; he suggested that people work harder in small communities.

These data from communities and schools and groups of persons make clear that the common "assumption that there is a direct coupling between the facilities or properties of schools and behavior and experience of students" is not true (Barker & Gump, 1964, p. 201). If versatility of experience is preferred over specialization, small schools are required; if specialization is sought, the large school is better. Density of population whether it is measured per room, per neighborhood, or per town is only one factor in an environment. Whatever the density level, the number of activities, choices, events, and resources, including people significantly influence outcomes. Very little, if any, research exists about family residential density and there is limited research at the community level. Most density studies reported are experimental studies or are based in schools.

## CONCLUSIONS

There is no simple relationship between population or room density and child exploration, play and experience generally. It is clear that object exploration and exploration of space display some common developmental patterns that are important to both the individual and the species and that require active participation on the part of the developing organism. It is also clear that the organization of the everyday environment can either increase or suppress active involvement of their inhabitants, even the children. The gradual increase in organism-environment *inter*action as development progresses seems to be a common thread whether the focus of the interaction is objects, people, or space. A more complex unifying theme can be found in the concept of control-participation. "Loose parts" are parts that may be controlled by the user; participation in an active way through interacting with an object, traversing space, assuming leadership in a situation is to exert some control over the object, space, or situation. The active interaction may be playful or serious but the effects of the control-participation on experience and developmental pattern appear to be comparable.

## REFERENCES

Adelberg, B. Z. *The activity ranges of children in urban and exurban communities.* Unpublished doctoral dissertation. University of Kansas, 1977.

Altman, I. *The environment and social behavior: Privacy, personal space, territory, crowds.* Monterey, California: Books-Cole, 1975.

Anderson, J. & Tindall, M. The concept of home range; New data for the study of territorial behavior. In W. Mitchell (Ed.) *Environmental Design: Research and practice,* EDRA 3/ AR8 Proceedings, U.C.L.A., 1972, 1.11–1.17. (microfilm).

Anderson, J. W. Attachment behavior out of doors. In N. Blurton Jones (Ed.), *Ethological studies of child behavior.* Cambridge: The University Press, 1972, 199–215.

Arnaud, S. H. Some functions of play in the education process. *Childhood Education,* 1974, *51*(2), 72–78.

Arnold, D. W., & Greenberg, C. I. Deviate rejection within differentially manned groups. *Social Psychology Quarterly,* 1980, *43,* 419–424.

Baird, L. L. Big school, small school: A critical examination of the hypothesis. *Journal of Educational Psychology,* 1969, *60,* 253–260.

Baldassare, M., & Fischer, C. The relevance of crowding experiments to urban studies. In D. Stokols (Ed.), *Perspectives on environment and behavior: Theory, research, and applications.* New York: Plenum Press, 1977, 273–285.

Barker, R. G. Ecology and motivation. In M. R. Jones (Ed.), Nebraska *Symposium on Motivation.* Lincoln: University of Nebraska Press, 1960, 1–49.

Barker, R. G. On the nature of the environment. *The Journal of Social Issues,* 1963, *19*(4), 17–38.

Barker, R. G. *Ecological psychology.* Stanford, California: Stanford University Press, 1968.

Barker, R. G., & Gump, P. V. *Big school, small school.* Stanford, California: Stanford University Press, 1964.

Barker, R. G., & Schoggen, P. *Qualities of community life: Methods of measuring environment and behavior applied to an American and and English town.* San Francisco: Jossey-Bass, Inc. 1973.

Barker, R. G., & Wright, H. F. *Midwest and its children: The psychological ecology of an American town.* New York: Row Peterson, 1955.

Baum, A., Aiello, J. R., & Calesnick, L. E. Crowding and personal control: Social density and the development of learned helplessness. *Journal of Personality and Social Psychology,* 1978, *36,* 1000–1011.

Beach, F. Current concepts of play in animals. *American Naturalist,* 1945, *79*(785), 523–541.

Bechtel, R. B. The undermanned environment: A universal theory? In D. H. Carson (Ed.), *Man-environment interactions: Evaluations and applications* (Part 2). Stroudsburg, Pennsylvania: Dowden, Hutchinson and Ross, Inc. 1974.

Berg, M., & Medrich, E. A. Children in four neighborhoods: The physical environment and its effect on play and play patterns. *Environment and Behavior,* 1980, *12,* 320–348.

Berlyne, D. E. *Conflict, arousal and curiosity.* New York: McGraw Hill, 1960.

Blaut, J. M., McCleary, G. S. Jr., & Blaut, A. S. Environmental mapping in young children. *Environment and Behavior,* 1970, *2,* 335–349.

Bower, G. H., Black, J. B., & Turner, T. Scripts in memory for text. *Cognitive Psychology,* 1979, *11,* 177–220.

Bradbard, M. R., & Endsley, R. C. How can teachers develop young children's curiosity? What current research says to teachers. *Young Children,* 1980, *35*(5), 21–32.

Bruner, J., & Connolly, K. Competence: The growth of the person. In K. Connolly, and J. Bruner, (Eds.), *The growth of competence.* London: Academic Press, 1974, 309–313.

Bruner, J., Jolly, A., & Sylva, K. *Play – its role in development and evolution.* New York: Basic Books, 1976.

Bruner, J. S., Olver, R. R., & Greenfield, P. M. *Studies in cognitive growth: A collaboration at the Center for Cognitive Studies.* New York: Wiley, 1966.

Chatelanat, G., & Schoggen, M. Issues encountered in devising an observation system to assess spontaneous infant behavior-environment interactions. In J. Hogg & P. Mittler (Eds.), *Advances in mental handicap research* (Vol. 1). New York: Wiley, 1980.

Coates, G. & Bussard, E. Patterns of children's spatial behavior in a moderate-density housing development. In R. C. Moore (Ed.), *Childhood city, man-environment interactions* (Vol. 3). Milwaukee: EDRA, 1974, 131–141.

Cohen, S., Glass, D., & Singer, J. Apartment noise, auditory discrimination and reading ability in children. *Journal of Experimental Social Psychology,* 1973, *9,* 407–422.

Coie, J. An evaluation of the cross-situational stability of children's curiosity. *Journal of Personality,* 1974, *42,* 93–116.

Csikszentmihalyi, M. *Beyond boredom and anxiety.* San Francisco: Jossey-Bass, 1975.

Dember, W. N., & Earl, R. W. Analyses of exploratory, manipulatory and curiosity behaviors. *Psychological Review,* 1957, *64,* 91–96.

Dolhinow, P. J., & Bishop, N. The development of motor skills and social relationships among primates through play. *Minnesota Symposium on Child Psychology* (Vol. 4). Minneapolis: University of Minnesota Press, 1970, 141–198.

Eckerman, C. O., & Rheingold, H. L. Infants' exploratory responses to toys and people. *Developmental Psychology,* 1974, *10,* 255–259.

Endsley, R. C. *Tactual access, stimulus dimensionality, and peer presence as determinants of young children's identification and transformational questions.* Unpublished manuscript, 1979.

Endsley, R. C., & Gupta, S. Group size as a determinant of preschool children's frequency of question asking. *Journal of Genetic Psychology,* 1978, *132,* 317–318.

Fagot, B. I. Variations in density: Effects on task and social behaviors of preschool children. *Developmental Psychology,* 1977, *13,* 166–167.

Gans, H. J. *People and plans: Essays on urban problems and solutions.* New York: Basic Books, 1968.

Glassman, J. B., Burkhart, B. R., Grant, R. D., & Vallery, G. G. Density, expectation and extended task performance: An experiment in the natural environment. *Environment and Behavior,* 1978, *10,* 299–315.

Goldberg, S., & Lewis, M. Play behavior in the year-old infant: Early sex differences. *Child Development,* 1969, *40,* 21–31.

Gray, M. D., Tracy, R. L., & Lindberg, C. L. Effects of maternal interference on the attachment and exploratory behavior of one-year-olds. *Child Development,* 1979, *50,* 1211–1214.

Groos, K. The value of play for practice and self realization. In D. Muller-Schwarze (Ed.), *Evolution of play behavior. Benchmark papers in animal behavior.* Stroudsburg, Pennsylvania: Dowden, Hutchinson & Ross, Inc., 1978, 16–81 (Original 1898).

Gump, P. V., & Adelberg, B. Behavior from the perspective of ecological psychologists. *Environment and Behavior,* 1978, *10,* 171–192.

Gump, P. V., & Friesen, W. V. Participation in nonclass settings. In R. G. Barker and P. V. Gump, *Big school, small school.* Stanford, California: Stanford University Press, 1964, 75–93.

Haggard, E. A. Some effects of geographic and social isloation in natural settings. In J. Rasmussen (Ed.), *Man in isolation and confinement.* Chicago: Aldine Press, 1973, 99–144.

Hart, R. *Chilren's experience of place.* New York: Wiley, 1979.

Hartup, W. W., & Lempers, J. A problem in life-span development: The interactional analysis of family attachments. In P. B. Baltes & K. W. Schaie (Eds.), *Life-span development psychology: Personality and socialization.* New York: Academic Press, 1973, 235–252.

Hauser, P. M. Urbanization: An overview. In P. M. Hauser & L. F. Schnore (Eds.), *The study of urbanization.* New York: Wiley, 1965, 1–47.

Henderson, B., & Moore, S. G. Measuring exploratory behavior in young children: A factor analytic study. *Developmental Psychology,* 1979, *15,* 113–119.

Hollos, M. Logical operations and role-taking abilities in two cultures: Norway and Hungary. *Child Development,* 1975, *46,* 638–649.

Hollos, M., & Cowan, P. A. Social isolation and cognitive development: Logical operations and role-taking abilities in three Norwegian social settings. *Child Development,* 1973, *44,* 630–641.

Hughes, M. Sequential analysis of exploration and play. *International Journal of Behavioral Development,* 1978,*1,* 83–97.

Huston-Stein, A., Friedrich-Cofer, L., & Susman, E. The relations of classroom structure to social behavior, imaginative play and self-regulation of economically-disadvantaged children. *Child Development,* 1977, *48,* 908-916.

Hutt, C. Exploration and play in children. In P. A. Jewell & C. Loizos (Eds.) *Symposium of the Zoological Society of London,* 1966, 61–68.

Hutt, C. Specific and diversive exploration. In H. W. Reese & L. P. Lipsett, (Eds.), *Advances in child development and behavior* (Vol. 5). New York: Academic Press, 1970, 119–180.

Hutt, S. J., & Hutt, C. *Direct observation and measurement of behavior.* Springfield: Charles C. Thomas, 1970.

Ingham, A. G., Levinger, G., Graves, T., & Peckman, U. The Ringelmann effect: Studies of group size and group performance. *Journal of Experimental Social Psychology,* 1974, *10,* 371–384.

Jacobs, B. A., & Moss, H. A. Birth order and sex of sibling as determinants of mother-infant interaction. *Child Development,* 1976, *47,* 315–322.

Jennings, K. D., Harmon, R. J., Morgan, G. A., Gaiter, J. L., & Yarrow, L. J. Exploratory play as an index of mastery motivation: Relationship to persistence, cognitive functioning, and environmental measures. *Developmental Psychology,* 1979, *15,* 386–394.

Kleiber, D. A., & Barnett, L. A. Leisure in childhood. *Young Children,* 1980, *35*(5), 47–53.

Kleinert, E. J. Effects of high school size on student activity participation. *NASSP Bulletin,* 1969, *53,* 34–46.

Langer, J. *The origins of logic: Six to twelve months.* New York: Academic Press, 1980.

Latane, B. A theory of social impact. Paper presented at *The Psychonomic Society,* St. Louis, Missouri, 1973.

Latane, B., Williams, K., & Harkins, S. Many hands make light the work: The causes and consequences of social loafing. *The Journal of Personality and Social Psychology,* 1979, *37,* 822–832.

Lazarus, R. S. & Cohen, J. B. Environmental stress. In I. Altman, & J. F. Wohlwill, (Eds.), *Human behavior and environment: Advances in theory and research,* Vol. 2, New York: Plenum Press, 1977, 90–118.

Loizos, C. Play behavior in higher primates: A review. In D. Morris (Ed.), *Primate ethology.* Chicago: Aldine Press, 1967, 176–218.

MacDonald, A. P., Jr. Manifestations of differential levels of socialization by birth order. *Developmental Psychology,* 1969, *1,* 485–492.

Maw, W., & Maw, E. W. Nature of creativity in high and low curiosity boys. *Developmental Psychology,* 1970, *2,* 325–329.

McMahon, M. L. *The relationship between environmental setting and curiosity in children.* Unpublished manuscript (M.A. thesis). MIT: Department of City and Regional Planning, 1966.

McReynolds, P., Acker, M., & Pietila, C. Relation of object curiosity to psychological adjustment. *Child Development*, 1961, *32*, 393–400.

Mendel, G. Children's preference for differing degrees of novelty. *Child Development*, 1965, *36*, 453–466.

Milgram, S. The experience of living in cities. *Science*, 1970, *167*, 1461–1468.

Miller, S. Ends, means, and galumphing: Some lietmotifs of play. *American Anthropologist*, 1973, 87–98.

Minuchin, P. Correlation of curiosity and exploratory behavior in preschool disadvantaged children. *Child Development*, 1971, *42*, 939–950.

Moore, R., & Young, D. Childhood outdoors: Toward a second ecology of the landscape. In I. Altman & J. Wohlwill (Eds.), *Human behavior and environment* (Vol. 3), *Children and the environment*. New York: Plenum Press, 1978, 83–130.

Morgan, D., & Alwin, D. F. When less is more: School size and student social participation — manning theory revisited. *Social Psychology Quarterly*, 1980, *43*, 241–252.

Murphy, L. B., & Moriarty, A. E. *Vulnerability, coping and growth*. New Haven: Yale University Press, 1976.

Nicholson, S. How not to cheat children: The theory of loose parts. *Landscape Architecture*, 1971, *62* (Oct.), 30–34.

Nunnally, J. C., & Lemond, L. C. Exploratory behavior and human development. In H. W. Reese (Ed.), *Advances in Child Development* (Vol. 8). New York: Academic Press, 1973, 60–109.

Pence, E. C., & Taylor, R. B. Level of manning and response to deviant behavior. *Environmental Psychology and Nonverbal Behavior*, 1978, *3*, 122–123.

Petty, R. M., & Wicker, A. W. Degree of manning and degree of success of a group as determinants of members' subjective experiences and their acceptance of a new group member. *JSAS Catalog of Selected Documents in Psychology*, 1974, *4*, 43, (Ms. No. 616).

Piaget, J. *Play, dreams and imitation in childhood*. New York: Norton, 1962.

Piaget, J. *The mechanisms of perception*. New York: Basic Books, 1969.

Prescott, E., & Jones, E. *Group day care as a child-rearing environmet*. Pasadena, California: Pacific Oaks College, 1967.

Rabinowitz, F. M., Moely, B. E., Finkel, N., & McClinton, S. The effect of toy novelty and social interactions on the exploratory behavior of preschool children. *Child Development*, 1975, *46*, 286–289.

Ramsey, B. *Systematic observation of the spatio-temporal behavior of preschool children under varyng conditions of spatial density*. Unpublished MA thesis, George Peabody College, Nashville, Tenn., 1975.

Read, P. B. Socialization research revisited. SSRC *Items*, 1980, *34*(2), 31–35.

Rheingold, H. L., & Eckerman, C. O. The infant separates himself from the mother. *Science*, 1970, *168*, 78–83.

Rheingold, H. L., & Eckerman, C. O. Fear of the stranger: A critical examination. In H. W. Reese (Ed.), *Advances in child development and behavior* (Vol. 8). New York: Academic Press, 1973, 185–222.

Rohe, W., & Patterson, A. H. The effects of varied levels of resources and density on behavior in a day care center. In D. H. Carlson (Ed.), *Man-environment interaction: Evaluation and application* (Part 3, Vol. 3). Stroudsburg, Pennsylvania: Dowden, Hutchinson & Ross, 1974, 161–171.

Schank, R., & Abelson, R. *Scripts plans goals and understanding*. Hillsdale, N. J.: Lawrence Erlbaum Associates, 1977.

Schiller, P. H. Innate motor actions as a basis of learning. In C. H. Schiller (Ed. and trans.), *Instinctive behavior*. New York: International Universities Press, Inc., 1957, 264–287.

Schmidt, D. E., Goldman, R. D., & Feimer, N. R. Perspectives of crowding: Predicting at the residence, neighborhood and city levels. *Environment and Behavior*, 1979, *11*, 105.

Schopler, J., & Stockdale, J. An interference analysis of crowding. *Environmental Psychology and Nonverbal Behavior,* 1977, *1,* 81–88.

Schuster, S. O., Murrell, S. A. & Cook, W. A. Person, setting and interaction contributions to nursery school social behavior patterns. *Journal of Personality,* 1980, *48,* 24–37.

Scott, J. P. *Early experience and the organization of behavior.* Belmont, California: Brooks/Cole, 1968.

Sherrod, K., Vietze, P., & Friedman, S. *Infancy.* Monterey, California: Brooks/Cole, 1978.

Smith, P. K., & Connolly, K. J. Social and aggressive behavior in preschool children as a function of crowding. *Social Science Information,* 1977, *16,* 601–620.

Stallings, J. Implementation and child effects of teaching practices in follow-through classrooms. *Monograph of the Society for Research in Child Development,* 1975, *40,* (Serial No. 163).

Torrance, E. P. Group size and question performance of preprimary children. *Journal of Psychology,* 1970, *74,* 71–75. (a)

Torrance, E. P. Freedom to manipulate objects and question-asking performance of six-year-olds. *Young Children,* 1970, *26*(2), 93–97. (b)

Vandenberg, B. Play and development from an ethological perspective. *American Psychologist,* 1978, *33,* 724–738.

Wachs, T. Utilization of a Piagetian approach in the investigation of early experience effects: A research strategy and some illustrative data. *Merrill-Palmer Quarterly,* 1976, *17,* 283–317.

Weisler, A., & McCall, R. B. Exploration and play—Resumé and redirection. *American Psychologist,* 1976, *31,* 492–510.

Why small town boys make good. *Time,* 1976, May 24 (Microfiche 85).

Wicker, A. Undermanning, performance and students' subjective experience in behavior settings of large and small high schools. *Journal of Personality and Social Psychology,* 1968, *10,* 255–261.

Wicker, A. Cognitive complexity, school size, and participation in school behavior settings: A test of the frequency of interaction hypothesis. *Journal of Educational Psychology,* 1969, *60,* 200–203.

Wicker, A. W., Kirmeyer, S. L., Hanson, L., & Alexander, D. Effects of manning levels on subjective experiences, performance, and verbal interaction in groups. *Organizational Behavior and Human Performance,* 1976, *17,* 251–274.

Willems, E. P. Forces toward participation in behavior settings. In R. G. Barker and P. V. Gump. *Big school, small school.* Stanford, California: Stanford University Press, 1964, 115–135.

Wohlwill, J. F., & Heft, H. Environments fit for the developing child. In H. McGurk (Ed.), *Ecological factors in human development.* Amsterdam: North-Holland Publishing Co., 1977, 125–137.

Wolfe, M. Childhood and privacy. In I. Altman & J. F. Wohlwill (Eds.), *Human behavior and environment:* (Vol. 3), *Children and the environment.* New York: Plenum Press, 1978, 175–222.

Wortman, C. & Brehm, J. Responses to uncontrollable outcome: An integrating reactance theory and the learned helplessness model. In L. Berkowitz (Ed.), *Advances in experimental social psychology* (Vol. 8). New York: Academic Press, 1975, 277–336.

Wright, H. F. *Children's behavior in communities differing in size,* Parts, 1, 2, 3, & Supplement. Report to Project Grant #H01G98 (NIMH). Lawrence, Kansas: Department of Psychology, University of Kansas, mimeo, 1969.

Wright, H. F. Urban space as seen by the child. *Courrier: Revue medico-sociale de l'enfance,* Sept.-October, 1971, *XXI*(5), 485–495.

Yarrow, L. J., Rubenstein, J. L., & Pedersen, F. A. *Infant and environment: Early cognitive and motivational development.* New York: Wiley, 1975.

# 5 Children, Crowding, and Control: Effects of Environmental Stress on Social Behavior

John R. Aiello
*Rutgers — The State University*

Donna E. Thompson
*Graduate School of Management*
*Rutgers — The State University*

Andrew Baum
*Uniformed Services University of the Health Sciences*

## INTRODUCTION

The last half century has witnessed an ever increasing concern of social scientists with the effects of crowding and other environmental stressors on human behavior. Initially, research was conducted on crowded animal populations, and evidence from these studies strongly implicated high density in the development of social and organic dysfunction (e.g., Calhoun, 1962; Christian, Flyger, & Davis, 1961; Myers, Hale, Mykytowycz, & Hughes, 1971). Early correlational studies of urban areas related different degrees of human population density to various indicators of social and physical pathology (e.g., Lantz, 1953; Plant, 1930; Shaw & McKay, 1942). Subsequent correlational investigations, some of which have been concerned with infants and children, have revealed that population density is positively related to such factors as infant morality, neonatal lethargy, juvenile delinquincy, short-stature, low body weight, and frequent illness (e.g., Booth & Johnson, 1975; Galle, Gove, & McPherson, 1972; Schmitt, 1966).

The purpose of this chapter is to provide a comprehensive review of research which has been directly concerned with the effects of high density conditions on the social behavior and health of children and adolescents. Throughout this chapter, we examine how control (and the *lack* of control) mediates this relationship. We also consider some recent research concerned with other environmental stressors, which may also impact on habitats for children.

## DENSITY EFFECTS IN NONRESIDENTIAL SETTINGS

We begin our review by focusing on studies conducted primarily by psychologists that deal with the impact of dense nonresidential environments (e.g., classrooms, playrooms, and playgrounds), which are repeatedly experienced by children for relatively brief periods of time. Most of this research has been inspired by practical consideration such as how the size and layout of classrooms and play areas influence the behavior of children. Almost all of the investigations have focused on nursery schools and very young children (age 2–5). Studies in this area have distinguished between two types of density conditions. Of the studies reported to date, *fifteen* have varied spatial density by observing a constant number of children in different size rooms (or areas), *four* have varied social density by observing different numbers of children in the same size room (space), and *two* have examined both social and spatial density.

### Decreases in Social Contact

These studies have generally found that when placed in either high social or spatial density conditions children engage in less social interaction, display more avoidance behavior and exhibit more withdrawal and solitary play (Bates, 1970; Hutt & Vaizey, 1966; Loo, 1972; Loo & Smetana, 1978; P. L. McGrew, 1979; W. C. McGrew, 1970; Preiser, 1972; Price, 1971; Rohe, 1976; Rohe & Nuffer, 1977; Rohe & Patterson, 1974; Shapiro, 1975; Slosnerick, 1974).[1] For example, Loo (1972) examined the effects of spatial density on 4- and 5-year-old middle class children. The children were divided into 10 groups of six and observed during free play in both a low-density condition (44.2 square feet per child) and a high density condition (15 square feet per child). Social interaction was recorded whenever an awareness of others was demonstrated through either play, talking, or observation. Degrees of social involvement were indicated by three categories: (1) solitary play: wherein a child showed no indication of social involvement, only showing interest in his or her own activity; (2) onlooker: wherein a child only observed

---

[1]Only three studies have failed to find this effect (Ginsburg & Pullman, 1975; Hutt & McGrew, 1967; and Smith & Connolly, 1972).

the activities of others; and (3) group involvement: wherein a child functioned as an integral member of a group. Results indicated that children exhibited significantly less social interaction and tended to engage in more solitary play than group play in the high density conditions.

In a more recent study, Loo and Smetana (1978) investigated the effects of spatial density on the free play behavior of 10-year-old boys from middle class to upper middle class backgrounds. Groups of five boys each were observed in either a low density room (52.1 square feet per person) or in a high density room (13.6 square feet per person). Although the frequency of positive group interactions (e.g., nonsolitary behavior, social interaction in a group and positive social overtures did not differ between the two density conditions, more avoidance behavior (e.g., escape, facing out, non-sitting) was displayed in the high density than in the low density condition.

P. L. McGrew (1970) observed the effects of both spatial and social density on the free-play behavior of 3- and 4-year-old middle class nursery school children. Spatial density was manipulated by making either 100% (low spatial density) of the playroom space available to the children or only 80% (high spatial density) available by partitioning off one end of the room with a barrier of benches and chairs. Social density in turn was manipulated by observing either 16–20 children (high social density) or 8–10 children (low social density) in the playroom at any given point in time. Four different experimental conditions resulted from these social and spatial density manipulations: (1) low social/low spatial density condition (89 square feet per child); (2) low social/high spatial density condition (77 square feet per child); (3) high social/low spatial density condition (51 square feet per child); and (4) high social/high spatial density condition (39 square feet per child). Observations were made of the following four categories of proximity behaviors: (1) contact (two or more children were in physical contact); (2) close proximity (two or more children were within three feet of each other); (3) intermediate proximity (two or more children were farther than three feet apart but occupied the same 7.2 × 7.2 ft. taped floor square); and (4) solitary proximity (one child occupied a taped floor square). An interesting pattern of results emerged with higher frequencies of close peer proximity behavior and increased amounts of solitary play being observed under the high spatial density conditions. This was particularly the case when high social density was combined with high spatial density.

Similar findings were reported by Preiser (1972) in his study of the effects of spatial density on the free play behavior of 3- and 4-year-old white, middle class children in a nursery school setting. Spatial density was manipulated by partitioning off one third of the floor space in the approximately 600 square feet nursery room. Observations of the children's behavior were made for two weeks preceding the use of the partition, two weeks during the reduction of space, and for two weeks following the removal of the partition. Consistent with the results of the two investigations cited above, social contact was found to decrease during the period of space reduction.

## Increases in Aggressive Behavior

Another area that has received a considerable amount of attention has been the relationship between density level and children's aggressive behavior. The results of a number of investigations have yielded equivocal results pertaining to this relationship. Most studies however have reported that children are more aggressive in higher density environments (Bates, 1970; Ginsburg & Pollman, 1975; Hutt & Vaizey, 1966; Loo, 1979; Loo & Kennelly, 1979; W. C. McGrew, 1972, Rohe, 1976; Rohe & Patterson, 1974; Shapiro, 1975). For example, Shapiro (1975) observed the behavior of 4-year-olds in half-day nursery school settings. Greater amounts of deviant (i.e., disruptive, aggressive, or unacceptable) behavior were found in crowded classrooms containing less than 30 square feet per child.

In an early study concerned with the effects of social density, Hutt and Vaizey (1966) observed 3- to 8-year-old brain-damaged, autistic and normal children in a free-play situation in a small group (6 or less), in a medium sized group (7 to 11), or in a large group (12 or more). Observations were made of the relative proportions of time the children spent in aggressive or destructive behavior (such as fighting or breaking toys) in a 27 ft. by 17.5 ft. playroom familiar to the students. Results indicated that aggressive behavior significantly increased for both the normal and brain-damaged children but not for the autistic children under the higher density conditions.

Similarly, in another investigation of the effects of social density, Bates (1970) observed two and three year old nursery school children in a free-play situation. This study took advantage of a naturally occurring social density manipulation in that the number of children present at any particular play session tended to vary regularly for several reasons. For example, while some of the children only attended the nursery school for half of the day, others attended a few days a week or on a full-time basis. Moreover, children were often absent because of illness or because they were out on family trips. Running observations were made of the children's behavior under three different social density conditions: (1) 10–15 children in the room (83 square feet per child): (2) 17–24 children in the room (51 square feet per child): and (3) 25–30 children in the room (40 square feet per child). With increased social density, both boys and girls were found to engage in more conflict interactions.

The effects of social density on the behavior and perceptions of five year old middle-class children were also investigated in a study by Loo and Kennelly (1979). Children were observed in either groups of four (low density condition) or groups of eight (high density condition) during free play in the same smaller playroom (9'9" × 13'5") used by Loo (1979) in her investigation of the effects of spatial density on social behavior. Significantly more aggression, activity, and anger were exhibited by the children in the high density condition than their counterparts in the low density condition.

Similar findings were reported in another recent study by Loo (1979). In this investigation, groups of six children each (who were five years of age and from middle class backgrounds) were observed during free play in either a low spatial density condition (43.4 square feet per child) or in a high spatial density condition (21.8 square feet per child). Consistent with the results reported above, more negative affect and aggressive behavior (e.g., anger, distress, physical aggression) were engaged in by the children in the high density condition than those in the low density condition.

Ginsburg and Pollman (1975) examined the effects of spatial density on the aggressive behavior of male elementary school children during unstructured playground activity. On different days the same group of children were videotaped on either a small playground area (low social density condition) or a larger playground area (high social density condition). Observations were recorded of: (1) the occurrence of an aggressive interaction (e.g., hitting, pushing, or kicking another child); (2) the duration of the aggressive interaction; and (3) the style of the aggressive interaction (i.e. whether or not two or more than two children were involved). Children were found to display higher incidences of aggressive behaviors on the higher density small playground but the fights were shorter in duration than those observed on the lower density large playground. However, this latter finding may be due to the differences in the styles of the interactions observed in the two different types of playground areas. More specifically, the majority of aggressive interactions on the larger playground involved only two children whereas more than two children were usually involved in those on the smaller playground. Typically though, these larger fights started out only involving two children. Consequently, the duration of the dyadic aggressive interactions on the smaller playground were significantly shorter due to the interventions of other children.

Other studies however, have found more equivocal results; either no differences between children under high and low densities (Price, 1971; Smith & Connolly, 1972) or less aggression under high density conditions for males and no differences for females (Loo, 1972), although in this study aggression was of a more playful type and was linked to motoric activity. One possible explanation for these inconsistent findings initially suggested by Smith (1973) is that aggression may result because of the frustration and competition experienced by the relatively larger number of children under high social density conditions when there is a limited number of toys and other distractor items present in the environment (i.e. resource scarcity).

Rohe and Patterson (1974) found that the amount of equipment available for use by children did mediate the relationship between density and aggression. In their study, films were made of the behavior of 2- through 5-year-old children in an activity room of a day care setting. Although the children's socioeconomic backgrounds differed, the majority were from families earning less than $8,000 year. The children were observed in four experimental conditions: (1) low density/high resources (48 square feet per child: normal and adequate supply of toys and materials); (2) low density/low resources (48 square feet per child: half of the toys and materials were available for use); (3) high density/high resources (24 square feet per child: normal and adequate supply of toys and materials); and (4) high density/low resources (24 square feet per child: half of the toys and materials were available for use). The findings indicated that combining high density and low resources yielded the most frequent occurrence of aggressive/destructive behavior. Therefore, it is possible that objects like toys may be used by children to ameliorate uncomfortable situations involving excess levels of stimulation from others. Furthermore, children will likely experience a sense of relative deprivation when too many others are competing for a smaller amount of toys and equipment or when there is too little space in which to be able to adequately use these toys.

## Increases in Competitive Behavior

Competitive behavior has also been shown to vary as a function of density level. Rohe and Patterson (1974) for example, found that children spent considerably more time in competitive play when they were in highly dense playrooms, particularly when these play areas contained very few toys. Consistent findings have been reported by Aiello, Nicosia, and Thompson (1979) and Rohe and Nuffer (1977).

Aiello et al. (1979) demonstrated that pronounced effects observed during exposure to high density conditions may also carry over into activities following exposure to crowded conditions. In this study, the *aftereffects* of a short-term crowding experience, involving close physical proximity on the cooperative behavior of 9- to 17-year-old children and adolescents were examined. During each experimental session, two groups of four children each were exposed to either a high density condition (where they sat in two small, 4' × 2.5', partitioned rooms) or to a low density condition (where they sat in two large 10' × 12', partitioned rooms). During this time their skin conductance level (a measure of physiological arousal) was measured. Following this, the students were taken to another room where they completed a post-experimental questionnaire related to their experience and played Kagan and Madsen's (1971) "circle matrix board" game, a measure of cooperation-competition in which they could win coupons that could be traded in for prizes (e.g. Twinkies, Devil Dogs) at the end of the day. Despite the fact that in terms of the available prizes to win children had all to gain from cooperating and nothing to lose, those who had been crowded were more competitive than those who were not crowded. Moreover, the students who had experienced the low density conditions displayed a distinct pattern of avoidance of direct conflict with each other while playing the game.

In an investigation of the mediating effects of partitioning on the behavioral responses of nursery school children to density, Rohe and Nuffer (1977) reported a similar finding of decrements in cooperative behavior in high spatial density conditions. A room divider was used to manipulate spatial density such that when it was closed (high density condition) the playroom space (22 ft. × 33 ft.) was reduced by half. Partitioning was varied by either using eight 4 ft. × 4 ft. partitions to divide the playroom into five separate activity areas or by leaving the playroom open. Behavioral observations of twelve children, ranging in age from 40 to 68 months were made in each of the four experimental conditions resulting from the manipulation of both spatial density and partitioning: low density/partitioning; low density/no partitioning; high density/partitioning; and high density/no partitioning. Cooperative behavior decreased under the high density conditions. However, the addition of partitions increased the amount of cooperative behavior observed under both the high and low spatial density conditions.

## Other Responses to High Density

Additional responses of children under high density conditions include: higher levels of stress-related arousal (Aiello et al., 1979); decreases in locomotion and gross motor activity (Bates, 1970; W. C. McGrew, 1972; Smith & Connolly, 1972); decreases in active play, e.g., running, toy changes, creative play (Loo & Smetana, 1978); increases in proximity (P. L. McGrew, 1970); greater frequency of interruptions (Loo, 1972); and more fearful behavior and more laughing (W. C. McGrew, 1972). For example, in a series of studies, W. C. McGrew observed the effects of density on the free-play behavior of nursery school children.

In McGrew's first experiment, four 3½-year-old children were observed under three naturally occurring spatial density conditions: (1) high density condition (33 square feet per child) wherein the children were observed inside their school during inclement weather; (2) medium density condition (52 square feet per child) wherein the children were observed on an outside concrete strip as well as inside when the grass was wet following inclement weather; and (3) low density condition (150 square feet per child) wherein the children were observed on the lawn and concrete strip as well as inside during clear weather when the grass was dry. Six different kinds of body movement were observed: Hand, arm, leg, gross body, other, and locomotion. As density increased, the amount of time spent in gross body movements and locomotor movements decreased while the amount of time spent in arm movements increased. The number of gross body movements also decreased significantly.

In the second experiment, both social and spatial density were manipulated. Nursery school children were observed during free play in four experimental conditions resulting from these manipulations; (1) high social/high spatial density condition (14–19 children; 37 square feet per child); (2) high social/low spatial density condition (14–19 children; 52 square feet per child); (3) low social/high spatial density condition (8–10 children; 74 square feet per child); and (4) low social/low spatial density condition (8–10 children; 86 square feet per child). Results indicated that whereas more laughing occurred in the high social density conditions, more fearful behavior (i.e., automanipulative behavior, digit suck, physical contact) was displayed in the high spatial density conditions.

## Age as a Moderating Factor of High Density Effects

All but two of the studies reported to date have focused on children between the ages of two and eight. Only Aiello et al. (1979) has directly compared responses and behaviors of children of various ages (9, 13, and 16). Loo (1978) however, has been able to compare the results of her three studies of 5-year-olds with that of her investigation of 10-year-olds (despite the confound that the former studies involved both boys and girls but the latter study employed only boys). She indicated that the effects of density on the behaviors and perceptions of children appear to diminish with age. Despite the fact that children of these two age groups did not report feeling differentially crowded in the high density conditions, the crowded environment resulted in more physical aggression, negative affect, distress, nonplay, and desire to leave the crowded room for the younger children. The older children exhibited more avoidance, no increases in aggression and anger, and generally more socially acceptable, nonaggressive attempts at avoiding each other in the situation. This comparison suggests that the detrimental effects of crowding are more potent for the young and that coping and adaptation mechanisms develop with age. These findings are consistent with the views of Evans (1978), who after reviewing physiological and behavioral effects of high density on human and animal development, concluded that young organisms are more severely affected by crowding than are adult organisms.

This developmental process may pertain however only to younger children. Our research with older children (Aiello et al. 1979) purposely employed a high spatial density condition that interfered with any avoidance strategy attempted by participants. We found that under these circumstances children and adolescents at three age levels were similarly affected by the exposure to crowding. Adolescents experiencing comparable stress-related arousal were just as bothered by the spatial intrusion, annoyed, tense, and uncomfortable due to the close physical proximity of others in the high density condition as were the younger children. The answer to the question of whether the discrepancies between Loo's observations and the data obtained in our research are a function of the age levels involved (9 through 16 in Aiello et al., 1979; 5 and 10 in Loo, 1978a) or the product of the specific density conditions established, will need to await further research.

## Sex as a Moderating Factor of High Density Effects

Fairly strong evidence for sex differences in response to crowding has been reported in studies involving adults (see Aiello & Thompson, 1980; Sundstrom, 1978 for reviews of this literature). Unfortunately many researchers examining the effects of density on children have either not used both sexes in their studies or have not analyzed for differences between the sexes when they were both employed. Of those investigations reporting data relating to both sexes, a good number have cited differences, but a clear pattern of these differences does not emerge from this literature (See Heft, this volume). For example, Loo (1979) found that girls were more affected by high spatial density conditions, felt more crowded, and expressed a greater desire to leave the high density room. On the other hand, Loo and Kennelly (1979) reported that boys were more affected by a high social density environment and engaged in more acting out, destructive, and angry behavior. Aiello et al. (1979) reported that males under high spatial density conditions experienced greater spatial discomfort, more stress-related arousal and exhibited more competitive behavior. Future research will have to clarify the nature of any differential effects that density has on children as a function of their sex.

## Personal Space as a Moderating Factor
## of High Density Effects

Four studies have been conducted (as of this writing) which have found that high density conditions differentially affect adults with close or far personal space preferences (Aiello, DeRisi, Epstein, & Karlin, 1977; Cozby, 1973; Dooley, 1978; Rawls, Trego, McGaffey, & Rawls, 1972). For example, Aiello et al. (1977) conducted the only study using a measure of an individual's directly observed personal space behavior during ongoing interaction to assess how spatial preferences mediate the effects of high spatial density conditions. Adults with far personal space preferences were found to experience greater stress-related arousal in the crowded environment and displayed more physiological, behavioral, and subjective indications of discomfort.

Personal space behavior has been found to develop rather consistently from early childhood to early adolescence (Aiello & Aiello, 1974; Tennis & Dabbs, 1975). As can be seen in Figure 5.1, children use more and more space

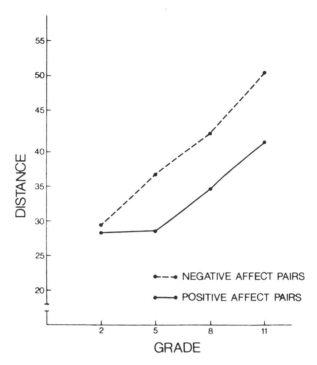

FIG. 5.1.    Interaction distances of reciprocated, positive and negative affect pairs at four grade levels (from Aiello & Cooper, 1979).

(absolutely as well as in proportion to their size) during interaction as they grow older. Since younger children have smaller personal space preferences, might they be less negatively affected than adolescents or adults under high density conditions?

Only one set of studies has assessed the role of personal space preferences as a mediator of high density for children (Loo, 1979; Loo & Kennelly, 1979; Loo & Smetana, 1978). Loo (1979) reported that 5-year-olds under high spatial density conditions were more verbally abusive and exhibited greater avoidance than their counterparts under low density conditions. Loo and Kennelly (1979) on the other hand found no differences as a function of personal space preferences for high and low social density conditions. Loo and Smetana (1978) however, in their study of 10-year-old boys under two spatial density conditions found that under the high spatial density conditions of personal space boys reported experiencing greater discomfort and disliking the crowded room to a greater extent. In contrast, under low spatial density conditions, close personal space boys engaged in a greater number of interactions. Loo (1978b) concluded nonetheless that personal space is a "weak differentiating variable in terms of density" (p. 383).

Strong caution must be urged in viewing the results of these studies. The personal space measure Loo used was assessed through a *simulation* procedure in which an adult experimenter would walk toward the child until the child felt that the adult was getting too close and at that point told the adult to stop. We have data from more than a dozen studies which indicate rather conclusively that there is very little relationship between projected or simulated personal space behavior and that which is actually exhibited during ongoing interaction (See Aiello & Thompson, 1980). Consistent with this, it should be pointed out that Loo (1978b) reported that personal space (approach distances) in her studies decreased with age among children (as was found by Meisels & Guardo, 1969 and Petri & Huggins, 1975, who also employed projective measures). It can be clearly observed that when these findings are compared with those obtained in studies where personal space behavior is directly observed during ongoing interaction (see Figure 5.1), they reflect a developmental trend that is precisely the *reverse* of true behavioral development. Research is needed to assess the role of actual personal space behavior as a mediator of children's reactions to high density conditions. As Evans and Eichelman (1976) suggested, there very well might be a connection between the size of an individual's personal space and the susceptibility to the effects of high density.

## Crowding and High Risk Children

In one of the earliest studies of the effects of density on children, Hutt and Vaizey (1966) reported that brain-damaged children exhibited considerably more aggression (twice as much as that of normal children) under increasing social density conditions. On the other hand, autistic children under these density conditions spent a much greater proportion of their time on the boundaries of the room, possibly reflecting an intensification of their isolation from others. Loo (1978b) reported that she had to abort a study focusing on the effect of two density conditions on the behavior of autistic children because during the session, "the children demonstrated autistic behaviors such as rocking, twiddling fingers, and hypnotic-like stares. Some cried unceasingly and helplessly." (p. 338). She noted that in previous research she had never seen such a high level of distress.

Using the same data base as Loo (1979), Loo (1978c) examined whether spatial density had differential effects on children who scored either high or low on dimensions of hyperactivity-distractibility, anxiety, hostility-aggressiveness, behavior disturbance, and motor inhibition. Her findings suggested that crowding has more severe negative consequences for children who are emotionally and behaviorally disturbed. This investigation indicated that high anxiety children and more impulsive children in particular were more stressed by the high spatial density conditions and exhibited emotionally-helpless responses as compared with the more adaptive and less negative responses of the healthy children. Taken together, the results of these studies point to the need for closer examination of children who are potentially more vulnerable to the effects of high density conditions.

## SUMMARY OF DENSITY RESEARCH IN SCHOOL AND PLAYGROUND SETTINGS

High social and high spatial density conditions have a considerable impact on the social behavior of children. Under these conditions children have been found under some circumstances to decrease their involvement with others by avoiding and withdrawing from them or under other conditions to exhibit more verbal and physical aggression and higher levels of competition, to decrease locomotion and gross motor activity, and generally to display more fearful behavior, and to experience more stress-related arousal.

Some research has begun to examine how situational changes may ameliorate some of the negative effects of high density. One study (Rohe & Patterson, 1974) found that providing sufficient quantities of resources (i.e., toys and equipment) resulted in reductions in aggressive and destructive behavior and increases in cooperative behavior. Another study (Rohe & Nuffer, 1976) demonstrated that strategic placement of partitions within high density environments can increase the amount of cooperative behavior of children.

It appears as though the consequences of high density conditions that involve either too many children or too little space are: excess levels of stimulation, stress and arousal; a drain on resources available; considerable interference; reductions in desired privacy levels; and the loss of control. The results of studies presently available (e.g., Loo & Smetana, 1979) also seem to provide some evidence that coping and adaptive mechanisms of children develop during the course of early and middle childhood years. The effects of high density may therefore be more harmful for younger children, since these capacities have not developed sufficiently to buffer them from the aversive effects of these conditions. While younger children increase their activity level, their group interaction, and their levels of aggression, older children use more avoidance strategies under high density conditions. When the situation is such that this escape strategy is rendered unavailable (i.e., they could not withdraw from the excess stimulation), stress levels experienced by children appear more comparable at the various age levels (e.g., Aiello et al., 1979). The few studies reported thus far which have focused on high risk children (e.g., Hutt & Vaizey, 1966; Loo, 1978c) provide some indication that the essential development of control mechanisms necessary for children to adapt to high density environments may be impeded, resulting in these children being more vulnerable to these conditions.

*very active busy*

The roles of sex and personal space as mediators of reactions to high density conditions, which has been so well established in the adult literature, have yet to be adequately addressed in research with children. Considerations of social structural factors such as social class and ethnicity, which have been so much a part of investigations into the effects of residential density, have been completely ignored in studies of school and playground settings. In fact only Rohe and Nuffer (1976) used children who were not from middle class families.

Another clear need in this area related to studies involving the effects of crowding rather than density. Only the recent studies of Loo (1979; Loo & Kennelly, 1979; Loo & Smetana, 1978) and Aiello et al. (1979) have asked children whether or not they felt crowded under high and low density conditions. The significance of this is nicely demonstrated by the fact that Loo (1979) found that only 14% of her high density condition 5-year-old children said that the room was crowded. This guided her in establishing the conditions necessary for additional crowding research. The importance of distinguishing between density and crowding has been well established (e.g., Stokols, 1972). In our research (Aiello et al., 1979) we purposely focused on children nine years of age and older because we discovered that children younger than this did not seem to really *know* what crowding meant.

Unfortunately only two studies (Aiello et al., 1979; Loo & Smetana, 1979) have investigated the effects of high density on children older than age eight. More work is needed with this older age group particularly if we wish to learn more about the development of coping and adaptation mechanisms of children under environmentally stressful conditions. Lastly, only one investigation has focused on *aftereffects* of a high density environment (Aiello et al., 1979). It may be as important or even more important, to determine the residual effects following exposure to high density conditions as it is to assess the effects of this environment while children are present.

*no study on this*

## EFFECTS OF RESIDENTIAL DENSITY ON CHILDREN'S SOCIAL BEHAVIOR

Investigations that have sought to assess the effects of residential density on the social behavior of children have unfortunately been quite rare. Most of the research focusing on residential density effects has tried to identify indicators of physical and social pathology. While these studies have suffered from a series of methodological problems that caution us to interpret their results as tentative, a number of effects have been reported rather consistently.

Quite a few of these studies, which vary widely with respect to the measures selected and controls employed, have reported a relationship between external or internal high density conditions and juvenile delinquency (Chilton,

1964; Galle & Gove, 1979; Galle, Gove & McPherson, 1972; Gillis, 1974; Schmid, 1969; Schmitt, 1957, 1966; Shaw & McKay, 1942; Wallis & Malliphant, 1967). For example, in their study of the linkages between population density and pathology in Chicago, Galle, Gove, and McPherson (1972) found that two types of density were related to juvenile delinquency. Unlike earlier sociological articles, this investigation statistically controlled for the usually confounding factors of ethnicity, socioeconomic class, occupation and education level. Four different types of density were examined: (1) Number of persons per room; (2) Number of rooms per housing unit; (3) Number of housing units per residential structure; and (4) Number of residential structures per acre.

The results of the Galle et al. (1972) study indicated that the most important component related to juvenile delinquency was the number of people per room. Number of housing units per residential structure was also related to juvenile delinquency. In fact, this type of density had a more significant "impact" on delinquency than it did on any of the other pathologies studied. In interpreting these findings, Galle and colleagues suggest two possible contributing factors to juvenile delinquency. The first is that children may receive less attention from their parents because of the size of larger families and rely more on their peers for guidance and support. Secondly, they speculate that in high density environments parents are more likely to be tired, harassed, and irritable. Children may choose to spend more time outside the home to escape the negative interactions that may result from their parents dispositions as well as other unpleasant factors that often characterize high density situations (e.g., lack of privacy, noise level). The authors further suggest that parents in turn, are likely not to discourage the children from spending a good deal of time outside of the home, since their leaving helps to reduce their own negative experiences with the high density living conditions.

Some support for the latter suggestion is found in the second of three large-scale sample surveys examining the social, personal, and health consequences of high density housing in Hong Kong conducted by Mitchell (1971). This study was based on a sample of families in urban areas. Five hundred and sixty-one husband-wife pairs were interviewed along with 2,631 other individuals who were married and living with their spouse, but whose spouse was not interviewed. Although he concluded that high density did not have a very significant effect on individuals and families, he did acknowledge that it had a clear impact on parent-child relationships. Parents with a child 18 years of age or younger living at home were asked, "How often do . . . your children . . . play outside the house and you do not know where they are?" The responses to this question indicated that the amount of surveillance that parents had over their children varied as a function of density. A higher proportion of parents living in higher density housing reported that they had no knowledge of where their children were playing. It is of interest to note that this finding was obtained even after two factors which have been related to parental control over children (education and family income) were controlled for statistically. It appears that in attempts to reduce some of the negative effects of high density, parents do not discourage their children from going outside of the home, thereby reducing the density. As a consequence however, they experience reductions in the control that they have over their children. Evidence that parents from high density environments experience lower levels of control over their children and have trouble keeping track of them has also been reported by Gove, Hughes, and Galle (1979), Loo (1980), McCarthy and Saegert (1979).

In their more recent investigation, Gove et al. (1979) provide direct support for the notion that parents in crowded households not only fail to discourage their children from leaving the home but that they also feel considerable relief when they are outside of the house as well. This interview study was conducted in Chicago. A total of 2,035 respondents were interviewed; approximately 25 interviews were gathered from 80 separate census tracts within the city limits. An interesting feature of this investigation is that the sample was selected so as to minimize the relationship between socioeconomic status, race and crowding. Overall, the findings indicated that both objective crowding (i.e. number of persons per room) and subjective crowding (i.e. perceptions of excessive social demands and a lack of privacy) were significantly related to poor child care. As indicated above, children in crowded households were experienced as an "irritant" and relief on the part of the parents was experienced when they were away from the household. In addition, crowded parents also reported not having very much knowledge concerning their child's friends and their parents, suggesting that they are also less aware of their child's activities outside of the home. It should be noted however, that as with much of the literature related to the indirect effects of residential density on children's social behavior, these findings have been questioned by other researchers in this area (Booth, Johnson, & Edwards, 1980).

One other area that may influence children's social behavior relates to the degree of interpersonal conflict in the home (see Booth, this volume, for a more complete discussion of this research). It is conceivable that these environmental conditions may exert either a direct effect on children through parent-child interactions or a more indirect effect on children through their exposure to a more generally negative atmosphere in the home. Some recent evidence provides some clues that higher density homes may contain higher levels of interpersonal strain.

The data from the Gove et al. (1979) study described above indicated that subjective crowding was associated with adverse relationships between parents and their children (e.g., lack of positive marital relations, parents not feeling close to one another, greater incidences of physical violence, irritability, withdrawal, ineffectual behavior and a variety of indications of poor mental health). Booth (1976) reported that while fathers and mothers played with their children as much in crowded households as those that were not crowded, parents in crowded homes hit their children more. Loo (1980) also found in her recent study of the effects of density in San Francisco's crowded Chinatown area, that dwelling density was significantly related to family problems relating to marriage and parenting responsibilities.

Research comparing high-rise, low-rise and single family housing units additionally provides some evidence of greater interpersonal strain and problems related to difficulties with space and children being "under foot" for families living in high-rise buildings (e.g., Becker & Friedburg, 1974). While only speculation can be offered concerning the effects of poor relationship in the home on early development of the social behavior of children (e.g., Cappon, 1972; Plant, 1930), the literature on high-rise, low-rise residential settings does indicate that younger children may be exposed more in the high density environment. Kumove (1966) found that preschoolers living in high density housing in Toronto spent more time inside than those living in lower density housing. Other studies have also found that fewer children play outside of high-rise than low-rise buildings (e.g., Maizels, 1961).

## Affiliation, Dependency, Aggression, and Social Behavior Problems

While it is necessary to draw inferences from most of the residential density research regarding how the social behavior of children is affected, a small number of studies have focused more directly on this type of behavior. The effects of long-term population density on the affective relationships and attitudes of students from three East African societies, which differed in their rates of population increase were examined by Munroe and Munroe (1972). Their results indicated that affiliative behavior (e.g., self-reported frequency of hand-holding with friends) decreased as population density increased. Waldrop and Bell (1964) reported that 2- and 3-year-old boys coming from large families in which the births were closely spaced exhibited greater dependency behavior. They initiated considerably more contact with teachers in their nursery school environment. In his study of the influence of crowding on children's social behavior, Murray (1974) found that fourth and fifth grade children from higher density homes were rated as more aggressive by their classmates. He also found that boys from these more crowded homes had records of more criminal offenses. Booth and Johnson (1975) also reported that children from crowded homes exhibited more acting out behavior in that their parents reported that they had been contacted more frequently by school authorities regarding problems with their child's social behavior.

## Other Effects on the Social Behavior and
## Affective States of Children

In a recent study, Saegert (1980) assessed the effects of residential density on the well-being of 312 low-income elementary school age children (75% of whom were black, 23% Hispanic-American, and 2% Anglo American) living in New York City Public Housing. The two aspects of density employed were the number of people per room in the apartment (range was 0.2 to 2.6 persons per room, with an average density of 1.12) and the building size. While half of the children lived in high density apartments (with densities of more than 1.013), the other half lived in lower density apartments (with densities of less than 1.013). Building size also included two levels, fourteen-story buildings ($n = 174$) and three-story buildings ($n = 83$). Measures of the children's psychological development and well-being were obtained from: (1) Teachers ratings of behavioral adjustment on a modified form of the Behar Behavior Rating Scale (Behar & Stringfield, 1974). An overall rating of behavioral adjustment was obtained along with subscale ratings for hostility, anxiety, and hyperactivity-distractibility; (2) The New York City Reading Achievement scores. The vocabulary scores, reading scores and totals were analyzed separately for both the number of months each child scored below or above the average performance for the child's grade level were scored and the number of months below or above the average performance of the child's own class were recorded. (3) Interviews with the children which addressed such issues as the children's experience of crowding and perception of space in the apartment, their acquaintance and friendship experiences, and whether or not they felt good, bothered or hassled, angry, and/or lonely in their home. One additional measure, which provided a partial replication of Rodin's (1976) procedure, was also employed. It consisted of the interviewer offering each child a toy at the end of the interview by asking, "Now I would like to give you a toy. Would you like to choose it or should I choose it for you?"

Taken together, the results of this investigation clearly demonstrate that the high residential density conditions had a significant impact on the psychological development and well-being of the children studied. The teachers' ratings indicated that when compared with their low density counterparts, children from high density apartments received higher overall behavioral disturbance scores, as well as higher anxiety and hyperactivity-distractability ratings. With regard to their reading scores, children from higher density apartments received lower vocabulary scores on both measures. The interview data related to household use patterns indicated that girls spent more time inside the higher density households than did boys and as a result, experienced the high level of apartment use more frequently. These data correspond with those obtained with adult females in dense dormitory environments. (e.g., Aiello, Epstein, & Karlin, 1975). In contrast, the data from the children living in lower density households indicate that boys spent more time inside than did girls. Another interesting finding was obtained from the childrens' responses when asked how much time they spend doing things with each person in the household. Not only did the girls in the high density apartments spend more time inside but they also reported doing things most frequently with the other people in the household when they lived in a high-rise building. Boys on the other hand, reported doing things with others most frequently in low-rise, high-density apartments.

The interview responses concerned with the children's reports of the frequency of their various affective experiences in their homes revealed that when compared with their counterparts in the low density households, the children in high density households reported feeling *angry* more often. Moreover, they also said they dealt with this anger by *acting out* whereas the children from the less dense homes reported that they tended to cope with anger by withdrawing. In addition, the children in high density households reported being *bothered more often by other people,* as well as being bothered more often while doing homework.

Several findings related to building size are also worth noting. The responses from the interview indicated that the children perceived the fourteen-story, high-rise buildings as more crowded than the three-story, low-rise buildings. When compared with their counterparts from the low-rise buildings, the children from the high-rise buildings also described the other tenants in their building as less friendly and as less likely to offer aid to someone in the hall needing help. They also reported feeling *less guilty* themselves about committing antisocial acts (e.g., fighting, vandalism).

## SUMMARY OF RESIDENTIAL DENSITY RESEARCH
## PERTAINING TO CHILDREN'S SOCIAL BEHAVIOR

There is considerably less known about the effects on children's social behavior of residential density than about this type of density effects in school and play settings. It is important to take into account when analyzing the nature of high density environments the setting-specific features of these environments (cf. Karlin, Epstein & Aiello, 1978). It is likely that the components of a crowded home environment will be very different from the components of a school or play setting. Crowded residential environments are likely to be characterized by excesses of social stimulation, problems with privacy, interference with goals and some loss of control. As Plant (1930) noted, the mental strain arising from constantly having to adapt to and get along with other people can be significant.

Two of the studies that have specifically been concerned with the effects of residential density on children's social behavior have found effects similar to that observed under high density school and play settings — children from crowded homes are more aggressive (Murray, 1974; Saegert, 1980). Evidence of this was obtained from peer-classmate ratings of level of aggression (Murray, 1974), as well as from interviews with children from high density households, who said they felt angry more and that they dealt with this anger by acting out (Saegert, 1980). We can only speculate about the possible connection between this relationship and the findings that related to children's social behavior problems in school and even the linkage to juvenile delinquency. The reports that parents from crowded homes strike their children more (Booth & Edwards, 1976) and have higher incidence rates of physical violence (Gove et al., 1979), would seem to bear more directly on this association.

Some investigators (e.g., Evans, 1978) have hypothesized that younger children would be more negatively affected by crowding stress. Others (e.g., Booth & Johnson, 1975) have suggested that spatial needs are greater for older children and yet their control over their home environment is limited so that they would be more affected. With regard to this latter point of view, Parke and Sawin (1979) reported a clear-cut developmental course for children's privacy behaviors in which the amount of privacy increases as the child develops. This parallels Wolfe and Laufer's (1974) findings that children develop greater and greater understanding of the concept of privacy and of its complexities as they age. At present, some research exists to support the contention that younger children are more adversely affected by density as well as to support the view that older children are more negatively affected by density. Future research will have to explore the vulnerability of children at various ages to crowding stress so as to provide needed information about this issue. Further research is also necessary to clarify how presently available evidence of poorer relations in crowded homes, and the feelings of parents that they lack control over their children and knowledge about their activities, affects the social behavior of children.

One additional direction for future research to explore is whether or not high-density residential settings result in decreases in children's feelings of control over their environment and any consequences which may follow from this loss. Research that is currently available is reviewed in the final section of this chapter.

## CONTROL AND CROWDING

All of these findings reflect a consistent impact of high density on children's behavior. In various ways and for a number of reasons, children are affected by high density in residential and nonresidential settings. Clearly, there is no single explanation for this impact nor any single solution for it. It is apparent to us, for example, that reduced parental contact and control over children in high density residential settings has consequences for both. Yet, this can account for only some effects. Other processes are implicated as well.

One of these other processes may be related to loss of control. General descriptions of the ways in which control is threatened by crowding have appeared (e.g., Altman, 1975; Baron & Rodin, 1978; Sherrod & Cohen, 1979) and there are reasons to suspect that control is a relevant concern for children as well.

Research on college students, for example, has suggested that loss of control over social experience in crowded settings may be responsible for crowding stress that is observed. We have found, for example, that residents of high social density dormitories were more withdrawn than their counterparts in less socially dense housing (e.g. Baum & Valins, 1977). In these settings, crowding was associated with avoidance of social contact, helpless-like behavior and a lower threshold for social overload. Crowded students more readily complained of loss of control in the dormitories and, over the course of the first three months of dormitory residence, appeared to pass through a reactance-helplessness sequence similar to the one proposed by Wortman and Brehm (1975) as a model of response to loss of control (e.g., Baum, Aiello, & Calsnick, 1978; Baum, Gatchel, Aiello, & Thompson, 1981).

In another series of studies, focusing on crowding caused by over-assignment to dormitory rooms, control was again implicated as a determinant of response to density by college students (e.g., Aiello, Baum, & Gormley, 1981; Aiello, Epstein, & Karlin, 1975; Baum, Shapiro, Murray, & Wideman, 1979; Reddy, Baum, Fleming, & Aiello, 1981). Initial studies found that students housed three-to-a-room (the rooms were designed for two) exhibited symptoms of crowding stress (Aiello et al., 1975; Baron, Mandel, Adams, & Griffen, 1976). Subsequent study, however, suggested that the problems associated with crowding were exhibited more by one of the three roommates. In most of these tripled rooms coalitions appeared to form—two students became close and "left the other out." The isolate roommate complained of a lack of control over what happened in the room and reported more crowding and related difficulty than did the other tripled residents (e.g., Aiello et al., 1981; Baum et al., 1979; Reddy et al., 1981).

These findings strongly support the notion that control problems are associated with crowding, at least among college students. Other studies addressing this find similarly supportive evidence (e.g., Rodin et al., 1978; Sherrod, 1974). The extension to young children is not supported by as much evidence, however. Yet, there are sufficient data to suggest that control is relevant for children exposed to chronic or episodic crowding.

The most unequivocal evidence for this conclusion are those studies we have already reviewed. It is reasonable to assume that control problems result from overcrowded households and play areas — increasing density will limit behavioral options and place others more frequently in the path of goal attainment. Further the aggressive response to high density observed in many studies may reflect attempts to reassert control and the withdrawal observed in other studies may reflect diminishing expectations for being successful in regaining control. The only direct evidence of this lies in the fact that Aiello et al.'s (1979) findings of competitive response following crowding are equivalent to those of students complaining of loss of control in dormitory settings (Baum et al., 1978).

Indirect evidence for a control-based interpretation of crowding among children is also obtained by considering studies of another environmental stressor — noise. Until recently there was little evidence to suggest that the physiological and control-related psychological effects of noise generalize from adults to children (e.g., Cohen, Glass, Phillips, 1977; Glass & Singer, 1972). The results of a major study of exposure to aircraft noise near the Los Angeles International Airport, however, has established the fact that children do show some of these effects (e.g., Cohen, Evans, Krantz, & Stokols, 1980).

This study considered adaptation to and consequences of attending school under aircraft flight paths over the course of two years. Quiet and noisy elementary schools were matched on a number of variables and the primary difference between them was the fact that the latter were characterized by peak sound levels of 95 dB(A) caused by airplane overflights. Children attending the quiet and noisy schools were tested in a quiet setting (noise-insulated trailer brought to the schools) providing the investigators with estimates of the effect of aircraft noise that persisted in quiet settings.

Findings from the first year of study indicated that exposure to aircraft noise had physiological and psychological consequences for the school children (Cohen et al., 1980). Children attending the noisy school showed higher systolic and diastolic blood pressure, particularly if they had attended the school for only one or two years. In addition, children attending noisy schools for less than two years were less distractable than were children attending quieter schools, while children attending noisy schools for more than two years were more distractable than those at quieter schools.

Results from continued study of these children provide additional informational about the impact of noise (Cohen, Evans, Krantz, Stokols, & Kelley, 1981). Children were tested again a year after initial testing, and results indicated that the noise remained bothersome for children attending schools situated beneath flight paths. Elevated blood pressure findings were not reported but this was apparently caused by the fact that a relatively high proportion of those initially exhibiting high blood pressure were lost to attrition (e.g., they moved away) and were therefore not considered a second time. However, distractability findings were similar and provide some evidence of the stability of the effects of noise on annoyance and distractability.

One measure that was considered in both studies that we have not mentioned dealt with issues of control and helplessness. Studies of noise with college students have found strong mediating effects of perceived control and helplessness-like effects of acute noise-exposure (e.g., Glass & Singer, 1972). Cohen et al. (1980, in press) have considered the role of control in response to aircraft noise by children and report data that allow important links to study of children exposed to other stressors.

In order to consider the susceptability to helplessness of children attending quiet and noisy schools, Cohen et al. (1980) gave each child two puzzles to work on for a brief (2 1/2–4 minutes) period of time. The first puzzle was a pretreatment manipulation—half of the children at each school received a solvable puzzle and half were given an unsolvable puzzle. Thus, at least half of the children failed to solve the first puzzle, and their response to initial success or failure on a second solvable puzzle was used as an index of helplessness. If children from the noisy school were more susceptible to the helplessness induction, they should have shown less persistence in the face of failure than the quiet school subjects.

The results of this effort generally suggested that children attending noisy schools gave up more quickly than did those attending quiet schools. However, this lack of persistence by noisy school subjects was complicated by the fact that these children were also more likely to fail to solve the pretreatment puzzle that was solvable. Subsequently, Cohen et al. (1981) asked the school children to work on a third solvable puzzle one year after initial testing. Again, noisy school children were more likely to fail on the task and took longer to solve it if they were successful. However, persistence differences, although in the predicted direction, were not significant. Analyses that considered whether children had succeeded in solving the pretreatment puzzle yielded the same findings. Thus, children from the noisy school performed more poorly on the puzzles than did children from the quiet school but the relative lack of persistence by noisy school subjects did not appear during the second testing. Cohen et al. attribute this to attrition in the sample; because lengths of enrollment in the noisy schools did not affect persistence during the first testing and because many of the most affected students were not available for follow-up testing, this attrition hypothesis appears to be the most likely explanation.

Despite the problems noted above, these data provide suggestive evidence that exposure to noise is associated with helplessness-like effects among children. In addition to the consistency of this finding with work on older populations, it also suggests another link with research indicating that children, adolescents, and college students exhibit symptoms of helplessness in the face of crowding (e.g., Aiello & Baum, 1979; Baum et al., 1978; Rodin, 1976).

For our purposes, the most important study linking crowding to helplessness was reported by Rodin (1976). Based on research indicating that chronic residential crowding involved a loss of control (e.g., Calhoun, 1962), she reasoned that prolonged exposure to high-density living would affect children's responses to choices and to the opportunity to exert control. In one study, Rodin placed children in a situation in which performing a simple response earned candy as a reinforcement. At various points in the session, the children were given the opportunity to gain control over the type of candy that they received. Controlling for a number of variables, Rodin found that children exposed to high residential density were less likely to exert this control than were those living in less dense environments.

These findings were strengthened by the results of a second study in which junior high school students were given either a success or failure pretreatment (solvable vs. unsolvable puzzles) and then asked to work on a second set of solvable puzzles. As in the Cohen et al. research, helplessness manifested itself in the form of an exaggerated response to failure pretreatment. Students living in high-density settings performed more poorly on the second set of puzzles than did students living in less crowded homes, and students given failure pretreatment performed more poorly than did those having solved the first puzzles. However, these effects were largely due to an interaction between density and pretreatment indicating that density did not substantially affect response to success pretreatment but that it was associated with large differences in response to failure. After experience with unsolvable puzzles, children from high-density homes showed considerable poorer performance than did students from lower density settings. Baron and Rodin (1976) have suggested that a similar process may occur in classroom and play environments. As class size increases, learned helplessness training begins to occur.

These findings are consistent with evidence that loss of control associated with crowding affects the behavior of young animals (e.g., Calhoun, 1970; Goeckner, Greenough, & Meade, 1973) and suggest that crowding may affect control-relevant responses by children. Considered with those reported by Cohen and his associates, they suggest that the intrusive aspects of environmental stressors may involve loss of control, facilitate children's perception that they often cannot control what happens to them and, consequently, enhance their acquisition of symptoms of helplessness. Clearly there are reasons to believe or reject this notion but available evidence indicates that it is at least a possibility worth exploring.

There is evidence that control is important to children and that lack of it may affect motivation to control the outcome (e.g., Dweck, 1975; Dweck & Reppucci, 1973). Thus the findings reported by Rodin (1976) and Cohen et al. (1981) should not be surprising. However, there appears to be some hesitation in directly applying the relationship between control and stress to children due to issues surrounding the relative importance of events and resources for children.

As an example of the reasons for this hesitancy, consider our review of the effects of crowding presented above. The evidence for the position that crowding has consequences for children is not strong. Resource shortages and interference due to crowding have been linked to negative social behaviors (e.g., Rohe & Patterson, 1974), but inconsistencies remain. It can be argued, however, that these inconsistencies are due less to the weak nature of crowding impact for children and more to the fact that adult experimenters may not be measuring those aspects of a child's world that are most strongly affected. The same problems for adults and children may not be expressed in the same way. When the major dependent measures are more finely tuned to the experiences of children, evidence of crowding impact may become clearer.

The question remains however, "do control-mediated stressors have more or less impact on children than they do on adults?" If children are generally less concerned with control or if the fact that others are responsible for them mitigates their relative lack of control in an adult world, one should expect the control inhibiting impact of environmental stress to be less severe for children. If, on the other hand, their low "baseline" level of control makes them more sensitive to further loss of control, or if their nascent physiological and psychological "beings" are more susceptible to stress, one would expect children to be equally (if not more seriously) affected by control-relevant stressors.

## REFERENCES

Aiello, J. R., & Aiello, T. D. The development of personal space. Proxemic behavior of children 6 through 16. *Human Ecology,* 1974, *2,* 177–189.

Aiello, J. R., & Baum, A. (Eds.) *Residential crowding and design.* New York: Plenum Press, 1979.

Aiello, J. R., Baum, A., & Gormley, F. P. Social determinants of residential crowding stress. *Personality and Social Psychology Bulletin,* 1981, *7,* 643–649.

Aiello, J. R., & Cooper, R. E. Personal space and social affect: A developmental study. Paper presented at the meeting of the Society for Research in Child Development. San Francisco, 1979.

Aiello, J. R., DeRisi, D. T., Epstein, Y. M., & Karlin, R. A. Crowding and the role of interpersonal distance preference. *Sociometry,* 1977, *40,* 271–282.

Aiello, J. R., Epstein, Y. M., & Karlin, R. A. *Field experimental research on human crowding.* Paper presented at the meeting of the Eastern Psychological Association, New York, April 1975.

Aiello, J. R., Nocosia, G., & Thompson, D. E. Physiological, social and behavioral consequences of crowding on children and adolescents. *Child Development,* 1979, *50,* 195–202.

Aiello, J. R., & Thompson, D. E. Personal space, crowding and spatial behavior in a cultural context. In I. Altman & J. F. Wohlwill (Eds.), *Human behavior and environment,* Vol. 3:

*Environment and culture.* New York: Plenum, 1980, 107–178.

Altman, I. *The environment and social behavior: Privacy, personal space, territory, and crowding.* Monterey, Cal.: Brooks/Cole, 1975.

Baron, R. M., Mandel, D. R., Adams, C. A., & Griffen, L. M. Effects of social density in university residential environments. *Journal of Personality and Social Psychology.* 1976, *34,* 434–446.

Bates, B. *Effects of social density on the behavior of nursery school children.* Unpublished doctoral dissertation, University of Oregon, 1970.

Baum, A., Aiello, J. R., & Calesnick, L. E. Crowding and personal control: Social density and the development of learned helplessness. *Journal of Personality and Social Psychology,* 1978, *36,* 1000–1011.

Baum, A., Gatchel, R. J., Aiello, J. R., & Thompson, D. E. Cognitive mediation of environmental stress. In Harvey, J. H. (Ed.), *Cognition, social behavior, and the environment.* Hillsdale, N. J.: Lawrence Erlbaum Associates, 1981, 513–533.

Baum, A., Shapiro, A., Murray, D., & Wideman, M. V. Interpersonal mediation of perceived crowding and control in residential dyads and triads. *Journal of Applied Social Psychology,* 1979, *9,* 491–507.

Baum, A., & Valins, S. *Architecture and social behavior: Psychological studies of social density.* Hillsdale, N. J.: Lawrence Erlbaum Associates, 1977.

Becker, F. D., & Friedburg, L. P. *Design for living: The resident's view of multi-family housing.* Center for Urban Development Research, Cornell University, Ithaca, New York, 1974.

Behar, L., & Stringfield, S. A. Behavioral rating scale for the preschool child. *Developmental Psychology,* 1976, *10,* 601–610.

Booth, A. *Urban crowding and its consequences.* New York: Holt, Rinehart, Winston, 1976.

Booth, A., & Edwards, J. N. Crowding and family relations. *American Sociological Review,* 1976, *41,* 308–321.

Booth, A., & Johnson, D. R. The effect of crowding on child health and development. *American Behavioral Scientist,* 1975, *18,* 736–749.

Booth, A., Johnson, D., & Edwards, J. In pursuit of pathology: The effects of human crowding. *American Sociological Review,* 1980, *45,* 873–878.

Bronzaft, A. L., & McCarthy, D. P. The effects of elevated train noise on reading ability. *Environment and Behavior,* 1975, *7,* 517–527.

Calhoun, J. B. Population density and social pathology. *Scientific American,* 1962, *206,* 136–148.

Calhoun, J. B. Space and the strategy of like. *Ekistics,* 1970, *29,* 425–437.

Cappon, D. Mental health in the hi-rise. *Ekistics,* 1972, *196.*

Chilton, R. J. Continuity in delinquency area research: A comparison of studies for Baltimore, Detroit, and Indianapolis. *American Sociological Review,* 1964, *29,* 71–83.

Christian, J., Flyger, V., & Davis, D. E. Phenoma associated with population density. Proceeding. *National Academy of Science,* 1961, *47,* 428–449.

Cohen, S. Environment load and the allocation of attention. In A. Baum, J. E. Singer, & S. Valins (Eds.), *Advances in environmental psychology,* Volume 1, *The urban environment.* Hillsdale, N. J.: Lawrence Erlbaum Associates, 1978, 1–29.

Cohen, S., Evans, G. W., Krantz, D. S., & Stokols, D. Physiological, motivational, and cognitive effects of aircraft noise on children: Moving from the laboratory to the field. *American Psychologist,* 1980, *34,* 231–243.

Cohen, S., Evans, G. W., Krantz, D. S., Stokols, D., & Kelly, S. Aircraft noise and children: Longitudinal and cross-sectional evidence on adaptation to noise and the effectiveness of noise abatement. *Journal of Personality and Social Psychology,* 1981, *40,* 331–345.

Cohen, S., Glass, D. C., & Phillips, S. Environment and health. In H. H. Freedman, S. Levine, & L. G. Reeder (Eds.), *Handbook of medical sociology.* Englewood Cliffs, N. J.: Prentice-Hall, 1979.

Cohen, S., Glass, D. C., & Singer, J. E. Apartment noise, auditory discrimination, and reading ability. *Journal of Experimental Social Psychology,* 1973, *9,* 407–422.

Cozby, P. A. Effects of density, activity and personality on environmental preferences. *Journal of Research in Personality,* 1973, *7,* 45–60.

Dooley, B. Effects of social density on men with "close" or "far" personal space. *Journal of Population: Behavioral, Social and Environmental Issues,* 1978, *1,* 251–265.

Dweck, C. S. The role of expectations and attributions in the alleviation of learned helplessness. *Journal of Personality and Social Psychology,* 1975, *31,* 674–685.

Dweck, C. S., & Reppucci, N. D. Learned helplessness and reinforcement responsibility in children. *Journal of Personality and Social Psychology,* 1973, *25,* 109–116.

Evans, G. W. Crowding and the developmental process. In A. Baum & Y. M. Epstein (Eds.), *Human responses to crowding.* Hillsdale, N. J.: Lawrence Erlbaum Associates, 1978, 117–139.

Evans, G. W., & Eichelman, W. Preliminary models of conceptual linkages among proxemic variables. *Environment and Behavior,* March, 1976, *8,* 87–116.

Fagot, B. I. Variations in density: Effect on task and social behaviors of preschool children. *Developmental Psychology,* 1977, *13,* 166–167.

Galle, O. R., & Gove, W. R. Crowding and behavior in Chicago, 1940–1974. In J. R. Aiello & A. Baum (Eds.), *Residential crowding and design.* New York: Plenum Press, 1979, 23–39.

Galle, O. R., Gove, W. R., & McPherson, J. M. Population density and pathology: What are the relations for man? *Science,* 1972, *176,* 23–30.

Gillis, A. R. Population density and social pathology: The case of building type, social allowance and juvenile delinquency. *Social Forces,* 1974, *52,* 306–314.

Ginsburg, H. J., & Pollman, V. *Variation of aggressive interaction among male elementary school children as a function of changes in spatial density.* Presented at the meetings of the Society for Research in Child Development, Denver, Colorado, 1975.

Glass, D. C., & Singer, J. E. *Urban Press.* New York: Academic Press, 1972.

Goeckner, D. J., Greenough, W. T., & Mead, W. R. Deficits in learning tasks following chronic overcrowding in rats. *Journal of Personality and Social Psychology* 1973, *28,* 256–261.

Gove, W. R., Hughes, M., & Galle, O. R. Overcrowding in the home: An empirical investigation of its possible pathological consequences. *American Sociological Review,,* 1979, *44,* 59–80.

Hutt, C., & McGrew, W. C. *Effects of group density upon social behavior in humans.* Paper presented at Association for the Study of Animal Behavior, Symposium on Changes in Behavior with Population Density, Oxford, England, July, 1964.

Hutt, C., & Vaizey, M. J. Differential effects of group density on social behavior. *Nature,* 1966, *209,* 1371–1372.

Karlin, R. A., Epstein, V. M., & Aiello, J. R. A setting-specific analysis of crowding. In A. Baum & Y. M. Epstein (Eds.), *Human responses to crowding.* Hillsdale, N. J.; Lawrence Erlbaum Associates, 1978, 141–179.

Kumove, L. *A preliminary study of the social implications of high density living conditions.* Toronto: Social Planning Council of Metropolitan Toronto, 1966.

Lantz, H. R. Population density and psychiatric diagnosis. *Sociology and Social Research,* 1953, *37,* 322–326.

Loo, C. M. The effects of spatial density on the social behavior of children. *Journal of Applied Social Psychology,* 1972, *4,* 372–381.

Loo, C. M. Density, crowding, and preschool children. In A. Baum & Y. M. Epstein (Eds.), *Human responses to crowding.* Hillsdale, N. J.: Lawrence Erlbaum Associates, 1978, 371–388. (a)

Loo, C. M. Behavior problem indices: The differential effects of spatial density on low and high scorers. *Environmental Behavior,* 1978, *10,* 489–510. (b)

Loo, C. M. Issues of crowding research: Vulnerable participants, assessing perceptions and developmental differences. *Journal of Population,* 1978, *1,* 336–348. (c)

Loo, C. M. A factor analytic approach to the study of spatial density effects on preschoolers. *Journal of Population,* 1979, *2,* 47–68.

Loo, C. M. *Chinatown: Crowding and mental health.* Presented at the Meetings of the American Psychological Association Convention, Montreal, September, 1980.

Loo, C., & Kennelly, D. Social density: Its effects on behaviors and perceptions of preschoolers. *Environmental Psychology and Nonverbal Behavior,* 1978, *2,* 226–249.

Loo, C., & Smetana, J. The effects of crowding on the behaviors and perceptions of 10-year-old boys. *Environmental Psychology and Nonverbal Behavior,* 1978, *2,* 226–249.

Maizels, J. *Two to five in high flats.* London: The housing centre, 1961.

McCarthy, D. P., & Saegert, S. Residential density, social overload, and social withdrawal. In J. R. Aiello & A. Baum (Eds.), *Residential crowding and design.* New York: Plenum Press, 1979, 55–75.

McGrew, P. L. Social and spatial density effects of spacing behavior in preschool children. *Journal of Child Psychology and Psychiatry,* 1970, *11,* 197–205.

McGrew, W. C. *An ethological study of children's behavior.* New York: Academic Press, 1977.

Meisels, M., & Guardo, C. Development of personal space schemata. *Child Development,* 1969, *40,* 1167.

Mitchell, R. E. Some social implications of high density housing. *American Sociological Review,* 1971, *36,* 18–29.

Munroe, R. L., & Munrow, R. H. Population density and effective relationships in three East African societies. *Journal of Social Psychology,* 1972, *88,* 15–20.

Murray, R. The influence of crowding on children's behavior. In D. Canter & T. Lee (Eds.), *Psychology and the built environment.* London: Architectural Press, 1974, 112–117.

Myers, K., Hale, C., Mykytowycz, R., & Hughes, R. The effects of varying density and space on sociality and health in mammals. In A. H. Esser (Ed.), *Behavior and environment.* New York: Plenum Press, 1971, 148–187.

Parke, R. D., & Sawin, D. B. Children's privacy in the home: Developmental ecological, and child-rearing determinants. *Environment and Behavior,* 1979, *11,* 87–104.

Petri, H. L., & Huggins, R. G. *Some developmental characteristics of personal space.* Paper presented at the meeting of the Eastern Psychological Association, New York City, 1975.

Plant, J. S. Some psychiatric aspects of crowded living conditions. *American Journal of Psychiatry,* 1930, *9,* 849–860.

Preiser, W. Behavior of nursery school children under different spatial densities. *Man-Environment Systems,* July, 1972, *2*(4), 247–250.

Price, J. L. *The effects of crowding on the social behavior of children.* Unpublished doctoral dissertation, Columbia University, New York: 1971.

Rawls, J. R., Trego, R. E., McGaffey, C. N., & Rawls, D. I. Personal space as a predictor of performance under close working conditions. *Journal of Social Psychology,* 1972, *86,* 261–267.

Reddy, D. M., Baum, A., Fleming, R., & Aiello, J. R. Mediation of social density by coalition formation. *Journal of Applied Social Psychology,* 1981, *11,* 529–537.

Rodin, J. Crowding, perceived choice, and response to controllable and uncontrollable outcomes. *Journal of Experimental Social Psychology,* 1976, *12,* 654–678.

Rodin, J., & Baum, A. Crowding and helplessness: Potential consequences of density and loss of control. In A. Baum & Y. M. Epstein (Eds.), *Human responses to crowding.* Hillsdale, N.J.: Lawrence Erlbaum Associates, 1978, 389–401.

Rohe, W. *Mediators of crowding: With a study concerning privacy and crowding in a day care center.* Unpublished master's thesis, Pennsylvania State University, 1976.

Rohe, W. M., & Nuffer, E. *The effects of density and partitioning on children's behavior.* Presented at the meetings of the American Psychological Association, San Francisco, 1977.

Rohe, W., & Patterson, A. H. *The effects of varied levels of resources and density on behavior in a day care center.* Paper presented at the annual conference of the Environmental Design Research Association, Milwaukee, WS, 1974.

Saegert, S. *The effect of residential density on low income children.* Presented at the meetings of the American Psychological Association Convention, Montreal, September, 1980.

Schmid, C. Urban crime areas. *American Sociological Review,* 1960, *25,* 527–542; 655–678.

Schmitt, R. C. Density, delinquency, and crime in Honolulu. *Sociology and Social Research,* 1957, *41,* 274–276.

Schmitt, R. C. Density, health and social disorganization. *Journal of the American Institute of Planners,* 1966, *32,* 38–40.

Shapiro, S. Some classroom ABC's: Research takes a closer look. *Elementary School Journal,* 1975, *75,* 437–441.

Shaw, C. & McKay, H. D. *Juvenile delinquency and urban areas.* Chicago: University of Chicago Press, 1942.

Sherrod, D., & Cohen, S. Density, personal control, and design. In J. R. Aiello, & A. Baum (Eds.), *Residential crowding and design.* New York: Plenum Press, 1979, 217–227.

Slosnerick, M. *Social interaction by preschool children in conditions of crowding.* Paper presented at the annual conference of the Midwestern Psychological Association, Chicago, 1974.

Smith, P., & Connolly, K. Patterns of play and social interaction in preschool children. In N. Blurton Jones (Ed.), *Ethological studies of child behavior.* Cambridge University Press, 1972, 65–95.

Stokols, D. On the distinction between density and crowding: Some implications for future research. *Psychological Review,* 1972, *79,* 275–277.

Sundstrom, E. Crowding as a sequential process: Review of research on the effects of population density on humans. In A. Baum, & Y. M. Epstein (Eds.), *Human responses to crowding.* Hillsdale, N. J.: Lawrence Erlbaum Associates, 1978, 31–116.

Tennis, G. H., & Dabbs, J. M. Sex, setting, and personal space: First grade through college. *Sociometry,* 1975, *38,* 385–394.

Wallis, C. P. & Maliphant, R. Delinquent areas in the country of London: Ecological factors. *British Journal of Criminology,* 1967, *7.*

Wolfe, M., & Laufer, R. The concept of privacy in childhood and adolescence. In D. H. Carson (Ed.), *Man-environment interactions: Evaluations and applications* (part two). Stroudsburg, PA: Dowden, Hutchinson, and Ross, 1975, 29–54.

Wortman, C., & Brehm, J. Responses to uncontrollable outcomes: An integration of reactance theory and the learned helplessness model. In L. Berkowitz (Ed.), *Advances in experimental social psychology* (Vol. 8). New York: Academic Press, 1975, 278–336.

# 6 Habitats for Children: An Ecological Perspective

James Garbarino
*The Pennsylvania State University*

## INTRODUCTION: ENVIRONMENTAL PRESS AND THE DEVELOPING INDIVIDUAL

*Environmental press* refers to the combined influence of forces working in a setting to shape the behavior and development of individuals in that setting. Environmental press arises from the circumstances confronting and surrounding an individual that generate psychosocial momentum tending to guide that individual in a particular direction. As we shall see, the child's environment is multifaceted and multileveled—a complex network of forces that affect the child through behavior settings.

From the perspective of ecological psychology, "behavior settings are coercive of behavior. People who enter settings are pressed to help enact its program (while at the same time using the setting for their own purposes)" (Gump & Adelberg, 1978, p. 174). Over time, individual behavior tends to become congruent with the situational demands of the environment. Environmental press implements this "principle of progressive conformity" (Moos, 1976).

However, environmental press is not a single or unitary force, but the resultant influence of numerous forces interacting within an environment. Various elements of a setting generate behavior-modifying forces that contribute to environmental press. Physical characteristics, for instance, may facilitate or impede access to desired destinations or alternate uses of existing space. Social patterns also may encourage or discourage various actions, reward or punish particular values or attitudes. Further, these various influences interact with and modify each other, so that physical attributes affect social variables and vice versa.

The presence, strength, and dynamic balance among environmental forces differs, of course, across contrasting settings. Contrasting environments therefore press toward different forms of behavior or directions for development. For example, small social environments (towns, groups, institutions) are associated with patterns of behavior different from large ones (Barker & Gump, 1964). Large secondary schools tend to discourage participation by students while small schools tend to encourage it (Barker & Gump, 1964; Garbarino, 1980b). Environments that separate residential concentrations of children from recreational settings by busy streets lined on both sides by parked cars generate both injuries to children and pressure on parents to provide regulation (Aldrich, 1979; Michelson & Roberts, 1979).

The balance of environmental forces is not the sole determinant of outcomes for an organism, of course. The individual organism itself figures significantly as well. While environmental press is the environment's contribution to individual-environment transactions, the individual brings to the situation an arrangement of personal resources and a level of development. Different people thus may react differently to the same environment. The big school-small school findings cited above, for instance (Barker & Gump, 1964; Garbarino, 1980b), applied most significantly to academically marginal students. Further, the same environment may interact differently with the same person at different times. For example, the same busy street that is life-threatening to a child of four may be a developmentally appropriate challenge for a 9-year-old, and a mild inconvenience for a teenager.

Inter-individual differences and intra-individual change require that we consider individual characteristics if we are attempting to predict outcomes of individual-environment interactions. All environments contain forces that support or undermine the processes of child development. These forces may work for or against assurance of the child's basic survival needs; for or against provision of emotional nurturance and continuity; for or against developmentally-appropriate attempts at self-determination—in short, for or against the creation of a positive environment for growth and development. Forces that support children represent opportunities for adequate, or even enhanced, developmental experiences, while the absence of such characteristics or the presence of threatening forces presents environmental risks to the developing child. To assess the role of residential density in environmental risk and opportunity we need a framework within which to systematically consider the dynamic interaction of individual organism and the social systems of the environment.

## AN ECOLOGICAL VIEW OF RESIDENTIAL DENSITY

To study the ecology of child development is to undertake the scientific study of how the child develops interactively with the immediate social and physical environment, and how aspects of the larger social context affect what goes on in the child's immediate settings. This distinguishes the current ecological perspective on human development (cf. Bronfenbrenner, 1979; Garbarino & Gilliam, 1980), from both ecological psychology (cf. Barker & Schoggen, 1973) and traditional human ecology (cf. Hawley, 1950). While there is little value to a "my ecological perspective is better than yours" argument, there is a significant difference here. Both of these latter ecological approaches focus on environmental systems without really attending to the role of the developing organism. Although there is growing interest among ecological psychologists in factors influencing the "life cycle" of behavior settings (e.g., Wicker, 1979), their studies — as Devereaux (1977) so aptly observed, have typically examined the inner life of human settings with little or no attention to how the primary economy of the community produces, maintains, and terminates those settings. Traditional human ecology, on the other hand, focuses on precisely that community role without really attending to how the settings themselves function (let alone the organisms in them). The principal contribution of recent ecological initiatives is thus to bring Kurt Lewin's classic formulation of human behavior (Behavior is a *function* of *P*ersons and *E*nvironment) nearer to fruition.

Working within this framework establishes the child as a developing person who plays an active role in an ever-widening world. Indeed, the very definition of development itself reflects this theme. Bronfenbrenner (1979) defines human development as:

> the process through which the growing person acquires a more extended, differentiated, and valid conception of the ecological environment, and becomes motivated and able to engage in activities that reveal the properties of, sustain, or restructure that environment at levels of similar or greater complexity in form and content. (pp. 27–28)

This has important implications for studying the effects of residential density on children. It suggests that there is both a mean gradient of appropriateness associated grossly with age, and a developmentally enhancing pattern specifically matched to each individual. Social policy can address the mean gradient, while the "clinical" action of caregivers and the "self-directive" action of the individual child can address the match of organism to experience. The newborn shapes the feeding behavior of its mother but is confined largely to a crib or a lap, and has limited means of communicating its needs and wants. The 10-year-old, on the other hand, influences many adults and other children located in many different settings, and has many means of communicating. The world of adolescents is still larger and more diverse, as is their ability to influence it. One of the common themes of these changes is the ever-increasing role of peers in the individual's environment.

The child and the environment negotiate their relationship over time. Neither is constant; each depends on the other in this reciprocal process. One cannot predict the future of either without knowing something about the other. Does a handicapped child stand a greater risk of being abused? It depends. Some environments are more "vulnerable" to the stresses of caring for such a child than are others (cf., Young & Kopp, 1980). Does economic deprivation harm development? It depends on how old one is when it hits, what sex one is, what the future brings in the way of vocational opportunity, what the quality of family life was in the past, what one's economic expectations and assumptions are, and whether one looks at the short-term or the long-run (cf. Elder, 1974; Elder & Rockwell, 1977). In short—it depends.

In addition to recognizing the transactive nature of development, an ecological framework also considers the multiple levels at which environmental influences originate (cf. Garbarino & Plantz, 1980). Bronfenbrenner describes the individual's environment as "a set of nested structures, each inside the next, like a set of Russian dolls" (Bronfenbrenner, 1979, p. 22). As we ask and answer questions about development at one level, this ecological framework reminds us to look at the next levels beyond and within the immediate setting to find the questions to ask and answer. For example, if we see husbands and wives in conflict over lost income we need to look outward to the economy that puts the husband out of work and welcomes the wives into the labor force, and to the culture that defines personal worth in monetary terms and blames the victims of economic dislocation for their own losses. In addition, we must look inward to the parent-child relationships that shift in response to the changing roles and status of the parents and to temperamental characteristics of the individuals involved (cf. Elder, 1974). Further, we must look "across" to see how the several systems involved (family, workplace, and economy) adjust to new conditions over time. These swirling social forces are the stuff of which ecological analyses are made, namely interlocking social systems.

Bronfenbrenner's framework posits four general types of environmental systems, categorized by their proximity to and immediacy of effects upon children. The following paragraphs present the four levels of environmental systems, their distinctive relationships to the developing child, and the crucial issue of the risks and opportunities these environments can represent for children (cf. Garbarino & Plantz, 1980). It is within this framework that we can seek to understand how the human density of children's habitats affects their development.

Most immediate to the developing child are *"microsystems."* These are the joint product of physical settings and behavioral interactions in which individuals experience and create day-to-day reality. Microsystems for children are the places they inhabit, the people who are there with them, and the things they do together. At first, most children experience only one, quite small microsystem—the home—involving interaction with one person at a time in relatively simple activities such as feeding, bathing, and cuddling. As the child develops, complexity normally increases; the child does more, with more people, in more places. As we shall see, however, the significance of the "objective" density of these settings depends upon their subjective meaning to the developing organism.

We know that the management of "survival needs" (eating, eliminating, etc.) is a critical task for the developing child's microsystem. Play, and later work, also figure prominently in the process of the microsystem from the early months of life. Playing, working, and loving — what Freud deemed the essence of normal human existence — are the principal classes of activities that characterize the child's microsystem. However, the extent to which these activities take place, their quality, and their level of complexity are variable. Developmental risk to the child derives from a microsystem characterized by a narrowly restricted range and level of activities, impoverished experience in playing, working and loving, or stunted reciprocity where genuine *inter-action* is lacking and either party seeks to avoid or be impervious to the other. Such neglect and rejection are developmentally dangerous (Garbarino, 1980a; Polansky, 1976; Rohner, 1975; Rohner & Nielson, 1978). In contrast, enduring, reciprocal, multi-faceted relationships that emphasize meeting survival needs, playing, working, and loving provide environmental opportunities for a child.

How are we to understand the meaning of density in microsystems? Here as elsewhere, it is not simply numbers that count but roles as well. Thus, a family microsystem of four people has different developmental significance if those four include two adults and two children versus one adult and three children, as well as if the children are widely spaced as opposed to tightly packed together. The ratio of adults to children affects the role density of the microsystem, and thus the pattern of interaction. It applies as well, and increasingly as the child grows up, to play groups outside the home. This rendering of household and play group composition permits us to incorporate the extensive research literature on single parents, family size and even, to some extent, ordinal position within an ecological view of density. If we add to this the evolving capacity of the developing child to manage, and indeed profit from larger and more complex microsystems we introduce a major psychological variable into the discussion of density. This issue becomes clearer in light of the other categories of social systems in Bronfenbrenner's conception of the human ecology of the child.

*Mesosystems* are the relationships *between* contexts (microsystems), in which the developing person experiences reality. Important mesosystems for children include relationships between home and school, home and neighborhood, home and play group, and school and neighborhood. The number of links, value consensus, and diversity between microsystems indicates the richness of the child's mesosystems. In this sense, a dense ecology is a positive influence.

The school-home mesosystem is of great developmental significance to the child. In general, we expect enhanced development where this mesosystem was "characterized by more frequent interaction between parents and school personnel, a greater number of persons known in common by members of the two settings, and more frequent communications between home and school, more information in each setting about the other" (Bronfenbrenner, 1979, p. 218). In short, mesosystem density tends to be good for a child.

The same number of microsystems can account for significantly different numbers of mesosystems, however. At one extreme we might have a child involved in four microsystems (e.g., home, school, neighborhood and church) but no mesosystems. The same number of microsystems could be associated with at least six mesosystems, however, if all the possible microsystem pairs were related behaviorally and phenomenologically. The latter child's environment is more socially dense, and probably more supportive of overall development. However, we must add the proviso "that such interconnections not undermine the motivation and capacity of those persons who deal directly with the child to act on his behalf. This qualification gives negative weight to actions by school personnel that degrade parents or to parental demands that undermine the professional morale or effectiveness of the teacher" (Bronfenbrenner, 1979, p. 218). Those familiar with contemporary schooling know that both of these often are problems, particularly in the urban environment. In contemporary communities, the quality of school-home mesosystems is variable. It seems here as elsewhere that Aristotle's Golden Mean prevails: in all things moderation.

When it comes to mesosystems, thus, high social density is good for children unless it "crowds" out those in the parental roles, an issue in peer group-home relations to be sure. In general, the stronger, more positive, and more diverse the links between settings, the more powerful and beneficial the resulting mesosystem will be as an influence on the child's development. A rich range of mesosystems is a developmental opportunity, a poor set of mesosystems produces impaired development—particularly when home and school are involved. Events in systems where the child herself does not participate but where things happen that have a direct impact on her parents, peers and others who do interact with her often determine the quality of the child mesosystems, however. Bronfenbrenner calls these settings "exosystems."

*Exosystems* are situations having a bearing on a child's development but in which the developing child does not herself actually play a direct role. The child's exosystems are those settings that have power over her life, yet in which she does not participate. They include the workplaces of parents (since most children do not have direct contact with them), and those centers of power, such as school boards and planning commissions, that make decisions affecting the child's day-to-day life. These exosystems enhance development when they make life easier for parents and undermine development when they make life harder for parents. The situation of latchkey children (who return from school to a household without adult supervision) is one example (Garbarino, 1980). Working parents often have few institutional allies and are often victimized by unsympathetic exosystems. Thus, exosystem opportunity lies in situations where there are forces at work outside the family on behalf of children and their parents. When children "have friends in high places" the opportunities for child development increase. The political initiative taken by the powerful Kennedy family on behalf of retarded children is an example. More typically, however, institutions (offices and structures) in the exosystem are generally of greater importance. Thus, the relevance of exosystems to our concern with density lies mainly in how they affect micro- and mesosystems.

One very important exosystem for children is the planning board. This group can play a significant role in determining how well the authorities incorporate interests of children into decisions about land use. Given that a physical environment attractive to children may be unattractive by adult standards, this is vital (Michelson & Roberts, 1979). For example, children may thrive on *both* "empty lots," which they fill with games, and on the integration of commercial with residential properties, which many adults see as economically disadvantageous. "Planning has, over the years, stressed the separation of uses. I think that many planners, particularly those working in the city, realize the fallacy of that policy, and that diversity is, in fact, a strength rather than a weakness" (Barker, 1979, p. 118).

Meso- and exosystems are embedded in the broad ideological and institutional patterns of a particular culture or subculture—how the ecological pieces fit together. These patterns are the *macrosystem*—the "blueprints" for that culture's ecology of human development, which reflect a people's shared assumptions about "how things should be done," including cultural criteria for experiencing various levels of density as "crowding." A macrosystem is the norms about how development proceeds, and the appropriate nature and structure of micro-, meso-, and exosystems. Conventional cultural and ethnic labels (e.g., Latin, Italian, Indian) suggest unique clusters of ideological and behavioral patterns. Beyond these labels, however, we need to operationalize and examine ideologies and behaviors and their implications for child development. In terms of their consequences for parents and children, we need to know, for example, how different cultures respond to economic crises that require residential crowding and how the school-home mesosystem works in two "different" ethnic groups. Having different labels does not mean that we necessarily have different macrosystems. For example, researchers report relatively little difference among American ethnic groups in defining child abuse (Giovanonni & Beccerra, 1979).

Environmental opportunity in macrosystem terms is a pro-child ideology and a set of institutions that supports and encourages healthy childrearing.

For example, a society's assumption that families stricken by economic or medical tragedy have a right to public support represents macrosystem opportunity. A strong political base of support for child services is another manifestation of macrosystem opportunity. A third is a commitment to gearing the density of children's environments to *their* developmental needs, rather than exclusively to the economic needs of adults. With significant shifts in the urban-rural composition of the population, and even shifts in the very meaning of "rural" living, such ideological issues grow in importance (Garbarino & Plantz, 1980).

What is environmental risk when it comes to macrosystems? It is an ideology or cultural alignment that theatens to impoverish children's microsystems and mesosystems, and sets exosystems against them. It can be a national economic policy that tolerates or even increases the chances of economic dislocations and poverty for families with young children. It can be institutionalized support for high levels of geographic mobility that disrupts neighborhood and school connections, and the social networks of parents. It can be a pattern of non-support for parents that tolerates or even aggregates conflicts between the roles of worker and parent. It can be patterns of racist, sexist, or other values that demean parents, thereby undermining the psychological security of their children and threatening each child's self-esteem. In general, macrosystem risk is any social pattern or societal event that impoverishes the ability and willingness of adults to care for children, and for children to learn from adults. Certainly, when broad social forces prevent or disrupt optimal levels and forms of density cited earlier they place children at risk.

To recapitulate, environmental influences on the child's development originate from systems at all four levels in the human ecology of the child. Systems at each level have distinctive characteristics relevant to a child's development, and therefore different criteria are appropriate for assessing their impacts on the child. Further, these effects may be either positive or negative — either opportunities or risks. And, while the family microsystem is usually the most important system for a child, the overall impact of the environment emerges from the dynamic balance among all influences over time. The density of a child's social ecology is thus variable. No simple or static approach will suffice. Does density matter? It depends.

## RESIDENTIAL DENSITY AS AN ECOLOGICAL ISSUE

Like nearly all "factors," density becomes a phenomenon only insofar as an individual experiences it. As noted earlier, Bronfenbrenner defines human development in terms of the developing person's conception of and access to the environment. Using this definition of development, the significance of density lies in whether or not it contributes to a "more extended differentiated and valid conception of the ecological environment," keeping in mind the general developmental principle that for "optimal" development, the child needs more diversity as she matures. Thus, we can evaluate residential density in terms of its contribution to development in general, and specifically in terms of its contribution to how well the child does in competently handling an ever-widening set of microsystems.

The general elements of human competence go beyond "adaptivity," as intelligence is defined by Caldwell, Piaget, Binet, and Simon and others. McClelland (1975) set forth a suggestive analysis suitable for the present purpose. In his view, competence (i.e., successful performance in specific social contexts) typically consists of the following abilities (McClelland, 1973, p. 10).

1. *Communication skills* — being able to communicate intentions and needs accurately by word, look, or gesture
2. *Patience* — being able to delay responses to permit accurate processing of information
3. *Moderate goal setting* — being able to accurately match abilities to situational factors, and thus set goals neither too high nor too low
4. *Ego development* — being able to cope with setbacks and effectively marshal one's resources.

McClelland's definition of competence suggests a fulcrum with which to move the problem of evaluating density. It permits us to evaluate parental behavior (or parent-child relations, or teacher-student relations) in light of a developmental criterion, namely, its contribution to the development of competence. It sets goals for the socialization process, as Inkeles (1966) and others have argued is necessary. To evaluate socialization practices we must know what will be demanded of people through the life course. The principal general goal of socialization is, of course, competence (as McClelland defines it). If we start with this conception of competence as the "currency" of development, we can then say that density is a significant developmental influence mainly through its effects on the social resources of the child. Thus, a high density family microsystem (i.e., a high child-to-adult ratio with close spacing) tends to inhibit the development of competence while a low density family microsystem (a low child-to-adult ratio with wide spacing) tends to enhance the development of competence. Thus family "size" is not a simple issue. Similarly, when the mesosystem is dense (i.e., many interconnections between microsystems) it enhances development (so long as it contains a diversity of roles).

The principal density issue with respect to exosystems is whether or not they promote helpful microsystems and mesosystems for children. The focal point of such concern is typically the neighborhood. Neighborhood character plays a significant role in determining the developmental appropriateness of the child's social experience (Garbarino & Plantz, 1980). The overriding issue is whether or not the neighborhood contributes to the child's development by providing an experience that is "socially dense." The fragmentary available evidence suggests that some neighborhoods encourage deep relationships between children and adults (particularly non-parental adults) and among children while others discourage such relationships in favor of superficial, fleeting contact. Looked at phenomenologically, the former is a very dense setting, while the latter is very sparse. The social protection that is provided by supportive, reciprocal networks was described well by Jane Howard when she said of her strong extended family: "But we are numerous enough and connected enough not to let anyone's worse prevail for long. For any given poison, our pooled resources can come up with an antidote" (Howard, 1978, 60).

"Ecological niches" reflect enriched or impoverished conditions of life for children and their families, and for urban environments. Neighborhoods are one of the principal niches where one finds the conditions of life that either collaborate to bolster parents or conspire to compound their deficiencies and vulnerabilities. Students of urban life generally agree that the cutting edge of the quality issue in urban settings, at least for families with young children, is the social and physical character of the neighborhood as an environmental unit (cf. Jacobs, 1961). This theme emerged in a series of discussions of "the child in the city" sponsored by the University of Toronto's project investigating the interface of urban environments and urban children (cf. Michelson & Roberts, 1979).

Like many other important and intuitively appealing concepts, "neighborhood" is elusive (cf. Keller, 1968; Warren, 1980), and the field of community studies has not reached agreement on how to identify one. For urban dwellers, the notion of neighborhood generally includes the concept of "walking distance." Morris and Hess (1975) use such a basis.

> What is the neighborhood? It is place and it is people. It has no defined size or even scale, although common sense limits do appear throughout history. The homeliest tests for neighborhood would include the fact that a person can easily walk its boundaries. It is not so large that going from one side to another requires special effort. Its physical size means that it is or can be familiar turf for everyone in it. (p. 6)

The search for an acceptable definition of neighborhood will continue. Clearly, both geographical and social concerns must be reflected in whatever definition we use. Aside from the problem of a definition is the issue of neighborhood quality, and how density affects the quality of the neighborhood as an ecological niche for families. Kromkowski highlights some essential sources and indicators of neighborhood character. In so doing, he presents criteria with which to evaluate the quality of the neighborhood as a social environment.

> The organic life of a neighborhood, created by the persons who live in a particular geographic area, is always a fragile reality. A neighborhood's character is determined by a host of factors, but most significantly by the kinds of relationships that neighbors have with each other. A neighborhood is not a sovereign power — it can rarely write its own agenda. Although neighborhoods differ in a host of ways, a healthy neighborhood has pride in the neighborhood, care of homes, security for children, and respect for each other. (Kromkowski, 1976, p. 228)

The level of material resources of a family affects the importance of its social resources. The financially well-off can purchase access to formal, institutionalized social resources on behalf of themselves and their children (Seeley, 1956). Poor families, lacking in material resources, rely more heavily on their informal social resources for encouragement, sustainment, and feedback.

The importance of the neighborhood to family life varies as a function of family economic resources (cf. Lewis, 1978; Smith, 1976). Rich people who are freer to inhabit a neighborhood of their own choosing can better "afford" a weak or disorganized neighborhood than can poor people, who are more dependent on informal social resources within their ecological niche. Economically impoverished families, of course, are more likely to live in neighborhoods consisting primarily of other impoverished and marginal families. This can have significant effects upon the nature and impact of peer relations. In some of these neighborhoods, active social networks supplement family resources in crucial and creative ways. An excellent study of such social richness amidst economic impoverishment is Stack's observations (1974) of the resiliant support networks operating in a poverty-stricken neighborhood and the elaborate rules and protocols for network functioning. The severity of their economic impoverishment was such that, over the long term, few of the people in her study could have maintained living quarters and avoided periodic starvation if required to exist in social isolation. It was the strength and flexibility of their active social networks that provided these people with some reasonable assurance of survival. The extreme neediness of the participants often overtaxed the networks, but the alternative was social and personal disaster. And, in this socially enriched, "dense" setting, children were largely protected from the stresses of the environment and parental crises and insufficiencies.

In other poor neighborhoods, individuals and families exist in isolation from each other, and the desolation of social impoverishment compounds the deprivation of economic impoverishment. Lack of contact with potent family support systems, a disinclination to seek help in solving problems, a lack of involvement in reciprocal helping relationships, and the other accouterments of social isolation and a socially "sparse" environment compound personal vulnerability (Garbarino, 1977; Garbarino & Sherman, 1980; Wolock & Horowitz, 1978). Even relations among children suffer. The ecological perspective highlights the risk to children of these economically impoverished families clustered in socially impoverished places — high-risk families in high-risk neighborhoods.

Among the many family issues that can be considered from a neighborhood perspective is the broad problem of child maltreatment. Research findings on the neighborhood correlates of child maltreatment lend credence to the proposition that neighborhood quality, its social density as we are using the term, has important implications for the quality of life among financially distressed families. This research illustrates one form of microsystem risk to child development associated with the social richness of the child's environment.

When Garbarino and Crouter (1978) compared neighborhoods with high rates of reported child maltreatment to neighborhoods having low rates, they found that a substantial proportion (about 50%) of the variation in rates of child maltreatment among 93 neighborhoods could be accounted for by the proportion of families characterized by inadequate income, single parenthood. At the same time, they noted that there were differences in rates of child maltreatment among areas with the same concentrations of low income, single parenthood, and transience. In some areas, termed "high-risk" areas, the actual rate of child maltreatment substantially exceeded the rate that would be predicted from their socioeconomic and demographic profiles. Other "low-risk" ones had rates substantially lower than socioeconomic and demographic characteristics would predict.

Garbarino and Sherman (1980) compared pairs of socioeconomically and demographically similar high- and low-risk neighborhoods. They found that high-risk areas were characterized by low levels of neighborly exchange, residential instability, restricted interaction among children, deteriorating housing, poor relations with institutions such as schools, and a pervasive pattern of social stress.

Garbarino and Sherman (1980) further conducted interviews with matched samples of parents and with local "observers" in one high-risk and one low-risk area to discover how people perceive high- versus low-risk neighborhoods. Although the areas were matched roughly on income, single parenthood, working mothers, and transience, the high-risk neighborhood was seen as a less supportive environment for family life both by "observers" (e.g., parish priests, visiting nurses, educators, and policemen), and by "participants" (mothers living in the area). In a well-matched samples of parents randomly selected from the two neighborhoods, those in the high-risk area had more stresses, less support, less adequate child care, and a less positive view of family and neighborhood life.

A test of the evaluations contained in a random sample of comments by a wide range of "observers" (using raters unaware of the purpose of identity of the neighborhoods) revealed a significantly more positive view of the low-risk areas (Garbarino & Sherman, 1980). Mothers in the low-risk area reported significantly more poeple taking an interest in their child and are more likely to be home to greet children returning from school. In general, mothers in the low-risk area made fewer demands on the informal support system and see themselves as having more resources to call upon in that informal support system. The interviews found significantly higher levels of social stress among the high-risk mothers, with more than twice as many being in the moderate or major crisis category. Virtually all the comparisons in mothers' ratings of day-to-day existence present a more positive picture of life in the low-risk neighborhood. Significant differences favor the low-risk area in the availability of child care, in the neighborhood as a place to rear children, and in the child as being easy to raise. Recent efforts to examine similar issues in rural environments (Rosenberg & Reppucci, in press) suggest the same issues predominate outside the urban context as well. A strong positive neighborhood offers optimal social density for the child.

## COMPARING RURAL, URBAN AND SUBURBAN ENVIRONMENTS

The traditional urban-rural dichotomy has become increasingly obsolete in the period following World War II (Photiadis, 1970; VanEs & Brown, 1974). The rise of the automotive society gave birth to new residential forms that have altered the foundations of both urban and rural life. The automobile and the cheap-energy economy it represented made possible new and attractive suburban, rural, and urban patterns that by their very existence undermined the older forms (cf. Kowinski, 1980; Wynne, 1977). However, the basic need of children and parents for enduring support systems has not diminished. If anything, the greater complexity and challenge of the contemporary socioeconomic order ("modern life") has increased the importance of these support system relationships. Furthermore, there are still gross differences between urban and rural social forms (Heller & Quesada, 1977; Huessy, 1972). There are even regional differences in density *within* the general category "rural life." Thus, for example, rural Midwest and New England communities are more densely packed than in the Rocky Mountains, where they are much more sparsely distributed (Huessy, 1972). Whether an environment is urban, rural, or suburban, children need a geographic expression of the human microcosm. This is axiomatic. They must have some physical reality (Milgram, 1977). Thus, urban children and parents continue to need their neighborhoods, rural families their villages, and suburban children and adults their small towns.

"My own speculation, at this point, is that a complete community of around 5000 people allows a child to get a rather good idea of what community relations are all about" (Aldrich, 1979, p. 87). While there exists an extensive literature which shows that the issue of optimal community size is a controversial one, most investigators are in agreement that wherever they live, children do best when they are set within a community microcosm that offers stable opportunities to observe and practice basic human roles (Aldrich, 1979). "Properly put together, a neighborhood provides children . . . some sense of familiarity and protection" (Schorr, 1979, p. 132).

The limited available research buttresses these conclusions. Investigators report that children in a small town have more knowledge of people and roles than do urban children living in a non-neighborhood, while those in a strong urban neighborhood stand somewhere in between the town and city (Gump & Adelberg, 1978). The small town tends to be "underpeopled" in that it has a low ratio of people to settings. As a community, it has the full range of community activities to maintain, and thus is very dense with respect to roles and mesosystems. The urban neighborhood generally is not a community; it can rely on the larger city for too many functions. People thus are drawn away from it and children see less of life's basic social functions. It is less socially dense. The strong urban neighborhood somewhat approximates the small town. The weak neighborhood has so little going on that it impoverishes the social experience and knowledge of children. In this the weak neighborhood parallels the large school—it discourages productive social experience, particularly for the child whose personal resources are marginal (cf. Garbarino, 1980b).

Just as the community context of the child's immediate setting is important in determining the richness of the child's social experience, so is the stability of that setting and context. We know from informal observation that neighborhoods are hard to transplant. Urban renewal projects must be wary of disturbing the "natural" social systems of the area. Indeed, when disaster strikes a community (e.g., flood or tornado) the biggest problem is how to recreate the *social* landscape (Nuttal, 1980; cf. Erikson, 1976). When the disaster results from social policy—e.g., highway or dam development requiring relocation—the same issues obtain. Warren (1968), for instance, reported that when government officials tried to relocate a small town because of a dam project, only one quarter of the original behavior settings survived the move. It became less socially dense. As Devereaux (1977) has demonstrated in his critique of ecological psychology, community changes are probably the principal forces affecting the quantity and quality of behavioral settings. We must see the child's environment from the perspective of changing commu-

nity structure — changes often wrought by technological developments working in conjunction with economic forces.

The automotive era has had its clearest and most profound effects on suburban living, where social sparseness appears to be a serious problem, as Van
Vliet's analysis in this volume documents. Wynne (1977) distinguishes between "old" and "new" suburbs. The former are small towns on the periphery
of a city having railroad stations (for commuting) as focal points. The latter
are bedroom communities without a primary economy that are dependent
upon automobile-based commuting. In 1956, about 80% of America's suburbs were of the old type. The figure for 1980 is about 45%. The new suburbs
seem to add little to a family's personal resources for child rearing and may in
fact detract, beause they lack enough community activities (formal and informal) to offer children a socially rich and varied existence. Those "post-
industrial" suburbs are technology intensive and often socially deficient
(Wynne, 1977).

The automotive era's main effects on cities have been movement away
from the core of old cities to newer cities and suburbs and increased noise and
accident hazards (Michelson & Roberts, 1979). The significance of these effects is general but does seem to differ as a function of the child's sex, age,
and history (Chapters 3 and 5 in this volume).

The new patterns work against older neighborhoods, which function
somewhat like small towns (Gump & Adelberg, 1978). They diminish the social resources of children — making these environments socially "sparse" — by
undermining their support systems in the day-to-day functioning of the ecological niche. Furthermore, the erosion of the urban tax base and increasing
concentration of high-risk populations have jeopardized schools, governments, businesses, and neighborhoods. Where this has happened, it has
weakened the natural advantages of the city, namely the opportunity for social density. We assume these problems affect some children more than
others, and are of greater concern for children otherwise at social risk. Other
chapters in this volume encourage such speculation.

What is the role density of modern residential settings? Density has a qualitative side, when viewed in terms of its implications for child development.
The density of roles — i.e., the relative homogeneity versus heterogeneity of
the setting — is an important issue. A heterogeneous setting is one in which
mulitple roles exist, while in a homogeneous setting are few or only one role.
In this and many other respects, homogeneity tends to be developmentally
stultifying. Within the family microsystem, for example, the same two adults
could represent a more homogeneous setting if both play the same role than if
they play different roles (e.g., two "fathers" may not be as good as a "father'
and a "mother"). In this sense, the latter is a more dense setting. Also, the
spectrum of roles to the immediate social environment of the child contributes to development. A dense setting (with respect to roles) may be develop-

mentally enhancing, as when the neighborhood contains shopkeepers, re-tired persons, and a variety of kinship and friendship relations.

Is there sufficient demarcation of residential units into socially dense community-like clusters? Or, are the boundaries so weak and the residential clusters so socially sparse as to deprive children of the diversity they need to facilitate optimal development (using Bronfenbrenner's concept of develop-ment)? The superficial, short-term relationships with adults thought to be even more common for children suggest that those children are spread too thin across too large a social field outside the family and caged in too small a social field inside the family. This concern leads to a related issue.

Do children have sufficient mesosystems to facilitate development? We suspect that the social division of labor characteristic of modern commu-nities makes for sparse mesosystems (cf. Bronfenbrenner, 1975). These im-portant mesosystems are largely controlled by the economic and ideological forces at work in the society promoting age segregation, specialization, and homogeneity.

All told, a refocusing of the density issues raises some important questions about the human ecology of socialization in our society. By emphasizing so-cial phenomenological considerations, an ecological perspective pinpoints the role diversity of settings and the connections between settings as critical issues in considering the relation of residential density to child development.

Few studies address these issues. We can review one that does, however, as a way of beginning to explore them. Garbarino and his colleagues (Gar-barino, Burston, Raber, Russell, & Crouter, 1978) studied the "social maps" of preadolescent and early adolescent children. The children and their mothers reported on the children's social networks — the web of relationships in which the child is embedded. The interview procedures used permitted a cataloging of who the child knew well, who took an interest in the child and the nature of the relationship — all in the context of socioeconomic and eco-logical factors, and from both the child's and mother's point of view. While a complete recounting of the results is beyond the scope of this paper, several findings are worth reporting here. First, rural children listed more people as part of their networks (16.8) than the urban (12.2) and suburban children (11.1). Furthermore, the rural children reported more interconnections in their network (with each person listed among the "ten best known" reportedly knowing 5.6 others, versus 4.2 for the suburban and 3.5 for the urban chil-dren). However, the urban children have the highest mean number of adults listed among the "top ten" who are seen at least once per month (2.3 versus 1.5 for the rural and 1.0 for the suburban children). These results from a small scale study are provocative and cry out for replication, expansion, and clarification. They tantalize us with the preposition that the rural-urban-suburban trichotomy may be an important influence on social density of chil-dren's social experience.

## CONCLUSION

As always in an exploratory discussion, the conclusion is that we know enough to ask questions but don't know enough to answer them. So it is with an ecological perspective on density. Having simply specified some of the questions (hopefully the more important and intelligent ones) and their accompanying hypotheses is an accomplishment in its own right. By conceptualizing density in phenomenological terms we open up the concept of social richness — a clustering of diverse roles united in a pro-child consensus. By focusing on social richness (and impoverishment) we open up the multiple levels of the child's environment. This provides an integrated view of social density and social spareness as correlates of alternative structural and value themes in the community, in the neighborhood, and in the family. All relate to the character of the child's social network and the fabric of day-to-day social experience. All argue that children are best served by environments that put them "in the thick of it" with adults and other children.

## REFERENCES

Aldrich, R. The influences of mann-built environment on children and youth. In W. Michelson, G. Levine & E. Michelson (Eds.), *The child in the city*. Toronto: University of Toronto Press, 1979. Pp. 78–101.

Barker, D. Comments on "the spatial world of the child." In W. Michelson, S. Levine & E. Michelson (Eds.), *The child in the city*. Toronto: University of Toronto Press, 1979. Pp. 117–118.

Barker, G., & Gump, P. V. *Big school, small school: High school size and student behavior*. Stanford, California: Stanford University Press, 1964.

Barker, R. G., & Schoggen, P. *Qualities of community life: Methods of measuring environment and behavior applied to an American and an English town*. San Francisco: Jossey-Bass, 1973.

Bronfenbrenner, U. *The ecology of human development*. Cambridge, Mass.: Harvard University Press, 1979.

Bronfenbrenner, U. The origins of alienation. In U. Bronfenbrenner & M. Mahoney (Eds.), *Influences on human development*. Hinsdale, Illinois: The Dryden Press, 1975. Pp. 485–501.

Devereaux, E. *A critique of ecological psychology*. Paper presented at the Conference on Research Perspectives in the Ecology of Human Development, Cornell University, Ithaca, New York, August, 1977.

Elder, G. H. *Children of the great depression*. Chicago: University of Chicago Press, 1974.

Elder, G., & Rockwell, R. *The life course and human development: An ecological perspective*. Unpublished paper. Boys Town, NE: Boys Town Center for the Study of Youth Development, 1977.

Erikson, K. T. *Everything in its path: Destruction of community in the Buffalo Creek flood*. New York: Simon and Schuster, 1976.

Garbarino, J. The human ecology of child maltreatment: A conceptual model for research. *Journal of Marriage and the Family*, 1977, *39*, 721–736.

Garbarino, J. Defining emotional maltreatment: The message is the meaning. *Journal of Psychiatric Treatment and Evaluation*, 1980, *2*, 105–110. (a)

Garbarino, J. Some thoughts on the effects of school size on adolescent development. *Journal of Youth and Adolescence,* 1980, *9,* 19–31. (b)

Garbarino, J. Latchkey children. *Vital Issues,* 1980, *30*(3), 1–4. (c)

Garbarino, J., Burston, N., Raber, S., Russel, R., & Crouter, A. The social maps of children approaching the transition from elementary to secondary school. *Journal of Youth and Adolescence,* 1978, *7,* 417–428.

Garbarino, J., & Crouter, A. Defining the community context of parent-child relations: The correlates of child maltreatment. *Child Development,* 1978, *49,* 604–616.

Garbarino, J., & Gilliam, G. *Understanding abusive families.* Lexington, Mass.: Lexington Books, 1980.

Garbarino, J., & Plantz, M. *Urban children and urban environments.* New York: ERIC Institute for Urban Education, 1980.

Garbarino, J., & Sherman, D. High-risk families and high-risk neighborhoods: Studying the ecology of child maltreatment. *Child Development,* 1980, *51,* 188–198.

Giovannoni, J., & Becerra, R. *Defining child abuse.* New York: The Free Press, 1979.

Gump, P., & Adelberg, B. Urbanism from the perspective of ecological psychologists. *Environment and Behavior,* 1978, *10,* 171–191.

Hawley, A. *Human ecology: A theory of community structure.* New York: Ronald Press, 1950.

Heller, P. L., & Quesada, G. Rural familism: An interregional analysis. *Rural Sociology,* 1977, *42,* 220–240.

Howard, J. *Families.* New York: Simon and Schuster, 1978.

Huessy, H. R. Tactics and targets in the rural setting. In S. E. Golann & Carl Eisdorfer (Eds.), *Handbook of community mental health.* New York: Appleton-Century-Crofts, 1972. Pp. 699–710.

Inkeles, A. Social structure and the socialization of competence. *Harvard Education Review,* 1966, *36,* 282.

Jacobs, J. *The death and life of great American cities.* New York: Random House, 1961.

Keller, S. *The urban neighborhood.* New York: Random House, 1968.

Kopp, C., & Young, J. *The human ecology of handicapped children.* Unpublished paper, Project REACH, University of California at Los Angeles, 1980.

Kowinski, W. Suburbia: End of the golden age. *New York Times Magazine.* March 16, 1980, 16 ff.

Kromkowski, J. *Neighborhood deterioration and juvenile crime.* (U.S. Department of Commerce, National Technical Information Service, PB-360 473), The South Bend Urban Observatory, Indiana, August, 1976.

Lewis, M. Nearest neighbor analysis of epidemiological and community variables. *Psychological Bulletin,* 1978, *85,* 1302–1308.

McClelland, D. C. Testing for competence rather than for "intelligence." *American Psychologist,* 1973, *28,* 1–14.

Michelson, W., & Roberts, E. Children and the urban physical environment. In W. Michelson, S. Levine, & A. Spina (Eds.), *The child in the city.* Toronto: University of Toronto Press, 1979. Pp. 410–477.

Milgram, S. *The individual in a social world.* Reading, Mass.: Addison-Wesley, 1977.

Moos, R. Evaluating and changing community settings. *American Journal of Community Psychology,* 1976, *4,* 313–326.

Morris, P., & Hess, K. *Neighborhood power: The new localism.* Boston: Beacon, 1975.

Nuttal, R. *Coping with catastrophe: Family adjustment to natural disasters.* Paper presented at Groves Conference on Marriage and the Family, Gatlinburg, Tennessee, May 31, 1980.

Photiadis, J. D. Rural southern Appalachia and mass society. In John D. Photiadis & Harry K. Schwarzweller (Eds.), *Change in rural Appalachia: Implications for action programs.* Philadelphia: University of Pennsylvania Press, 1970.

Polansky, N. Analysis of research on child neglect: The social work viewpoint. In Herner and Company (Eds.), *Four perspectives on the status of child abuse and neglect research.* Washington, D.C.: National Center on Child Abuse and Neglect, 1976.

Rohner, R. *They love me, they love me not.* New Haven, CT: HRAF Press, 1975.

Rohner, R., & Nielsen, C. *Parental acceptance and rejection: A review of research and theory.* New Haven, CT: Human Relations Area Files Press, 1978.

Rosenberg, M. S., & Reppucci, N. D. Child abuse: A review with special focus on an ecological approach in rural communities. In T. Melton (Ed.), *Rural psychology,* in press.

Schorr, A. The child and the community. In W. Michelson, S. Levine, & E. Michelson (Eds.), *The child in the city.* Toronto: University of Toronto Press, 1979. Pp. 128–134.

Seeley, J. R. Alexander, R., & Loosley, E. L. *Crestwood Heights.* New York: Basic Books, 1956.

Smith, C. J. Residential neighborhoods as humane environments. *Environment and Planning,* 1976, *8,* 311–326.

Stack, C. *All our kin: Strategies for survival in a black community.* New York: Harper and Row, 1974.

VanEs, J. C., & Brown, J. E. The rural-urban variable once more: Some individual level observations. *Rural Sociology,* 1974, *39,* 373–391.

Warren, D. Support systems in different types of neighborhoods. In J. Garbarino, S. Stocking and Associates (Eds.), *Protecting children from abuse and neglect.* San Franciso: Jossey-Bass, 1980. Pp. 61–93.

Warren, S. *The relocation of Ozawkiy, Kansas.* Unpublished manuscript, University of Kansas, 1968.

Wicker, A. W. *An introduction to ecological psychology.* Monterey, Ca.: Brooks/Cole, 1979.

Wolock, I., & Horowitz, B. *Factors relating to levels of child care among families receiving public assistance in New Jersey.* Paper presented at the National Conference on Child Abuse and Neglect, New York, N.Y., April, 1978.

Wynne, E. *Growing up suburban.* Austin, Texas: University of Texas Press, 1977.

Young, M., & Kopp, C. *Handicapped children and their families: Research directions.* Unpublished paper, University of California, Los Angeles, 1980.

# 7

# Quality of Children's Family Interaction in Relation to Residential Type and Household Crowding

Alan Booth
*University of Nebraska-Lincoln*

## INTRODUCTION

Interest in the importance of housing environments on the lives of inhabitants is waxing with the current concern with environmental issues. Interest in the pathological effects of housing goes back at least to the mid-nineteenth century when physicians and social service workers were attempting to explain the rampant disease found in cities (Martin, 1967). Renewed interest in the effects of crowding was peaked by research on non-humans which demonstrated that remarkable increases in pathology were caused by compressed living conditions (cf. Calhoun, 1962).

The intent of this chapter is to review what we know about two aspects of the housing environment: housing type and household crowding. By housing type we mean whether a residence is a single-family dwelling, a duplex, row house, low-rise, apartment, high-rise, and so on. Household crowding, on the other hand, refers to conditions inside the dwelling such as the number of rooms or the amount of space per household member. Many writers tend to think of housing type and household crowding to be almost interchangeable aspects of the built environment. But, as van Vliet-- argues in detail elsewhere in this volume, they are not. Therefore, they are treated as separate aspects of the child's development.

In addition to focusing on the micro-environment, we limit our attention to the affect of housing on family relations and the decision to have children. The reader is referred elsewhere in this volume for an analysis of how the environment affects the child's relation with peers (see the chapter by van

Vliet––), and influences the child's health, attitudes and development (see the chapters by Aiello and Baum, Heft, Shannon and Aldrich).

It is not unreasonable to expect the micro-housing environment to have substantial affect on the decision to have children, and on the relationships between family members. After all, the household and its immediate sur-roundings constitute the primary environment of children. It is the exclusive environment for most young children, and only as children reach school age do their social arenas expand to include the neighborhood and larger commu-nity. As such it is the environment most likely to affect the life of a young per-son. In addition, the environment most likely to affect the decision to have a child is the micro-housing environment.

Given that the dwelling is the most salient aspect of the built environment for children and their parents, what sort of influence could we expect it to have? The condition of the dwelling (safety, cleanliness, noise, cold) has been shown to have an affect (cf. Wilner, Walkley, Pinkerton, & Tayback, 1962). The design of the micro-housing environment can also be seen as having an influence on such things as criminal victimization (Newman, 1973) and the quality of social interaction (cf. Festinger, Schachter, & Balk, 1950). The re-search on dwelling type and household crowding also gives us reason to be-lieve that these features of the micro-environment influence the lives of their younger inhabitants.

## RESIDENCE TYPE AS AN ASPECT OF THE CHILD'S ENVIRONMENT

A consideration of dwelling type commonly brings to mind extreme forms of housing, such as the suburban single-family dwelling and the central city high-rise. But of course there are variations in-between: from duplexes, town houses and row houses, to two-and-three-story walk-up apartments; four-dwelling apartment buildings and apartment complexes containing hundreds of dwellings. Thus, it seems that not only the floor containing the household is a relevant factor, but the number of dwellings in the building is also a di-mension to take into account. The floor and number of units are somewhat related, but not entirely. A several-hundred-unit complex may be spread out over several acres or concentrated on a few thousand square feet in the form of a high-rise. Thus, the floor and the number of units should be viewed as separate dimensions that may have somewhat different consequences. A third dimension that could impinge on the child's life is the presence or ab-sence of community areas such as hallways, play areas, sidewalks and so on that are associated with his or her dwelling. While it is a dimension that is of-ten related to floor level and number of units, it is not synonymous with these factors. There is reason to believe that community areas may have a unique effect on young inhabitants. No discussion of dwelling type would be complete without some consideration of people's housing preferences. The majority of families with small children prefer single-family dwellings, yet for a number of reasons, many children are reared in apartments, town houses and other types of units. The consequences of living in a dwelling which is not one's first choice needs to be explored. We begin our discussion by considering some of the ways the three dimensions of housing type and housing preferences might affect children. Some propositions are presented. The extant research is then critically examined to see to what extent our ideas are supported. We then draw conclusions about the effects of housing type on family life and detail the research that remains to be done to obtain a more complete understanding of the relationships under consideration.

## Floor, Number of Units, Community Areas and Housing Preference

The floor containing the dwelling would have a direct bearing on the difficulty parents experience supervising young children. The higher the floor, the harder it is for parents and children to communicate directly with each other. A child in trouble has difficulty getting his or her parents' attention, and a youngster who is not behaving properly has difficulty receiving directions from his or her parents. Therefore we would expect the floor containing the dwelling to have an effect on child-parent relations: parents of children on the upper floors of a high-rise may have less control over their children and experience more problems with them than parents in other types of dwellings. These problems may, in turn, be a source of marital discord.

The number of dwelling units in a building has consequences for the number of community facilities available to residents. Units with more dwellings, due to economies of scale, are likely to have day-care centers, laundry facilities, play areas, and stores. Some of these (day-care centers and play areas) facilitate child care, and others make it easier for parents of small children to shop, do the laundry and other household tasks which, in turn, may facilitate parent-child relations. Of course such facilities in large heterogenous complexes can become havens for delinquent activity, causing both parents and children worry about their personal safety. It should be noted that community facilities are probably more characteristic of new buildings than old ones, and of suburban developments located some distance away from shopping malls than of developments in the central city.

The number of units in a building also has consequences for the number of people with whom both the parents and the children have contact each day. The greater the number of dwellings, the more extensive the opportunities for contact. Perhaps opportunities for contact are more extensive in large highrises than in any other dwelling type because of the concentration of units.

While the number of people in a spread-out complex may be as great, the potential for contact while entering or leaving is less.

There is more than one possible consequence of having a large number of potential contacts. On the one hand, such contacts can enrich social relations by providing the mechanisms to form friendships and acquaintanceships and to establish voluntary organizations. Children are more likely to find same-age playmates in a building containing many units than one having few units. Parents are more likely to find like-minded adults with whom they can share baby-sitting or get advice on how to handle child-rearing problems (Litwak, 1969).

On the other hand, contact with large numbers of people may bring about excessive physical and mental stimulation as proposed by Milgram (1970). Mechanisms may be called into play that are designed to limit interaction to people who have some direct bearing on the satisfaction of personal needs, thus limiting communication with neighbors. Limiting interaction, in turn, breaks down the informal networks of control — the feeling of responsibility for what goes on outside the household (Booth, 1981). Vandalism and other crime may result and residents may experience a decline in personal safety because bystanders will not intervene (Newman, 1973; Rainwater, 1966; Yancey, 1972). These events are especially likely to occur if there is high residential turnover and if the population is heterogenous (Gillis, 1980). For the child, this means increased worry and risk of personal attack. For the parents it means anxiety over the child's welfare. If parents try to keep the children indoors in order to minimize the risks, elevated parent-child conflict could result from the children's desire to go outside, and the parents' wish to limit their offspring's activity.

The number of community areas adjacent to the dwelling is the third dimension of housing type to be considered. Community area includes hallways, stairways, elevators, lobbies, parking lots and garages, play areas, sidewalks, and so on. Even walls may be thought of as community areas because they are shared with other families, and one family's floor constitutes another family's ceiling. A large apartment complex is apt to have the greatest number of community areas and a single-family dwelling the least — perhaps none. Town houses may share two walls, driveway and swimming pool, but not the yard and garden or garage.

Children who use community areas are obligated to learn public behavior at an early age and practice it every time they leave the dwelling. This includes small things such as respecting community property, keeping noise down, observing conventions of elevator use and staying out of potentially unsafe areas (garage, furnace room). As a consequence, parental demands on children in multiple units as compared to single-family dwellings would be greater. The parents' struggle to inhibit the play activities of small children so that their noise does not disturb the neighbors can place a strain on the parent-child relationship. Moreover, if parents accompany the children so that they may directly supervise their activities, each hour outside is time that cannot be devoted to household duties or other work. Such neglect can be the source of marital discord. If the children go out unsupervised, parents not only worry about whether they are disturbing the neighbors, but also about their safety — another source of stress. The presence of a great many community areas immediately adjacent to the dwelling could diminish individual privacy. While the importance of privacy for well-being is unclear (Booth, Johnson, & Edwards, 1980), to the extent such a need is important, it would be less well met where community areas are in abundance. Most of these problems do not face residents of single-family dwellings.

This brings us to housing preference, another factor with the potential for influencing the quality of family relations. Michelson (1977, p. 337) in his study of housing preference has shown that people in households with a particular composition and life style prefer particular types of housing. The type of house preferred by the majority of intact families with dependent children is the single-family dwelling. In addition, Michelson (1977, pp. 273–302) demonstrated that when the actual living conditions depart from personal preference, dissatisfaction resulted, except when there was a prospect of moving in the near future to a preferred dwelling. Thus, parents with small children who reside in an apartment, but prefer to live in a town house or single-family dwelling, may show signs of stress that could have adverse consequences for the quality of all family relations.

The dimensions of dwelling type and housing preference as they relate to common housing designations are shown in Table 7.1. Given that the dimensions of dwelling type seem to find their extremes in the single-family dwelling and the high-rise, and that the potential problems for family relations created by the floor of the dwelling, number of units, the number of community areas, and housing preference would appear to be greatest for the high-rise

TABLE 7.1

|  | Number of Floors | Number of Units | Number of Community Areas/Unit | Preference by Families with Dependent Children |
|---|---|---|---|---|
| Single-Family Dwelling | Low | Low | Low | High |
| Duplex | Low | Low | Med | Moderate |
| Town House — Row-House | Low | Med | Med | Moderate |
| Walk-Up Apartment | Medium | Med | High | Low |
| low-rise | Low | High | High | Low |
| high-rise | High | High | High | Low |

our hypothesis would be that relations are most strained in families living in high-rises, and least in single-family dwellings. We review the research with the idea of testing this basic proposition.

## Research on the Effects of Residence Type

The research on the effects of housing type is not extensive and the studies typically focus on only one or two dimensions of dwelling type. For example, an early study by Fanning (1967) focused on single-family and walk-up apartment dwellings. He studied the incidence of physical ailments and psychological strain on a military base in a female population who had no choice in their residence. Those residing in apartments on upper stories reported more symptoms of stress than those living on lower levels and in single-family units. The fact that the women studied had no choice in dwelling type may implicate the inconsistency between housing preference and situations as a source of stress. The import of Fanning's work for our concern with family relations is that the strain observed may cause decrements in mother-child relations directly, and indirectly affect the parent-child bond by straining the husband-wife tie.

Mitchell's (1971) study of housing in Hong Kong extends Fanning's work by demonstrating the effect of the floor containing the dwelling across a wider range of housing types. Families living on higher floors reported more strain and reduced parental control. Other aspects of dwelling type were not examined.

In a study comparing the sociability of Chicago families in the suburbs with those in the central city in two housing types (apartments and single-family dwellings) Choldin (1980) found that apartment-dwelling families in large suburban projects had as many or more local social involvements than did residents of single-family dwellings. He notes that apartment dwellers in the central city in comparison to single-family dwelling residents are more transient, and therefore, less likely to visit neighbors, belong to neighborhood organizations and the like. But in the large suburban projects (in spite of the transience), laundry facilities, swimming pool, play areas and other community areas facilitate interaction with neighbors. Of course the remote location from shopping and recreation areas outside the project and the homogeneity of the population are also essential ingredients. Nevertheless, the importance of number of units is clearly demonstrated.

Some of the most extensive work on housing type has been done by A. R. Gillis who studied residents of public housing projects containing a range of dwelling types in Calgary and Edmonton, Alberta, Canada. In a carefully controlled multivariate analysis, Gillis (1977) showed that the floor on which people live has an effect; women who live on higher floors and on the first floor manifest more psychological strain than females on other levels. Such effects were not found among the men. These relationships were not attenuated by household composition variables, socioeconomic status, or problems with child supervision, feelings of isolation, or preference for staying at home. Women living on the ground floor appeared to feel more vulnerable. The exact basis of the feeling was not discernible from the data at hand. Gillis speculates that living on higher floors may be stressful for women because it is unesthetic and a reminder that they do not live in a single-family dwelling. Or it may mean that women are more subject to vertigo or acrophobia. Regardless of the source, the meaning of this data is clear. The mother's stress could be translated into strained child-parent relations.

In another study using the same data set, Gillis (1980) analyzes the effect on psychological strain of the number of dwelling units in the building. By itself, the variable had no effect. But when it was combined with a variable that assesses the extent to which residents perceive themselves as dissimilar from their neighbors (life style, child-rearing practices, marital status, life cycle, socio-economic status, ethnicity), an effect was observed. Individuals who viewed their neighbors as being dissimilar to their own family and who resided in buildings containing many units, showed psychological strain to a greater extent than residents in other circumstances. The relationship persisted after controls were introduced. While the effects of the number of units and heterogeneity need to be explored in other settings (e.g., non-metropolitan areas, private developments), the findings are suggestive for our review. If the number of units produces psychological strain when neighbors are seen as dissimilar, then family relations are apt to be adversely affected.

In a study of school children living in a rapidly-growing suburb of 250,000 near a Canadian city, Gillis and Hagan (1982) demonstrated that housing type (ordered so as to roughly approximate number of units in the building) was a predictor of police contact, rather than the amount of crime. Apparently juvenile delinquency is more visible in buildings with large numbers of units. Residents are more likely to complain to the police regardless of the actual level of adolescent deviant behavior. Thus, buildings with larger numbers of dwelling units are more likely to draw the attention of the police. This work, along with that of Yancey (1972) and Rainwater (1966), indicates that dwelling type and the associated dimensions of design are related to the incidence of reported juvenile delinquency. Families in which offspring have contact with the police are probably subject to more conflict and larger numbers of such families should be found in buildings containing many units.

Data from a study of 560 Toronto families is the basis of a report that concludes our review of the dwelling-type literature (Edwards, Booth, & Klobus-Edwards, 1980). In this report the authors compared families residing in single-family dwellings with those living in simple multiple dwellings (duplexes, triplexes, row houses), and with those living in complex multiple dwellings (low-rise and high-rise apartments). While the data do not permit examination of the separate dimensions of housing type outlined earlier, the three categories represent a rough progression in the number of floors, units and community areas. The multivariate analysis, where controls were introduced for age, education, socioeconomic status and household crowding, did reveal that dwelling type had modest effects on the residents. Edwards and his colleagues (1980) found stress to be associated with residence in multiple dwellings. Men reported more symptoms of psychiatric impairment and females indicated having their desire for privacy thwarted more often. This differs from the Gillis' (1977) finding that shows women, not men, residing on higher floors to report more symptoms of psychological strain. The inconsistency cannot be explained by the difference in the indicators of stress. With the exception of the privacy item in the Toronto data, the indicators were quite similar. Gillis' measures of dwelling type are more refined in that he examines floor and number of units directly, whereas the Toronto data-set taps them indirectly. Clearly, more research is needed.

While dwelling type did not influence whether or not parents played with their children the day preceding the interview, it did seem to affect parent-child relations adversely in other ways, at least for the father. Fathers residing in apartments were more likely to strike their child and feel that their children fight a lot. Such differences were not reported by the mothers in the sample. The quality of the data in the Toronto study was such that it was possible to see the extent to which reports of striking were reflected in signs of abuse. The children in the study were medically examined and one of the procedures was to check for bruises, abrasions, cuts, and burns that could be evidence of child abuse. No relation was found between reports of spanking and signs of abuse. The authors concluded that spanking and quarreling are not pathological, but merely reflect stress. The decrement in father-child relations is consistent with the elevated stress among males reported above.

Edwards and his colleagues (1980), in addition report that marital relations (arguments, threats to leave home, feeling less loved than before) in multiple dwellings tend to be poorer than in single-family units for both husbands and wives. The authors speculate that multiple dwelling residents may feel that raising children in such environs is less than ideal and that these circumstances symbolize the inability of one or both parents to provide sufficiently well to acquire a single-family dwelling. This disenchantment may account for the heightened stress and conflict reported by the respondents residing in multiple dwellings. The authors caution, however, that the amount of variance explained is a few percentage points and that the effects should be regarded as insignificant.

## Conclusion

Certainly the research on the effects of dwelling type is not conclusive. The research needed to make it more conclusive is described later. Nevertheless, certain trends are apparent:

1. Residing several stories above the ground seems to cause mild stress in women and perhaps men. Such stress may be manifested in marital discord and a decline in parent-child relations for the father.
2. The number of dwelling units in a building, and perhaps the number of community areas, may:
a. be a stressor for the inhabitants, especially if they view their neighbors as different from themselves. The stress may be reflected in decrements in family relations as described above.
b. stimulate social interaction among children at the neighborhood level.
3. Differences between housing situation and housing preference may explain some of the adverse consequences reported by dwelling type studies.

## Further Research on Housing Type

All research worthy of the name leads to further investigation. Each of the studies reviewed above adds to our knowledge about the effects of the microenvironment on children. But these gains lead to refinements in the questions and lay before us new issues to be resolved. In the following paragraphs I attempt to detail some of these issues.

From the analysis presented above it is evident that housing type is not a unidimensional variable. Each dimension (floor of residence, number of units in the building, number of community areas, and housing preference) may have quite different effects. Housing preference is an attitude of the resident, while the other three dimensions are qualities of the residents' dwelling. Moreover, one may live on the second floor of a high-rise or a walk-up. The number of community areas may be different for an older high-rise in the central city than for a recently constructed one in a suburban development. In future examinations of the effects of housing type, each of these dimensions should be measured for each resident.

Assessing the unique and combined influences of each dimension will not be easy. For one thing, because the probability of living on a higher floor is greater for residents in buildings with a large number of units, multicollinearity may be high. This makes the use of most multivariate techniques more difficult. Furthermore it is quite possible that these dimensions affect the quality of life only when they interact with one another. Possible two- and three-way interactions should be explored in detail.

In addition to the independent variables reflecting family relations and the decision to have children, the effect of the housing-type dimensions on an array of mental and physical health measures should also be explored. Finally, the paucity of studies that deal with the quality of sibling relations is indicative that special attention should be devoted to this aspect of family life.

There are three other factors that should be taken into account as control variables in future analyses of the influence of housing type on the lives of children. They are: neighborhood heterogeneity, residential mobility, and the housing market. We already noted the effect of heterogeneity detected by Gillis (1980) in his analysis of the number of units in the building containing the resident's dwelling. Heterogeneity at the neighborhood level should continue to be taken into account in subsequent studies. Residential mobility can also deter the formation of ties with neighbors and inhibit the development of a sense of who is a stranger and who belongs in the area. Neighboring and the sense of recognition can provide a relaxed micro-environment where problems that may be created by the dwelling itself are easily ameliorated (Newman, 1973). On the other hand, high turnover can enhance any effects residential features might have. Finally, I would suggest that the nature of the housing market should be taken into account. The family relations of people living in a dwelling they do not like, and one which is creating problems for them, are much more likely to be harmed if they know they are trapped in their surroundings indefinitely than if they believe they are likely to move in a few weeks or months. Kennedy's (1975, p. 149) finding that public housing tenants who had little opportunity to achieve their housing goals expressed a high degree of dissatisfaction is consistent with the proposition. Thus, investigations of housing type should be encouraged in cities where the housing market is tight, as well as in the more open North American communities.

## HOUSEHOLD CROWDING AS AN ASPECT OF THE CHILD'S ENVIRONMENT

### Stress, Withdrawal, and Other Models

Investigations of non-human crowding consistently suggest that stress is the mechanism accounting for the pathology that is associated with congested conditions. Crowding appears to set biological and social mechanisms to work which stress the animal and thereby diminish reproductive capacity. Because of the methodological problems in making interspecies comparisons (Mazur, 1973), it would be foolhardy to make simple extrapolations to human families. While the stress model may give us a clue as to where to look, we must carefully examine family interaction in order to speculate as to what mechanisms might be at work, if any.

For our purposes it is useful to conceive of household crowding as the condition where interaction is intensified because of room or space limitations. Interaction refers to verbal and nonverbal communication as well as to accommodating the movements of others. In a crowded household, then, we would expect many more exchanges to be necessary to conduct daily tasks such as fixing and eating meals, cleaning, tending children, and watching television. The intensified interaction would more often bring family members into competition for space and facilities and into the more strained aspects of family life such as disciplining a child or a spousal argument. It is, of course, possible that families develop ways of organizing their lives under crowded conditions which minimize being drawn into competitive or combative situations. By establishing rules for the use of the kitchen or bathroom, or arbitration procedures for handling conflict, the effect of compressed conditions may be ameliorated.

On the other hand, if families are unable to organize their lives to cope with congested conditions, the ensuing competition and conflict would be stressful since they represent an unusual amount of stimulation to the individual. Interaction by itself (without the competition and conflict) could be a stressor as each act requires thought and motion. A more or less continuous stream of interaction without respite could tax family members enough to constitute a stress.

If intensified interaction were a stressor, what could we expect to find among crowded families in addition to an elevated level of conflict? The research of Selye (1956), Levi (1971) and others have detailed the physiological response to intense or prolonged stress. Very simply, the initial physiological response to stress becomes a stressor in itself. Prolonged stress will decrease virility, maternity, and foetal development, lower disease resistance, and enhance structural damage. The affect on married couples would be to have fewer children. The children they did have would be more sickly, and develop more slowly physically. Since sick children spend less time in school, intellectual development would be influenced. Moreover, learning research has shown stress to cause a deterioration in learning. Such performance is reflected in rigidity, inability to learn from previous experience or from new information, increases in errors made, decreases in speed of performance, and decline in perseverance (cf. Hokanson, 1969, pp. 124–125). The poor performance may lead to feelings of helplessness and a lack of control which can make children even more vulnerable to the effects of crowding—an idea which Aiello and Baum develop in detail elsewhere in this volume. In short, a child under more or less constant stress at home may do poorly in school.

Another response to intensified interaction between family members as a result of crowding is withdrawal. Family members may withhold affection and reduce the number of joint activities (eating meals together, playing, etc.) as a way of avoiding the heightened interaction, competition and conflict. Withdrawal might also include the permanent or temporary absence of a parent or sending away offspring to live with others. Withdrawal might also include drinking or drug use and excessive sleeping or television watching.

A variation of the model proposing that the heightened interaction caused by compressed household conditions creates conflict, competition, withdrawal, or stress is advanced by Freedman (1975). He suggests that heightened interaction, rather than creating adversity, merely intensifies the relations and conditions that already exist. If relations between family members are already poor, crowding will result in further decrements. If family relations are rich, compressed living conditions will enhance them. The available research allows us to examine the veracity of this alternative explanation.

Of course it is quite possible that modern crowded household conditions have no effect at all. First of all, families may never approach the levels of crowding observed among non-humans. The most congested slum housing may not approach the level of crowding experienced by the rats in Calhoun's (1962) famous experiment. Perhaps the only human experiences that come close are slave ships or concentration camps (cf. Hocking, 1970). Second, for much of history, humans have lived in dwellings more crowded than we find in modern western societies (Mitchell, 1971). Cromagnon caves, North American Indian long houses, and pre-industrial European cities were far more congested environs than modern cities. In short, the human species has had thousands of years of experience living in congested conditions. The human threshold for tolerating intense interaction and its concomitants may be far higher than the constraints imposed by modern housing. Our review of the extant research is aimed at sorting out the relationship between crowding and family relations.

## Research on the Effects of Household Crowding

There can be no question that children are sensitive to the amount of space in their environs and the number of people in that space. Studies showing that people are physiologically aroused by compressed surroundings (Aiello, Epstein, & Karlin, 1975) and that individuals adjust social activities to accommodate variations in the amount of space and the number of people (cf. Sommer, 1969), rely largely on college student populations. There is little doubt younger persons are also affected by crowded conditions. The few laboratory studies that focus on children testify to the veracity of this assertion. Both Loo (1972) and Hutt and Vaizey (1966) show that crowding increases withdrawal among groups of children at play. In the laboratory, however, child sensitivity to crowding cannot be translated into pathological family relations in the home. Experimental subjects are usually constrained in a novel situation and do not have the freedom needed to accommodate changes in space and people.

Studies focusing on the effect of household crowding tend to show that compressed conditions have minute or no effects on family relations. We should begin our review by mentioning studies in which the unit of analysis is the census tract, block, or other community area, as they constitute a significant portion of the early research on crowding. Galle and his associates (1972), in a comparison of high- and low-density community areas, show people-per-room to be positively related to juvenile court appearances and the number of youths receiving public assistance. While not measures of family relations, court appearances and public assistance may be correlated with poor family ties (Loring, 1955). On the other hand, in a study of city blocks, Choldin and Roncek (1976) found household crowding to have trivial relationships to crime and birth rates—variables only indirectly related to our concerns. While both studies conform to the highest standards for such research, there are problems associated with drawing inferences about individuals from ecological units. The fact that positive correlations are obtained between crowding and decrements in family relations for community areas does not necessarily mean that individuals living in crowded dwellings have family ties of lower quality than non-crowded people.

The limitations of aggregate analyses are addressed in field surveys where people who actually spend their lives in congested homes are compared with those who do not. There are five major surveys that examine the effect of household crowding on some aspects of family relations: Felson and Solaun (1975); Mitchell (1971); Booth (1976); Verbrugge and Taylor (1976), and Gove, Hughes, and Galle (1979).

Felson and Solaun limited their investigation to fertility. In Columbia, South America, a comparison of families in dwellings that could not be expanded (by adding rooms) with those residing in units where expansion was possible, revealed that the former had fewer children. The housing market was so tight that most families could not expect to change dwellings in order to accommodate child-bearing preferences. Thus, household crowding appears to influence the decision to have children in a constrained housing market.

In his study of Hong Kong families, Mitchell (1971) used square footage per person as a measure of household crowding. He found that crowding had no adverse effect on communication between spouses, marital happiness, or number of marital quarrels reported after controlling for education. The amount of space, independent of floor level, was related to the tendency for parents to be unaware of where their children were playing. The compressed conditions in the household encouraged parents to give their offspring greater freedom of movement which led to the observed loss of parental control. Thus, Mitchell notes a slight adverse effect of crowding on child-parent ties.

Like the Hong Kong survey, the Toronto survey of 560 families (Booth, 1976) also provides information on household crowding. Scales were created to assess both people's perception of being crowded and objective conditions. The objective scales reflected such factors as multiple use of rooms; the amount of time each day when the number of people exceeded the number of rooms, the amount of time an individual spent in a room also occupied by other people, and the relative number of rooms the family had compared to other families of a similar size and composition.

From questions aimed at obtaining a detailed history of pregnancy outcomes and queries regarding coital frequency, contraceptive use and unpro-
tected intercourse, along with medical examination data, Booth and his colleagues were able to analyze the effect of crowding on the decision to have
children. After controls for the number of years the wife lived with her current spouse, previous marriages and religious affiliation, crowded household
conditions were found to have no effect on the number of induced abortions,
sexual activity, contraceptive use, or the number of pregnancies. Of course,
Toronto's housing market was not as limited as that of Columbia. Toronto
families had more opportunities to adjust housing to family planning decisions.

The effect of household crowding on spousal relations was explored in detail in the Toronto study. While the feeling of being crowded was sometimes
mildly related to decrements in relations between the married pair, objective
conditions were not. The feelings of being loved, spousal arguments, threats
to leave, withholding sex, and the incidence of marital and extramarital intercourse were unaffected by household crowding.

The extent to which fathers and mothers played with their children was
similarly unaffected by crowded household conditions. However, there was a
tendency for parents in crowded homes (as assessed by both perceived and
objective measures) to hit their children more than those in less crowded
households. As in the analysis of household type, no evidence was found that
this behavior became abusive.

The indicator of the quality of sibling relations (the incidence of quarrels)
was not affected by crowding insofar as fathers were concerned, but mothers
in crowded households reported a higher incidence of conflict than did those
in uncongested homes. Again, the effects were modest, explaining only one
percent of the variance.

To test for extreme withdrawal, parents were asked whether any young
children were living with relatives, guardians, or in an institution, and if so,
the reason for the arrangement. No effects were found. Children who were
not at home for reasons of criminal incarceration, incorrigibility, unfit parents, or economic deprivation were as likely to come from uncrowded homes
as congested ones.

For most indicators of the quality of family life, the Toronto study showed
crowding to have little or no influence. Even in those cases where effects were
detected, they were very modest. Thus, with the possible exception of spanking, crowding did not seem to heighten conflict or withdrawal among family
members, nor did it affect decisions to have children. Nor was there evidence
that crowding intensified existing conditions, as Freedman (1975) proposed.
"The effects of crowding were more severe for people whose lives were already stressful only in a minority of cases. And crowded individuals whose
lives were not complicated by stressful life circumstance never evidenced

greater health or well-being than their uncrowded counterparts." (Booth, 1976, p. 103)

Verbrugge and Taylor surveyed a sample of houseowners in Baltimore and found that crowded housing did have modest adverse effects. People in congested homes (where the number of people-per-room was high) were more apt to report "conflicts over space, irritation about noise, and dissatisfaction with the amount of privacy a person has" (Verbrugge & Taylor, 1976, p. 13). Whether these factors contributed significantly to decrements in the quality of family ties, or are just minor annoyances, cannot be determined from the evidence presented. One noteworthy finding, however, is that those who had resided in their home for longer periods were less negative about crowding. This suggests that if crowding does have an effect, it is short-lived, as people accommodate their lives to their surroundings.

Drawing on interviews from a sample of more than 2000 Chicago residents, Gove and his colleagues (1979) examined the effects of household crowding as measured by people-per-room and two experiential variables on a variety of factors, including family relations and child care. They concluded that crowded household conditions have important adverse effects. In a review of the Chicago study, Booth and his colleagues (1980) demonstrated that the Chicago findings are quite similar to the field studies conducted by Mitchell (1971) and Booth (1976). They show that the experiential measures of crowding are also measures of many of the dependent variables and cannot be used to assess the effect of crowding. When the effects of the experiential variables are removed, people-per-room has either very modest or no effect on family relations. While it is difficult to distill the effect of people-per-room from the way Gove and his associates present their data, it would appear that the independent variable may influence the extent to which the parents know their children's playmates. The effect is small, accounting only for a few percentage points in the explained variance.

## Conclusion

While a number of tentative conclusions can be drawn from the studies of household crowding, there are unresolved issues that bear further research. The remaining issues are detailed in the next section of the chapter. On the basis of the extant research, however, it is evident that:

1. Household crowding has very limited, if any, effects on family relations. No consistent pattern of effects can be noted for any aspect of family ties: spousal, parent-child, or sibling. In those instances where adverse effects are observed, they are quite small and probably temporary.
2. The decision to have children is not affected by household crowding in North American cities, but may be influenced in other parts of the

world where opportunities to move to more spacious homes are severely limited.

## Further Research on Household Crowding

With some exceptions, the survey studies of the effect of crowding tend to show that household crowding has little influence on pathology. However, each of these studies has important limitations that may be masking the effects of crowding. These problems are: little variance in the independent variable; a crowding measure that does not reflect relative needs for space; insufficient assessment of people's experience with crowded environs; and consideration of whether people have a choice in housing — whether the housing market is tight or open. While individually these problems may not be significant, collectively they could be masking significant effects.

The three North American surveys have limited variance in the measure of crowding. While people-per-room is as low as "less than one," the upper limits are three or four people per room, quite commodious by world standards. And then, there are only a few cases at the upper end of the range. It is quite possible that household crowding does not create pathology until the number of people-per-room is much higher. While the Mitchell (1971) survey does deal with crowded conditions that are more severe, the amount of space available per person is not as easy to translate into a measure reflecting opportunities for privacy as an assessment based on number of rooms. Thus, what is needed is a study that uses a rooms-based measure where variance in crowding is much more extreme.

While people-per-room is a commonly used measure of crowding, it has basic conceptual and methodological defects. Conceptually, it means that all members of the household require the same number of rooms. This means that four persons in a four-room household are as crowded as eight people in an eight-room dwelling, and that four unrelated adults need the same number of rooms as a couple with two small children. This is untenable on its face. Small children do not need the same number of rooms as adults, and a married couple does not have need for the same number of rooms as two unrelated adults. Further, room-needs do not increase proportionally to the people gained. As a case in point, a three-room household may meet the space needs of a married couple with no children. The addition of four children is not likely to increase the space needs to nine rooms (the number of rooms needed to keep people-per-room constant). Because household composition influences space demands, people-per-room is limited as a measure of these demands. Moreover, because people-per-room is a ratio variable, there are problems in interpreting the correlations between crowding and pathology (Fuguitt & Lieberson, 1974; Schuessler, 1973).

A crowding measure that circumvents the problems inherent in the people-per-room measure was introduced in the Toronto study (Booth, 1976, p. 24–32). Reflecting room excess or deficit (termed "rooms deficit" for reasons of parsimony), the measure indicates the number of rooms a family has relative to other families of similar size and composition. Suppose families composed of mother, father, and three children have an average of 6.0 rooms in their household. Families of that size with only 5.0 rooms would have a room deficit score of − 1.0, and those living in 8-room-households would have a + 2.0 room deficit score. The measure is computed for a population by regressing the number of rooms in a household on the number of people in the household and the composition of the household (e.g., married couple, married couple with children, married couple with children and other relations, unrelated adults, etc.). By this process the predicted number of rooms for households of a given size and composition is computed. Each household's score is obtained by subtracting the number of rooms predicted for its size and composition from the actual number of rooms in the household. Negative values indicate fewer rooms, and positive ones more rooms than the average for households of the same size and composition.

The advantages of rooms-deficit over people-per-room are remarkable. First differing space demands of household statuses (husband, child, boarder), and household types (nuclear family, unrelated individuals) are taken into account in the development of the measure. Second, the measure is orthogonal to number of people in the household, thus overcoming one of the problems of people-per-room. Third, rooms deficit allows one to take into account that household crowding is a relative phenomenon varying with social classes and sub-cultures in the degree of household density tolerated by inhabitants before expending resources to move to less congested housing.

Because room deficit is derived from the average space needs of different types of households and can be computed for different sub-cultures, it more precisely measures relative space deprivation in a way that takes into account what people have learned to expect from their society. This element is missing from the people-per-room measure. While the preliminary work using the room deficit measure was fruitful (Booth, 1976), it needs to be more fully explored in a study where the variance in household crowding is more substantial.

Only two of the surveys took into account people's prior experience with household crowding as a factor that may mediate the influence of congestion on pathology. Whether individuals experienced household crowding as a child was examined in the Toronto study (Booth, 1976, pp. 47–52), and the length of time people had resided in their crowded dwelling was a factor in the Baltimore study (Verbrugge & Taylor, 1976). The data from both studies suggest that some experience with living in crowded environs reduces any impact this might have. Apparently people learn to adapt to compressed living conditions. Whether people successfully adapt to conditions of extreme crowding needs to be investigated further.

Finally, with the possible exception of the Hong Kong study, the survey investigations took place in communities where the housing market was open. Generally, people in these North American cities who wish to reside in a larger home, and have the necessary resources to do so, move. Felson and Solaun (1975) found that families living in small apartments in Bogota, Columbia restricted their fertility since the option of moving to larger quarters was not available. Thus, it is important to assess the import of household crowding in a setting where people's ability to move to larger quarters is restricted. If household congestion does have an effect, it should occur among families who are unable to move to a more spacious dwelling.

Given the limitations associated with variance in the independent variable, the measures of crowding, assessing prior experience, and the housing market in the five surveys reported earlier in this chapter, studies are needed which surmount these deficiencies and permit a more precise estimation of the impact of crowded housing. Studies of families residing in industrial cities where variance in crowding is more extensive, and the housing market tighter than in North American cities, are called for. Urban areas in such countries as Japan and Israel would be good candidates for study. As in the case of housing type, a wide range of dependent variables should be assessed. The proposed research on housing type and household crowding would have important policy implications for land use policy, population distribution and housing design. Most city governments have housing codes that regulate these matters. The outcome of the proposed investigations would provide guidelines for such policies as well as provide basic information on the effect of the micro-environment on children.

## REFERENCES

Aiello, J. R., Epstein, Y. M., & Karlin, R. A. Effects of crowding on electrodermal activity. *Sociological Symposium*, 1975, *14*, 43–47.

Archer, J. Effects of population density on behavior in rodents. In J. Crook (Ed.), *Social behavior in birds and mammals*. New York: Academic Press, 1970. Pp. 169–210.

Booth, A. *Ubran crowding and its consequences*. New York: Holt, Rinehart, Winston, 1976.

Booth, A. The built environment as a deterrent: a reexamination of defensible space. *Criminology*, 1981, *18*, 557–570.

Booth, A., Johnson, D., & Edwards, J. In pursuit of pathology: the effects of human crowding. *American Sociological Review*, 1980, *45*, 873–878.

Calhoun, J. Population density and social pathology. *Scientific American*, 1962, *206*, 134–146.

Choldin, H. Social participation in suburban apartment enclaves. In V. Karn & C. Ungerson (Eds.), *The consumer's experience of housing*. London: Gower Publishing, 1980.

Choldin, H., & Roncek, D. Density, population potential and pathology: A block level analysis. *Review of Public Data Use*, 1976, *4*, 19–30.

Edwards, J., Booth, A., & Klobus-Edwards, P. Housing, stress and family problems. *Social Forces,* 1982, *61,* 241–258.

Fanning, D. Families in flats. *British Medical Journal,* 1967, *18,* 382–386.

Felson, M., & Solaun, M. The fertility-inhibiting effect of crowded apartment living in a tight housing market. *American Journal of Sociology,* 1975, *80,* 1410–1417.

Festinger, L., Schachter, S., & Back, R. *Social pressures in informal groups: A study of human factors in housing.* New York: Harper, 1950.

Freedman, J. *Crowding and behavior.* San Francisco: W. H. Freeman, 1975.

Fuguitt, G., & Lieberson, S. Correlations of ratios or difference scores having common terms. In H. Cosner (Ed.), *Sociological methodology.* San Francisco: Jossey Bass, 1974, Pp. 128–144.

Galle, O., Gove, W., & McPherson, J. Population density and pathology: What are the relationships for man? *Science,* 1972, *176,* 23–30.

Gillis, A. High-rise housing and phychological strain. *Journal of Health and Social Behavior,* 1977, *18,* 418–431.

Gillis, A., & Hagan, J. Density, delinquency and design: formal and informal control and the residential environment. *Criminology,* 1982, *19,* 514–529.

Gillis, A. *The urban environment and individual unease: An empirical look at Wirthian logic.* Research Paper No. 110, Center for Urban and Community Studies, University of Toronto, 1980.

Gove, W., Hughes, M., & Galle, O. Overcrowding in the home: An empirical investigation of its possible pathological consequences. *American Sociological Review,* 1979, *44,* 59–80.

Hocking, F. Extreme environmental stress and its significance for psycho-pathology. *American Journal of Psychotherapy,* 1970, *24,* 4–26.

Hokanson, J. *The physiological basis of motivation.* New York: Wiley, 1969.

Hutt, C., & Vaizey, M. Differential effects of group density on social behavior. *Nature,* 1966, *209,* 1371–72.

Kennedy, L. W. *Adapting to new environments: Residential mobility from the mover's point of view.* Major Report #3, 1975, Center for Urban and Community Studies and Department of Sociology, University of Toronto.

Levi, L. *Society, stress and disease: The psychological environment and psychosomatic disease.* Toronto: Oxford University Press, 1971.

Litwak, E., & Szelenyi, I. Primary group structure and their functions: Kin, neighbors and friends. *American Sociological Review,* 1969, *34,* 465–481.

Loo, C. The effects of spatial density on the social behavior of children. *Journal of Applied Social Psychology,* 1972, *2,* 372–381.

Loring, W. Housing characteristics and social disorganization. *Social Problems,* 1956, *3,* 160–168.

Martin, A. Environment, housing and health. *Urban Studies,* 1967, *4,* 1–21.

Mazur, A. A cross-species comparison of status in small established groups. *American Sociological Review,* 1973, *38,* 513–530.

Milgram, S. The experience of living in cities. *Science,* 1970, *167,* 1461–1468.

Mitchell, R. Some social implications of high density housing. *American Sociological Review,* 1971, *36,* 18–29.

Mitchell, R. Ethnographic and historical perspectives on relationships between physical and socio-spatial environments. *Sociological Symposium,* 1975, *10,* 25–42.

Newman, O. *Defensible space.* New York: Macmillan, 1973.

Rainwater, L. Fear and the house-as-home in the lower class. *Journal of the American Institute of Planners,* 1966, *32,* 23–31.

Schuessler, K. Ratio variables and path models. In A. Goldberger & O. Duncan (Eds.), *Structural equation models in social science.* New York: Seminar Press, 1973, Pp. 201–228.

Selye, H. The stress of life. New York: McGraw-Hill, 1956.

Sommer, R. *Personal space: The behavioral basis of design*. Englewood Cliffs, New Jersey: Prentice-Hall, 1969.

Verbrugge, L., & Taylor, R. *Consequences of population density: Testing new hypotheses*. Baltimore: The Johns Hopkins Center for Metropolitan Housing and Research, 1976.

Wilner, D., Walkley, R., Pinkerton, T., & Tayback, M. *The housing environment and family life*. Baltimore, the Johns Hopkins Press, 1962.

Yancey, W. Architecture, interaction, and social control: A case of a large-scale housing project. In J. Wohwill & J. Carson (Eds.), *Environments and the social sciences*. Washington: American Psychological Assn., 1972. Pp. 126–136.

## END NOTE

1. For a detailed review of the non-human studies see Archer (1970) and for a more abbreviated examination of the research see Booth (1976, 1–5).

# The Role of Housing Type, Household Density, and Neighborhood Density in Peer Interaction and Social Adjustment

## 8

Willem van Vliet--
*The Pennsylvania State University*

### INTRODUCTION

It is not unusual for social scientists to study aspects of children's social adjustment and peer interaction in relation to the environment. In these studies, the environment is generally conceptualized in terms of social relations. For example, investigators have focused on effects of family structure, social class, ethnic background, school organization, and various other institutional contexts. A common characteristic of these studies is a concern with implications of differences in the types of environments in which children are embedded. The comparisons are between children in different types of social "systems," for example, between children from broken homes and children from intact families, between working- and middle-class children, or between children in "open" and "traditional" schools.

With few exceptions, there has been little systematic consideration of how the *number* of social relationships within any given social environment may have independent effects on children's social adjustment and peer interaction or how this numerical factor might intervene in or interact with the *types* of social relationships through which children are integrated in their social milieus. In many instances, the types of relationships which children have may be *more* important for their social maturation than is the number of their relationships. However, it should be carefully noted that this does not imply that, therefore, the number of relationships is *un*important. For example, the number of children in the same age group in a neighborhood may facilitate or hinder the formation and maintenance of viable friendships. In early sociological writings, Durkheim (1893) has examined in detail the implications of density for social organization, and Simmel (1908) has provided us with a discourse on the significance of group size for the nature of interpersonal relations and the quality of individual functioning. Wirth (1938), in an influential article, has analyzed the consequences of size, density, and heterogeneity of population on social interaction and personality development; consequences which, he argued, are predominantly negative. These early discussions have found extension in numerous sociometric studies and research on density effects. However, sociologists have not applied these lines of thought with respect to children. Psychological studies have focused more specifically on children, but have been restricted primarily to investigations of density effects under controlled laboratory conditions and in institutional settings[1] (e.g., Aiello et al., 1979; Loo, 1972; McGrew, 1970). The meaning of density in children's daily lives remains a relatively unexplored issue.

Elsewhere in this volume, density is conceptualized as a factor which may help to generate opportunities as well as risks for the developing child (see the chapter by Garbarino). In that discussion, attention is directed to the extent and ways that density may enrich the child's developmental experience and support the integrative functioning of the family, school, and other systems environing the child. Density is conceived of in terms of the connections between children and these systems. In this conceptualization, density of people and the number of relationships may be inversely related and, in some instances, the number of people may be entirely inconsequential for the density of linkages joining children and settings. However, in other instances the number of people may carry significance, and in this chapter the concern is with implications for children of density in this numerical sense. This delimitation is deceivingly simple; it subsumes, as we shall see later, a broad range of operational definitions. Common to these is, however, reference in one way or another to the actual or possible number of social relations in a given space.

In this chapter, I first discuss the role of peer interaction and social adjustment in children's development. Following this discussion, a review of the literature on effects of housing type, household density, and neighborhood density on peer interaction and social adjustment indicates the often inconclusive and at times contradictory nature of the research results that have been obtained. It is argued that the divergent findings are, in part, a reflection of both the lack of methodological standardization in density studies and the common failure to include proper consideration of contextual fac-

---

[1]A notable exception is the research by Roger Barker and other ecological psychologists on the implications of overmanning and undermanning (e.g., Barker & Gump, 1961; Wicker, 1968). In these studies, discussed elsewhere in this volume, density is conceived in terms of the number of children per available role (role density) rather than the number of children per environmental unit which will be the concern of this chapter.

tors. The diversity of density measures adopted in research is also seen as a necessary inquiry into the broad spectrum of density conditions affecting the child's residential experience. Results of a study of the effects of a heretofore little examined density condition, namely child density in the neighborhood, illustrate the potential value of further exploration of density factors impinging on children's development. The findings of this study — showing that high densities may, in fact, have positive effects as well — are discussed with reference to a conceptualization of neighborhood density as an attribute of the field of opportunities for social development; a conceptualization which offers a perspective on some contradictions seemingly apparent in studies of density effects. This conceptualization underlines the importance of including in research on density a consideration of contextual factors which may alleviate or exacerbate any effects that occur. This point is further amplified by a typology of basic planning principles which identifies four fundamental environmental contexts for conditions of neighborhood density. These environmental contexts are viewed, in turn, as evolving within and being inextricably interwoven with a more encompassing framework comprised of social, cultural, political, and economic factors. The chapter concludes with a summary of the main points.

## The Importance of Peer Interaction and Social Adjustment

In this section, I briefly discuss the roles of peer interaction and social adjustment in children's development. This discussion provides a backdrop for a review of the literature on the effects of density on these two factors.

What is the significance of peer interaction? Are isolated children "at risk" for maladjusted behavior? Do they have diminished opportunities for the development of social competence? The burgeoning literature on children's peer interaction and friendships is indicative of the growing interest in the functions which different forms of peer interaction may have in the various developmental processes through which children and adolescents go. Rubin (1980, pp. 4–6) has identified three distinctive functions of peer interaction for children. First, peer interaction provides opportunities for the acquisition of social skills, a wide repertoire of techniques for establishing and managing social interactions. Second, relationships with peers serve as a frame of reference in which children can meaningfully compare themselves to others. Such social comparisons, it has been argued, are essential for the development of a self-concept (Mead, 1934). Third, interaction with peers satisfies strong early-felt needs for a sense of group belonging. In a related vein, Piaget (1932) has suggested that the capacity of moral reasoning emerges out of experiences of mutual respect among peers as opposed to the unilateral respect more typically associated with interactions between children and adults.

What are, one wonders, the implications of a scarcity of peers on these developmental processes. Do children who live in low-density neighborhoods lack adequate opportunities to learn social skills? Do they conform more to parental norms than do children in relatively high-density environments where peer pressure may form a more powerful influence? Do they grow up to be different personalities? Growing up means transition in manifold ways. During the period of adolescence in particular, there is typically a considerable reorganization of the social and emotional spheres of life. Circumstances of this sort usually result in greatly increased dependence on support from others, especially those who are facing or have recently faced similar events in their own lives (Coleman, 1980). In which ways and to what extent do different levels of child density affect young people's support systems?

Here, it is not possible to examine in depth the existing evidence for the significance of peer interaction and its relation to children's social adjustment. Let us, therefore, briefly review some of the findings researchers have come up with.

In discussions of human behavior, one always has to be cautious in drawing analogies from studies of animals. Such research may have heuristic value though, and may highlight potentially critical issues. In this light, Harlow and Harlow's (1962a, 1962b) experimental research with rhesus monkeys is valuable in hinting at the apparent significance of peer interaction for adequate social development. In these investigations, infant monkeys were deprived of peer contact. Vigilance and hyperaggressiveness characterized those animals not having had contact with age mates through the first four to eight months of life. Referring to similar work involving maternal deprivation, the investigators noted that monkeys can be successfully raised without a mother, provided they have other infant monkeys to play with; monkeys with a mother but without age mates could not be successfully raised, even if their mother was entirely normal. These findings led Harlow and Harlow (1962b) to suggest that the infant-infant system is a sine qua non for later adjustment in all spheres of monkey life.

As noted, due care should be taken when interpreting findings from animal studies. Extending the above argument on the social isolation of young monkeys to children's lives is, in many ways, subject to the same criticisms as inferring human pathological implications of high-density conditions from the "behavioral sink" found by Calhoun (1962) in experiments with rats. Nevertheless, a number of studies seem to indicate that for children a sparsity of human ties may result in impaired social development and poor adjustment. Comparisons of children raised exclusively in foster homes and foster children raised initially in institutions, for example, showed that the latter had more problem behaviors, lesser school achievements, and were more isolated and less capable of entering into meaningful social relationships (Goldfarb, 1943). Other studies of social deprivation during childhood point out similarly negative implications for developmental outcomes (e.g., Davis, 1947; Jaco, 1954; Clarke & Clarke, 1976).

These findings are of limited generalizability in view of the small number and rather extreme nature of the cases involved. Nevertheless, they are in line with results from other studies which have found children's social functioning in interaction with peers to be related to adjustment in later life. For example, socially incompetent children are more likely to drop out of school (Ullman, 1957), exhibit aggressive behaviors (McCandless, 1967), and engage in delinquent activities (Roff et al., 1972; Freedman et al., 1979). In one study, successful peer relations in childhood were found to be very good predictors of adult mental health; other measures such as teacher ratings, IQ, grade point average, attendance records, and anxiety scores were not (Cowen et al., 1973). Further support for a relationship between poor peer adjustment in children and psychiatric problems in later life is provided by a number of other investigations (Kohn & Clausen, 1955; Michael et al., 1957; Pritchard & Graham, 1966; Roff, 1963; Watt et al., 1967), whereas there is also some evidence that inadequate relations with peers in childhood may carry over into adult social life (Maas, 1968; Roff, 1961). Noteworthy are the results of one study in which a random sample of 1,000 men enlisted in the U.S. army was classified by army psychiatrists as being normal, or suffering from mild psychoneurosis, severe psychoneurosis, or psychosis. Of those who reported having had no friends between the ages of four and ten, none was classified as normal and 85% as severe cases; for those who reported five or more friends during the same childood period the corresponding figures were, respectively, 39.5% and 27.8% (Lantz, 1956).

The importance of peer interaction is further underlined by the function of peers as tutors (Allen, 1976) and role models reinforcing or modifying social behaviors (Salmon, 1969; Hartup & Lougee, 1975). Furthermore, support has been found for a relation between peer interaction and the development of moral reasoning (Keasey, 1971), the establishment of role-taking capability (Gottman et al., 1975) and personal identity (Hewitt, 1976), the extension of home range (Hart, 1979), and adolescent life satisfaction (Feldman & Gaier, 1980).

It should be stressed that the impressive evidence for a correlation between peer relations and social adjustment does not necessarily imply a causal effect of the former on the latter. It might well be that children interact little with peers because they are poorly adjusted.[2] Furthermore, peer interaction may

---

[2]There is also a contamination of variables when social adjustment is defined in terms of social competence which may be translated into having social skills or friends (Foster & Ritchey, 1979). The assessment of children's social skills raises a number of yet unresolved methodological issues which call for caution in statements linking social competence and adjustment to peer interaction (Curran, 1979; Green & Forehand, 1980). Furthermore, it is likely that many times children can and do develop into mature and responsible adults without extensive peer interaction.

have negative implications as well. It has been found to be related to, for example, vandalism (Lisko, 1973), some types of drug use, and other delinquent behaviors (Schaefer, 1980; Huba & Bentler, 1980). However, as Ruben (1980, pp. 11-12) notes, the potential harmfulness of peer relations only serves to underline their importance. Peers do matter.

The preceding discussion has linked peer interaction to social adjustment and has provided indications of the significance of peer relations for children's development. Whether or not peer interaction and social adjustment are affected by residential density is quite another question to which we will now turn.

## EFFECTS OF DENSITY ON PEER INTERACTION AND SOCIAL ADJUSTMENT

The following review is restricted to research on effects of density as measured by objective indices. Not included, therefore, are considerations of crowding or children's subjective appraisal of these density conditions.[3] Also excluded are studies of density effects under contrived conditions and in institutional settings. This delimitation helps to provide some focus to an otherwise diffuse field and has the added advantage of directing attention to variables more readily amenable to manipulations intended to alleviate possibly adverse effects.

The review is organized into three sections. First, I examine effects of housing type on children's peer interaction and social adjustment. Strictly speaking, housing type is entirely unrelated to density conditions inside the home or the neighborhood. However, numerous investigators have defined density in terms of space limitations and, as apartments tend to be smaller than houses, there has been a tendency to equate apartment living erroneously with living under high-density conditions. In actual practice, apartments do often provide comparatively cramped living quarters, to be sure, and also make for relatively high external densities by accommodating a large number of households on a limited land area. However, high densities, either inside the dwelling or in the neighborhood, are not *inherent* in apartment living. Confounding density and housing type obfuscates the effects which these variables may have independently of each other. In an attempt to sort out these effects, I first review research on effects of housing type on peer interaction and social adjustment and, secondly, examine the evidence for effects of density inside the home. The third section of the review covers effects of neighborhood density.

---

[3]See Stokols (1972) for a perspicuous discussion of this distinction.

## Housing Type

While there are several major housing types and numerous variations within each, parents and housing-policy officials have been most concerned about adverse effects of multistorey living. As compared to children living in other housing types — particularly single family dwellings — apartment children would suffer more often from ill-effects of their housing conditions on their health and well-being. Let us examine the evidence with respect to social adjustment and peer interaction. Are apartment children more often maladjusted? Do they have fewer friends?

The literature is replete with assertions regarding the negative effects of apartment living on children's social adjustment. For example, apartment children would be more aggressive, because they cannot get back quickly to the safe shelter of their homes and, in order to survive, must learn to be tough. Young apartment children would be more neurotic and bored and would develop a greater dependence on their parents who restrict their mobility because of the difficulty of supervising them outside the home. Older apartment children, on the other hand, would roam around freely and, through peer influence, would more likely become engaged in vandalism and other delinquent behaviors. The evidence supporting these allegations appears to be largely anecdotal in nature and based on the personal experiences which observers have had in professional roles such as housing manager (Macey, 1959), engineer (Downing & Calway, 1963), radio reporter (Grégoire, 1971), child welfare worker (Pearse, 1968), medical officer (Gunn, 1968), and psychiatrist (Cappon, 1972). The majority of the studies dealing with hypotheses like those named above are characterizable by a lamentable lack of scientific rigor in the operationalization of concepts, the selection of respondents, the gathering of data, and the control of external variables in the analysis.

These deficiencies, discussed in more detail elsewhere (van Vliet--, 1983a), do not negate the possibility of adverse effects of apartment living on children's social adjustment; there merely indicate that there has been no thorough investigation of such effects. Further research needs to identify the relevant features of different housing types and examine their effects on children's social adjustment in conjunction with extraneous variables as, for example, children's age, building height, and culture-bound housing norms.

The influence of apartment living on peer interaction and friendship formation is a moot point in the literature. British surveys conducted in the early 1940s expressed a concern that apartments limit children's social contacts (Cooney, 1974; Gittus, 1976: Chapter Two). This concern is echoed in later writings by Jephcott (1971), Young (1976), and Grégoire (1971) who suggested that apartments inhibit spontaneous social interaction and limit the possibility of receiving friends at home. Also, Rosenberg (1968) has suggested that apartment living would result in anonymity and social isolation. The evidence, however, is mixed.

Stevenson et al. (1967) found that parents in apartments insisted more rather than less on seeing their children's friends at home. This enabled them to have some control over possible bad influences which they could not supervise outside their homes. While the conclusion of one large Yugoslavian study was that, for many children, relations with friends stopped at the apartment entrance (Kara Pesic et al., 1975, p. 78), Filipovitch (1975) failed to find any negative effects of apartment living on children's social interactions, and Farley (1977) found that children who had moved to high-rise apartments had *more* rather than fewer friends as compared to children who had moved to houses, although the difference had diminished one year after the move. Williamson (1978, p. 128) reported that German parents living in high rises considered the building structure a deterrent to their children's friendship formation. This, however, was not the case in his twin study in Italy where no such relation with building type was found, apparently because the home was the locus of family oriented activities which dominated over children's interactions with peers. This contrasts with some other studies which have found that apartment children spend *less* time with the rest of the family than children living in houses (Farley, 1977, p. 115; Hagarty, 1975, p. 144); these outcomes, however, may be better explained as a result of self-selection or cultural differences than as an effect of the housing situation.

The research findings summarized above fail to lend support to the notion that apartment living has deleterious effects either on children's social adjustment or on their interactions with peers. A majority of statements to the contrary appears to be based on casual observations or methodologically deficient research. The existing evidence points out inconsistent effects — sometimes positive, other times negative — suggesting that housing type interacts with extraneous variables such as household size and composition, child-rearing values, and age of the child.

## Household Density

In a number of studies, juvenile delinquency has been selected as an indicator of social pathology. It is a somewhat dubious measure of social adjustment as it may mirror as much or more of the behavior of administrative officials as it does the behavior of young people. Nevertheless, bearing this qualification in mind, let us look at the findings obtained in these studies.

Following an early British report of a positive relation between overcrowding and juvenile delinquency (Burt, 1925), Carr-Saunders and Manheim (1942) compared 7 to 17 year old boys brought to juvenile court in London with a matched sample of boys attending the same schools; they found that boys in the delinquent group more often lived in crowded households. A similar finding was obtained in another British study of a sample of 16 to 20 year old adolescents (East et al., 1942). Morris (1957) found the mean number of offenses recorded in police charge books to be positively related to the mean number of persons per room and to the proportion of households in wards living with two or more persons per room. Using London boroughs as the areal unit of analysis, Wallis and Maliphant (1967, p. 255) reported that detention in penal institutions for a sample of 914 offenders in the 17 to 20 year age group was positively related to the proportion of the population living with more than 1.5 persons per room and to the number of persons per room. Bloom (1966, p. 316) examined the relation between various density measures and the number of charged delinquents in the active files of the county probation department as a proportion of the population age 18 and under in census tracts of a medium-sized U.S. city. He found negative correlations with the proportion of vacant housing units and, unexpectedly, with household size. Finally, Hassan (1977) compared the average floor area per person for 90 juvenile delinquents living in Singapore public housing with the average floor area for all public housing residents. The delinquents came from homes with higher densities, but, it appears, also from poorer families; the relation, therefore, might well have been a spurious one with social class as the underlying variable.

The above studies have been valuable by calling attention to the general ecological context of juvenile delinquents in regard to conditions of residential density. However, given the possibility of confounding influences of important extraneous variables, the specific findings do not clarify the relation between household density and delinquent behavior. A number of studies have attempted to control for such influences. In a multivariate analysis, Lander (1954) found that a positive relation between overcrowding and juvenile delinquency vanished after effects of social class related variables such as educational attainment, rent level, and housing condition were partialled out. However, this study has been criticized on methodological grounds (Gordon, 1967), and in a replication based on data from Indianapolis census tracts overcrowded housing was found to be the strongest predictor of juvenile delinquency rates in a series of partial correlations controlling for 17 different variables (Chilton, 1964, p. 80). Schmitt (1966) examined census tracts in Honolulu and, after introducing controls for income and education, found a moderate positive relation between the person per room ratio and the rate of juvenile delinquency. After partialling out effects of social class, Galle et al. (1972) found the persons per room ratio for 75 community areas in Chicago to be positively related to the number of 12 to 16 year old boys brought before the county family court. However, in a study of census tracts in Edmonton, Canada, juvenile delinquency was found to be unrelated to the proportion of dwellings with more than one person per room after removing effects of income and ethnic background (Gillis, 1974). Similarly, Freedman (1972) obtained delinquency figures for more than 300 Health Areas in New York City and, holding social class and ethnicity constant, detected no relation with the person per room ratio. Finally, Herbert (1977, p. 93) in a study of census tracts in Cardiff, England, used the proportion of households sharing a dwelling, households with five or more persons, and households with more than 1.5 persons per room as independent variables in a stepwise multiple regression to predict the number of 10 to 19 year old offenders, contacted by police and receiving some kind of sanction, as a proportion of the total population in that age group in the same census tract. The proportion of households sharing a dwelling was the only density variable entering the equation, following the percentage of male unemployed, low social class, single parent, and sex ratio, and explaining a mere 2% of the variance.

To sum up, the evidence for effects of household density on juvenile delinquency is equivocal. After introducing controls for social class, population composition and other extraneous variables that might explain the positive relation reported in early studies, some more recent studies indicate continued support for a positive relationship (without establishing causality), whereas others do not. However, the question may not be whether or not a relation exists, but rather which specific relationships exist under which specific circumstances. Note that the seven more sophisticated studies were carried out in seven different cities in four different countries and employed six different measures of household density, in addition to using different delinquency measures and different areal units of analysis and introducing different controls. It is unclear to what extent and in which ways the diversity of samples and measures explains the differences in research results; it should not, however, contribute to comparability of findings. This is a point to which we return a little later.

Various investigators have employed other measures which may be taken as indicators of social adjustment. In the 1930s, Usher and Hunnybun (1933) and Plant (1937) suggested that high household densities have deleterious effects on children's social development. They noted, for example, that children from crowded homes tended to exhibit aggressive behaviors. However, their findings are difficult to interpret because the density conditions were not clearly specified and their observations were based on children from families which had sought their consultation of existing personal, social, or economic problems. Thus, any children living without problems in high-density households did not enter the picture. In a more carefully executed study of 250 British elementary school children, high household densities were found to be related to more aggression, extroversion, and neuroticism (Murray, 1974). The relation held only for boys though, and was reversed for girls. The findings may have been confounded because the negatively affected boys lived also in worse housing and in worse neighborhoods, but they are in line with the results of a recent study by Saegert (1980). In this investigation, teachers rated elementary school children living in New York City Public Housing Authority housing ($N = 312$) on scales measuring their hostility, anxiety, and hyperactivity-distractability. Living in homes with higher densities was positively related to all three behavioral disturbance measures. As in Murray's (1974) study, boys were more negatively affected than were girls. Children in high-density households also reported that they felt angry more than those is less crowded homes. In addition, children from the more crowded homes dealt with anger more often by acting out, while those in less crowded conditions tended to withdraw (Saegert, 1980, p. 21; see the chapter by Aiello for a more extended discussion of this study).

These results tie in with scattered findings from several other studies. In France, Chombart de Lauwe et al. (1959) found that misbehaviors by children, as reported by their mothers, increased sharply beyond a threshold of approximately 8 square meters per person or 2.3 residents per room. In another survey of households in Chicago, parents in high-density homes also mentioned problems with their children more often than did parents in less crowded households (Gove et al., 1979), and in a Toronto-based study it was found that parents in homes with higher densities tended to strike their children more often (Booth & Edwards, 1976). In a reanalysis of data from the Quality of Life Survey conducted in 1971 at the University of Michigan Institute for Social Research, the number of persons per room was found to be inversely related to parents' enjoyment of children, after controls for stage in the life cycle and social class (Baldassare, 1979, 116). However, after removing also effects of the number of children living in the dwelling, only a weak relation between household density and enjoyment of parenthood remained. Finally, a related finding comes from a study of households in Hong Kong. In more crowded conditions, parents did not discourage their children from leaving the home; the parents in such households were less knowledgeable about their children's whereabouts, and appreciated the alleviation of forced interaction with their children (Mitchell, 1971). Comparable observations were made by Hassan (1977) in an investigation of density effects in Singapore households.

The results of these various studies would appear to offer some support for a relation between high levels of household density and the incidence of maladjustment and behavior problems in children. The relationships found may not always be impressive in terms of statistical significance, but in any case one would expect household density to be but one of a number of, in most instances probably more important, determinants of children's social adjustment; when taken together, the findings seem to form a fairly consistent pattern which may be more significant than the magnitude of their statistical significance.

Nevertheless, there are several important unresolved issues. In most of the above studies, social adjustment is measured by teacher ratings, parent perceptions, or legal standards. This raises the question to what extent these measures are accurate and valid indicators of children's social adjustment. Tension between parents and children, for example, may be as much a manifestation of the parents' frustration with high-density conditions in the home as a result of children's inability to cope in those situations. Recent literature reviews indicate that children's social competence and adjustment may be assessed in multiple ways, each of which may yield different results (Foster & Ritchey, 1979; Green & Forehand, 1980). Research which is to clarify the relation between density and children's social adjustment would benefit from building on the insights contained in that literature.

Another question relates to the process(es) through which household density may affect children. As noted by Michelson and Roberts (1979), explanations of *how* those effects occur, if they occur, are not well articulated. Consequently, testing of theoretically derived hypotheses is rare, leaving potentially emerging issues unconfronted.

Furthermore, it is unclear which the thresholds are beyond which adverse effects occur. Floor space standards recommended by the American Public Health Association (1950) are around three times higher than those considered acceptable in some European countries. Clearly, the critical levels are culture-bound and situation-specific (cf. Mitchell, 1971; Saegert, 1980).

One point, often overlooked by researchers intent on finding negative effects of density, concerns the possibility of deleterious influences resulting from an excessive amount of space in the dwelling. Evidence for this is provided by the work of Chombart de Lauwe et al. (1959) which indicated an increase in social pathologies *below* a certain level of household density. Also noteworthy in this connection is the relationship found in some studies between rates of admission to psychiatric facilities and various other measures of social isolation in the home (Galle et al., 1972; Bloom, 1966).

In comparison with studies of effects of household density on children's social adjustment, research on effects of household density on children's interaction with peers is conspicuous by its absence. The results from one investigation suggest that, in high-density households, parents tend to restrict their children's freedom to bring friends into the home (Davis et al., 1974). These findings seem to be in line with two other investigations in which boys were found to be out in the street more often if they lived in more crowded homes (Mitchell, 1971; Hassan, 1977). Again, it is unclear which are the thresholds and which are the conditions that make them critical. The problem has scarcely been studied.

Now let us turn to neighborhood density and examine its possible effects on children's social adjustment and interaction with peers.

## Neighborhood Density

In a number of ecological studies, various measures of external density have been correlated with rates of juvenile delinquency. As noted earlier, the latter may be a poor indicator of social adjustment in view of its connotations which are legal rather more than behavioral, but it is the only indicator of social adjustment investigated in relation to neighborhood density. The results of these invesigations are inconclusive. Some of the earlier studies suggested a positive relationship between high neighborhood densities and juvenile delinquency. In their classic work, Shaw and McKay (1942, pp. 43–90) showed that delinquency rates were highest in the central city and decreased towards the urban fringe, but their explanation did not stress the relation between this gradient and residential density. In a follow-up study of 1,349 boys who had left school at the minimum statutory age, those convicted between the ages of 8 and 18 were found to live in wards with higher population densities (Ferguson, 1952). In another investigation, it was found that the number of persons per acre in wards was positively related to police recorded criminal offenses committed by the under-17 population in those wards (Morris, 1957). Similar findings are presented by Wallis and Maliphant (1967) who found the distribution of 17 to 20 year old detainees from London boroughs to be positively related to the number of people per acre, and Bloom (1966, pp. 316) who reported a negative relation between the number of single family dwellings as a proportion of all housing units in census tracts and the number of charged delinquents as a proportion of the population age 18 and under. Housing type as a density measure in the latter study is likely to correlate strongly with social class and age distribution of the population, undermining the relation with juvenile delinquency. However, the lack of control for confounding influences hampers the interpretability of all of the above studies.

In some more recent investigations, researchers have attempted to partial out such external effects. Schmitt (1966) found a modest correlation after controlling for income and education, as did Levy and Herzog (1974) in a study with social class and population heterogeneity held constant, but Freedman (1972) and Galle et al. (1972) detected no such relation (although, in the latter study, juvenile delinquency was positively related to the number of housing units per residential structure). Gillis (1974) reported a weak relation between neighborhood density and juvenile delinquency, outweighed by effects of building type and insignificant with the effects of income and national origin removed. More recently, Herbert (1977) has indicated that in Britain population groups which have moved from inner cities to peripheral estates have taken their behavioral characteristics with them, so that the distribution of offender rates in the typical British city now shows clusters in both central and peripheral locations. Finally, Hagan et al. (1978) found a relation between a measure of housing density and police perceptions of "offensible space," that is areas perceived by the police as having a disproportionate incidence of juvenile delinquency and associated with more police-initiated preventive action. Results from these studies, as well as work of others (Sengel, 1978; Shichor et al., 1979), caution that the effects of density are not necessarily simple and direct. In short, there is meager evidence that high neighborhood densities *per se* contribute to juvenile delinquency. Furthermore, the correlational nature of the relations found by some researchers does not preclude an explanation based on the notion of "self-selection" (Bell, 1958). The need to examine density effects within the context of a broader set of factors is a recurrent theme in this chapter and one to which I return later.

There has been virtually no research on the effects of neighborhood density on children's relations with peers. The architect Alexander (1967) has emphasized the presence of a minimum number of children as a condition for the formation of peer groups. He proposed a number of untested design solutions that would promote, if not determine, the amount and quality of local social interactions. In a similar vein, Jacobs (1960) has discussed the beneficial role of high densities in the socialization and protection of children. Sennett (1970), a sociologist, sees the development of individual identity and social competence as occurring in sequences, each of which can be resolved only by coping satisfactorily with internal and external conflicts. Such conflict situations would be promoted by heterogeneous high-density situations.

While there is little empirical research substantiating these claims, the evidence that exists does point out negative effects of low-density, typically suburban environments. Popenoe (1977), in his comparison of adolescents' social lives in Vällingby, Sweden, and Levittown, Pennsylvania, observed that friendships in the latter, as compared to those in the former, were shaped by locality constraints rather more than by common interests. Gans (1967) studied teenagers' evaluations of Levittown, New Jersey, through a content analysis of essays written in response to a question about what they liked and disliked about living in Levittown, and what they missed from their former place of residence. Gans concluded that the likes and dislikes reflected, in large part, the absence of social opportunities and lack of public transportation, making it difficult to meet friends.[4]

Also relevant are research findings reported by Berg and Medrich (1978) which seem to indicate that the friendships of children living in low-density neighborhoods are more formal in nature than those of children from neighborhoods with higher densities. In the low-density neighborhoods, visits to friends were not spontaneous, as they usually required a planned trip, often with the parents. Friendships were also more "privatized" and involved fewer children of a smaller age range. Berg and Medrich are careful to note that the different spatial accessibility of other children was not the only difference between the low- and high-density neighborhoods. However, the results of their study are in keeping with the observations of Popenoe (1977) and Gans

---

[4]However, neighborhood density was *not* specifically singled out for study as a factor which might potentially affect peer interaction.

(1967); relatively high densities seem to be conducive to the formation and maintenance of relations with peers.[5]

This raises an interesting question. How does it accord, one may ask, with the allegedly negative effects of high densities on social adjustment suggested by some of the ecological studies of juvenile delinquency (Schmitt, 1966; Levy & Herzog, 1974)? One possible answer is suggested by the critical mass perspective which will be discussed later. Another answer may lie in a feature characterizing the field of density studies generally: the diversity of research methodologies. Let us examine some aspects of this lack of methodological standardization.

## DENSITY EFFECTS RECONSIDERED

The preceding review provides no evidence that living in apartments or under "high" densities results in deleterious effects on children's social adjustment or their interaction with peers. In principle, the absence of evidence may be due to three reasons: there has been no research at all, the topic has not been studied; there has been sound research, failing to demonstrate effects not attributable to extraneous variables; there has been research with inconsistent findings for want of conceptual and methodological qualities. It would appear that, by and large, the studies reviewed above fall in the third category. To support this assertion, I illustrate in the following the lack of methodological standardization that has prevented accumulation of knowledge on the topic at hand. Furthermore, attention is directed to contextual factors which may counter-balance or aggravate effects of housing type and density and which, therefore, need to be incorporated in research designs.

It would go beyond the scope of this chapter to present a full-scale analysis of the methodological aspects of all pertinent studies. It would also be unnecessary, as the purpose here is to bring out the diversity of approaches taken in investigations of density effects. In this light, it suffices to scrutinize a little more closely one crucial step in the research process, viz. the operationalization of variables. Even when limiting oneself to the independent variables only, one cannot help being impressed by the variety and ingenuity of the measures that have been employed.

To begin with housing type, in the literature, the terms apartment building, high rises, multifamily housing, and flats are used almost interchangeably. The loose usage of these terms is reflected in the operational definitions. Among those used for high rises are the following: buildings higher than safety ladders can reach, higher than 50 feet, higher than 75 feet, higher than four stories, higher than six stories, and higher than eight stories. The British

---

[5]See note 4.

Bureau of the Census has used a definition of flat regardless of building height (Kendall & Hill, 1952), and there are almost as many definitions of multifamily housing as there are national census bureaus (cf. U.S. Department of Housing and Urban Development, 1978; Statistics Canada, 1978; U.N. Statistical Office, 1979). Others have managed to stay clear of this terminological morass by avoiding any operational definition, giving free play to the readers' interpretation. A further feat is accomplished by those offering conclusions about the effects of living in apartments (alias high rises, etc.) without consideration of comparative data from other housing types.

The situation with respect to density is not very different. Table 8.1 gives an overview of the arsenal of density measures at the disposal of investigators. To give but a few examples, household density has been defined as the number of possible relationships between household members divided by the square footage of floor space, the square footage of residential floor space per occupant, the number of rooms per household, the number of people per room, and the number of persons per bedroom. Operational definitions of neighborhood density include, among others, population per net residential acre, number of people per gross acre, number of people per square kilometer, number of persons per 10,000 square feet of living space, and average number of dwellings per acre. Among the areal units of analysis are census tracts, boroughs, and wards of a vastly different spatial scale, and denominators in density ratios may be, for example, acres, square miles, or square kilometers (see Table 8.1).

Add to the above the variety of dependent variables singled out for study, their different operationalizations, the differences in sampling procedures, and — last but not least — the different age groups of children, and there is little reason to expect anything but inconsistent results from studies of the effects of housing type and density on children's social adjustment and peer interaction. Among the factors further confounding findings from research are extraneous variables which set the context for the child's residential experience. Some of the obvious ones include demographic and socioeconomic characteristics such as age, sex, family income, and parents' educational level. Research also indicates the need to consider household composition, building height, and the ability to schedule activities at home (Mitchell, 1971), interactions between household density and density in school (Rubin, 1980) and neighborhood (Sobal, 1980), and flexibility of the housing market (Michelson, 1977). Common sense suggests additional variables which may interact with density levels to modify any relationships found to exist. Still other variables such as parental relations and perceived control may have intervening effects as they themselves are affected by density. The point is obvious, and there is no need to belabor it. Density effects vary according to the values of a complex constellation of variables.

At the same time, Table 8.1 indicates the broad spectrum and multivariegated nature of density conditions in children's residential experience.

Curiously, density of children in the neighborhood is not among the measures selected for study of their significance in children's behavior and development. In the research reported below, this factor was specifically singled out for examination of its possible relation to various aspects of children's friendship behavior. The findings are of interest empirically, as they indicate the possibility of positive effects of high densities, and also theoretically, as they serve to illustrate a conceptualization of neighborhood density as a factor contributing to children's field of opportunities for social interaction.

## Neighborhood Density and Friendship Behavior: An Empirical Examination

While there are studies galore of children in a variety of environments, there are relatively few investigations of either city or suburban settings as habitats for children. In these investigations, the terms "urban" and "suburban" are used rather loosely to describe two supposedly different types of environment; furthermore, there has been no systematic comparison of city and suburban environments as being possibly two distinctly different places to live for children, providing them with different opportunities, and perhaps affecting their development (van Vliet––, 1981, 1983b).

What is it about city and suburban environments that makes them different from each other? What, if any, are the implications of these differences for children? In one study which sheds some light on these questions, child density was extracted as one "objective" environmental dimension. Although this dimension discriminated between high- and low-density neighborhoods corresponding strongly with areas administratively labeled as being, respectively, "city" or "suburb," it cut across this dichotomy and at times differentiated children's environmental experiences where the city-suburban distinction failed to do so. Below, I first briefly describe the background of this research before presenting some of its results.

Fourteen to sixteen year old high-school students ($N$ = 148) — attending schools in Metropolitan Toronto selected because of their "typical" city and suburban locations — filled out during regular class hours a questionnaire in which they were asked, among other things, to evaluate their neighborhood.[6] The responses, solicited by a mixture of open- and closed-ended questions,

[6]The research reported here is taken from a broader investigation of children's environmental experiences conducted for a doctoral dissertation in the Department of Sociology at University of Toronto (van Vliet––, 1980a). Part of the data were collected for a pilot study for the Whole City Catalogue at the Child in the City Programme, University of Toronto, and obtained with the kind cooperation of Martha Friendly and Fred Hill. William Michelson provided very thoughtful advice. The research was made possible by a fellowship awarded within the framework of a bilateral exchange program between Canada and The Netherlands. The support of the Social Sciences and Humanities Research Council and the Department of External Affairs of Canada is gratefully acknowledged.

TABLE 8.1
Operational Definitions of Density Used in the Literature*

| Reference | Operational definition |
|---|---|
| Bossard (1951) | • number of possible relationships between household members divided by the square footage of floor space |
| Morris (1957) | • proportion of population in wards living in dwellings with more than 2 persons per room<br>• mean number of persons per room<br>• number of people per acre in wards |
| Schmitt (1957) | • population per net residential acre<br>• average household size<br>• dwelling units in structures with 5 or more people per room<br>• number of married couples without own household |
| Schmitt (1963) | • number of people per gross acre<br>• square footage of residential floor space per household<br>• square footage of residential floor space per occupant<br>• average household size<br>• number of rooms per household |
| Winsborough (1965) | • number of people per community area |
| Bloom (1966) | • proportion of housing units occupied by more than one person per room<br>• proportion of single family dwellings in census tracts<br>• household size |
| Schmitt (1966) | • number of people per net residential area<br>• households with 4 or more members as a proportion of all households<br>• dwelling units with more than one person per room as a proportion of all units<br>• dwelling units in structures with 2 or more units as a proportion of all units |

| Wallis and Maliphant (1967) | • proportion of population in boroughs living in dwellings with more than 1.5 persons per room |
| | • number of people per room |
| | • number of people per acre in boroughs |
| Ministry of Housing (1970) | • number of persons per acre |
| Mitchell (1971) | • number of people per square foot in home |
| Freedman (1972) | • number of people per residential area |
| | • average number of people per room |
| Galle et al. (1972) | • number of people per acre |
| | • number of people per room |
| | • number of housing units per structure |
| | • number of rooms per housing unit |
| | • number of residential structures per acre |
| Zehner and Marans (1973) | • average number of dwellings per gross acre |
| Gillis (1974) | • number of persons per room within a household |
| | • number of people per square unit of space with a given area of residential land |
| Levy and Harzog (1974) | • number of people per square kilometer |
| | • number of people per room |
| Carnahan et al. (1974) | • median number of persons per room |
| | • dwelling units with more than one person per room as a proportion of all units |
| Webb et al. (1975) | • number of people per acre |
| | • number of people per room |
| | • number of people per dwelling |
| | • number of dwellings per acre |

*(continued)*

TABLE 8.1 *(continued)*

| Reference | Operational definition |
|---|---|
| Booth and Johnson (1975) | • a measure of room deficit<br>• a summary measure composed of (1) the number of hours the mother was at home and awake when the number of people is equal to or greater than the number of rooms; (2) the number of hours the mother was at home and awake when the number of people in the room with the respondent was two or more; and (3) whether the kitchen was set in the wall of another room<br>• a summary measure composed of (1) housing type; (2) number of households in the block face containing the child's household and on the block opposite; (3) whether or not the space adjacent to the child's household was shared with non-household members; and (4) street width as an indicator of the amount of automotive traffic adjacent to the household |
| Herbert (1977) | • households with 5 or more persons<br>• households with more than 1.5 persons per room<br>• households sharing a dwelling |
| Patterson (1978) | • number of residents per room |
| Essen et al. (1978) | • households with more than 1.5 persons per room |
| Nelson (1978) | • number of residents per acre |
| Baldassare (1979) | • number of persons per room<br>• number of persons per residential acre in census tracts |
| Gillis (1979) | • number of persons per bedroom<br>• number of people per acre<br>• number of dwelling units per building |
| Gove et al. (1979) | • number of persons per room<br>• proportion of households with more than one person |

| | |
|---|---|
| Chapin and Kaiser (1979) | • number of dwelling units per acre of land actually in use or proposed to be used for residential purposes<br>• number of dwelling units on net residential land plus traversing streets, alleys, and drives, one-half of bounding streets, and one-quarter of bounding street intersections<br>• number of dwelling units per acre of land area in use or proposed for development as a neighborhood area, including residential land, areas for local shopping, schools, and public open spaces, and land taken up in streets |
| Borukhov (1979) | • fraction of net residential land covered by buildings<br>• total floor area divided by net residential land<br>• floor area of each dwelling unit<br>• number of rooms per dwelling unit |
| Fox et al. (1980) | • a logarithm of the number of dwelling units per acre |
| Verbrugge and Taylor (1980) | • household size<br>• number of persons per room<br>• number of persons per 10,000 square feet of living space<br>• population on both sides of street face<br>• street population per 1000 feet<br>• population for blocks in "neighborhoods" as defined by respondents<br>• population density per acre for blocks in "neighborhoods" as defined by respondents |
| Saegert (1980) | • median split on the density distribution of the number of persons per room |

*Excluding definitions of density under experimental conditions or in institutional settings such as schools or dormitories. Also not included are subjective appraisals of objective density conditions.

were supplemented with information on the students' home environments. Here, the most relevant of these environmental data is child density which was determined by dividing the square land area of the census tract in which a student's home was located into the number of 15 to 17 year old children living in that census tract.[7] Thus it was possible to obtain for each individual child an objective figure for the number of children he or she could find in his or her neighborhood. Inspection of Table 8.2 shows that the city and suburban children lived in environments which differed significantly from each other qua child density. A one-way analysis of variance indicated that, on the average, the city neighborhoods contained about five times more children than did the suburban neighborhoods, $F(1,137) = 138.1, p < .0001$.

The most significant city-suburban difference was found in the frequency of complaints about a lack of neighborhood friends generated by the open-ended question, "What do you dislike most about your neighborhood?" Quite clearly, the city children enjoyed the company of friends much more often than did the suburban children ($X^2 = 15.2, df = 1, p < .0001$). Probing beyond the relatively crude city-suburban dichotomy, the children mentioning "a lack of friends" in response to the above question lived in neighborhoods with levels of child density which were significantly lower than those in neighborhoods of children not making this complaint. Results of a one-way analysis of variance showed that the neighborhoods of those not complaining about a lack of friends typically contained a larger number of 15 to 17 year olds, $F(1,137) = 16.2, p < .0001$. The data also point out an inverse relationship between the mentioning of a lack of friends and the actual number of neighborhood friends which the children reported. As the actual number of friends increased, the frequency of complaints about a lack of friends decreased (Table 8.3). Not surprisingly, the number of neighborhood friends correlated positively with the level of child density in the neighborhood.

The children were also asked whether they had ever participated in each of 14 different activities including, for example, going to a library, hanging around the street, shopping, doing volunteer work, and attending sports events. If the answers were in the affirmative, a next question inquired about their companions, if any, for each of these activities. The number of activities engaged in with "friends" or "the whole family" yielded index scores which were used as the criterion variables in one-way analyses of variance which showed significant city-suburban differences. The suburban children shared, on the average, fewer activities with friends, $F(1,146) = 4.3, p < .04$, and more with the rest of the family, $F(1,143) = 8.3, p < .004$. This is a behavior pattern which accords with a family-centered lifestyle typically found in traditional residential suburbs (Bell, 1958).

The following discussion transcends the specific context of the findings

---

[7]Age breakdown used by Statistics Canada.

TABLE 8.2
Child Densities in City and Suburban Neighborhoods (15 to 17 Year Olds)

| | Number of Children in the Child's Neighborhood | | | |
|---|---|---|---|---|
| | Low[1] | Medium[2] | High[3] | N |
| City | 16% | 27% | 58% | (64) |
| Suburb | 75% | 25% | — | (84) |

[1]Between 17 and 73 children per KM² in the Census Tract in which the child lives.
[2]Between 108 and 113 children per KM² in the Census Tract in which the child lives.
[3]Between 131 and 1051 children per KM² in the Census Tract in which the child lives.
$X^2 = 74.6, df = 2, p < .0001$

presented above. To begin with, I put forward a conceptualization of neighborhood density as a factor contributing to opportunities for interactions with peers; interactions which may manifest themselves in well-adjusted as well as delinquent behaviors. Second, a typology of planning principles is proposed as one possible way of identifying basic environmental contexts of neighborhood density conditions. Finally, it is argued that the environmental context of children's residential experience is inextricably interwoven with a more encompassing framework comprised of personal, social, cultural, economic, and political factors.

## DENSITY AS OPPORTUNITY

The above findings indicate the possibility that the physical environment, specifically the level of child density, may function to facilitate or hinder the formation and maintenance of friendships. Such influences are suggested by the relationships that were found to exist between child density and the fre-

TABLE 8.3
Mentioning of Lack of Friends in Neighborhood
by Actual Number of Friends in Neighborhood

| | Actual Number of Friends in Neighborhood | | |
|---|---|---|---|
| | <4 | 4–7 | >7 |
| mentions lack of friends | 48% | 24% | 18% |
| does not mention lack of friends | 52 | 76 | 82 |
| N | (21) | (58) | (38) |

$X^2 = 6.2, df = 2, p < .04$

quency of complaints about a lack of neighborhood friends, the actual number of friends, and the number of activities shared with friends. Obviously, one has to be careful in inferring causality in these relationships. For example, it might be that, through a process of self-selection, parents with child-rearing values stressing affability and sociability choose to locate in neighborhoods which seem to offer a good potential for such traits to develop—neighborhoods with relatively high child densities. Children in such families would presumably be more strongly inclined to develop friendship relations. While it is likely that the physical and social environment interact to produce conditions which are more *or* less conducive to children's relations with peers, the influences of the social and physical environment appear to operate in different ways.

The physical environment may be viewed as providing in different degrees opportunities for children's social interactions. The physical environment poses questions concerning the possibilities for social contact. Are there other children in the neighborhood? How far away do they live? Are there any meeting places? In this light, child density can be considered an attribute of the field of opportunities for children's social development. Ceteris paribus, higher densities provide more opportunities for social interaction than do lower densities.[8] This simple notion is also implied by the construct of "institutional completeness" of communities, developed by Breton (1964) in a longitudinal study of the social integration of immigrants as measured by the number of their relationships with representatives of the absorbing community. A theoretical parallel is provided by the concept of critical mass which proposes that density has an "enabling" effect, making possible the emergence of diverse activities; the higher the density, the more varied the range of opportunities that is generated (Fischer, 1976; cf. Mumford, 1961). The implication for children's social interactions is enhanced social choice and a diminished role of spatial constraints in molding the pattern of peer relations.[9]

---

[8]Note that the effects of density on peer interaction may follow a curvilinear relationship. The present study provides no information in regard to an optimal density level; there are, no doubt, multiple optima as a function of contextual factors to be discussed later. Furthermore, it is important to point out that the theoretical perspective expounded here is not an exclusive approach to the study of effects of neighborhood density; neither is it necessarily appropriate for the study of household density or other types of density. See the chapter by Wohlwill for a review of various alternative and supplemental perspectives.

[9]The origin of the idea that opportunities have a certain spatial range and require a certain population threshold goes back to the German geographer Von Thünen who formulated in 1826 a model of concentric zones which expressed accessibility of agriculture products to the city. Christaller (1933) developed this line of thought further in central place theory which assumes a hierarchical hexagonal pattern for the distribution of goods and services. This theory holds that, as distance from the center increases, population densities decrease, and each unit of settlement accordingly supports an incrementally decreasing amount of retail trade, employment, community services, and so on.

While the physical environment is bound to affect also the nature of peer interactions—for examle, the degree of spontaneity (cf. Berg and Medrich, 1978)—the qualitative aspects of peer relations would seem to be primarily a function of sociocultural and personal factors. From a planner's standpoint, these factors may be seen as constituting children's propensity to make use of the opportunities available to them in a given physical environment and as predisposing and preconditioning them as to the manner in which this is done. In other words, whether or not the potential for social interaction associated with high densities is indeed realized and the particular quality of the relations that come about is, in large part, contingent on factors which constrain children from or motivate them to initiate and sustain contacts with peers.

Along these lines, it is not difficult to see how high densities may have positive as well as negative implications for children. Densities support opportunities for both socially acceptable and deviant behaviors. The nature of peer interactions, made possible by the propinquity of other children (i.e., density), needs to be examined within the context of the norms governing those interactions.

Commenting earlier on methodological aspects of density studies, I stressed the need to include a consideration of contextual factors. This need is further accentuated by the conceptualization of neighborhood density as contributing to diverse opportunities which may or may not be utilized, dependent on, for example, the child's familial and economic context. The remainder of this chapter is an amplification of this point. First, a typology of basic planning principles will identify fundamental patterns and dimensions of the environmental context of neighborhood density. Following this, it is argued that this environmental context should be studied in conjunction with a broader set of social structural and other factors constituting the overarching societal context.

## CHILD DENSITY IN CONTEXT: I

Several authors have noted the importance of spatial segregation in environmental research (e.g., Geruson & McGrath, 1977, p. 171; Sommer, 1969, p. 153). Spatial distance, implied by spatial segregation, is a simple and powerful concept with which to approach the relation between children and their environment. Michelson (1976, p. 47), for one, has suggested that the notion of spatial separation be taken as the most fundamental environmental concept. It is fundamental because at all spatial levels people are, in different ways and in different degrees, separated in space from other people and from places of human activity. For population groups with a limited mobility—as, for example, children—accessibility of friends and available community facilities and services gains further in importance.

|  | Dispersal | Concentration |
|---|---|---|
| Integration | X  0  △<br><br>△  X  0<br><br>0  △  X | X0          X0<br>△            △<br><br>    X0<br>     △ |
| Segregation | 0  X  △<br><br>0  X  △<br><br>0  X  △ | XX        00<br>X          0<br><br>   △△<br>    △ |

FIG. 8.1  Typology of basic planning principles. Symbols represent hypothetical categories of variables along the demographic, morphological, and functional dimensions.

Spatial separation seems relevant with respect to at least three environmental dimensions:

a. *demographic,* that is, related to population characteristics such as age, social class, and ethnic background;
b. *functional,* that is, related to the uses to which land is put, for example, residential, retail, and industrial; and
c. *morphological,* that is, related to the form and structure of artifacts, for example, housing types such as single family dwellings and apartment buildings.

Attributes along each of these dimensions may be organized into four distinct environmental situations. These four situations are contained in a matrix formed by two continua dichotomized by two basic planning principles: dispersal-concentration and integration-segregation (see Fig. 8.1).

The matrix, presented in Fig. 8.1, yields four "ideal types" in the sense of analytical constructs.[10] In reality, these ideal types are rarely found in their pure forms. However, children's environments tend to approximate one rather than another of these four patterns. The typology has value as a heu-

---

[10]The use of ideal types in the social sciences, exemplified by Max Weber's classic work on bureaucracies, involves the abstraction from reality of those characteristics judged to be essential for the creation of a caricatural framework within which actual situations may be typified. The environmental ideal types distinguished in Figure 1 are a further simplification of reality in that the visualization of the four patterns does not bring out that (variations of) these patterns exist simultaneously along all three dimensions (i.e, demographic, functional, and morphological) and are often closely intertwined.

ristic device which identifies—along three dimensions—"extreme" types of environments. Should children's experiences in such environments differ in minor ways only, we should expect to find even more minimal differences in comparisons involving less contrasting environments. Should, however, the environmental opposites furnished by the typology be associated with clear differences in children's experiences, this may provide some indications regarding environmental features that might usefully be studied in more finegrained investigations (van Vliet--, 1981). At the same time, the three-dimensional typology emphasizes that effects of neighborhood density are likely to vary according to the presence or absence of other environmental conditions. The need to study density effects within the context of these and other factors is further elaborated upon in the concluding section of this chapter.

## CHILD DENSITY IN CONTEXT: II

A persistent theme in this chapter has been the need to study density within the context of extraneous variables which may exacerbate or alleviate any effects that occur. This observation does not detract from the potential significance of residential density in children's daily lives. It serves to indicate that density should be considered a composite element of a more encompassing framework comprised of a range of personal, social, cultural, economic, political, *and* environmental factors.

The typology of basic planning principles clarifies the role of neighborhood density amidst a broader set of environmental factors. It points out that children are spatially segregated, in varying degrees, from other children with respect to age, social class, ethnic background, and so forth. Effects arising from patterns along this demographic dimension need to be studied in relation to different patterns along the functional and morphological dimensions. To complicate matters further, different patterns of segregation-integration may reinforce or counterbalance effects resulting from a given density level. This situation is illustrated by a recent study of neighbor interaction among a national sample (Fox et al., 1980). In this investigation, the frequency of meeting with neighbors at home was found to be positively related to neighborhood density, *provided that public open space was present.* When it was absent, density affected neighboring negatively. In much the same vein, Baum et al. (1978) have examined how features of the neighborhood—specifically, the presence or absence of stores—may mediate effects of high-density conditions.

While variables along the demographic, functional, and morphological dimensions should be viewed as being interrelated and constituting the environmental context for children, these dimensions, in turn, need to be considered within a broader framework of personal, social, political, and other factors. Certainly, age would appear to interact with density in regard to social relations. Children are less mobile than most adults and, therefore, more dependent on the local environment for opportunities for social interaction. Hence, neighborhood density—particularly density of peers—is important to children. For the elderly, density seems to carry a comparable significance (Patterson, 1978). Maternal employment status may be a relevant variable within the familial context. Full-time, employed mothers do not have as much time, for example, to chauffeur their children (Stone, 1972). Suburban children rely more heavily than city children on maternal transportation and typically lack adequate public transportation. Their mobility in such situations would appear to be limited. This, in turn, may affect their relations with peers. Some evidence for this comes from the Toronto study, mentioned before, in which maternal employment and suburban location were found to interact in such a manner as to reduce the number of activities children shared with friends.

A final point to stress is that the multidimensional density patterns, identified earlier, evolve situated within a context of decision-making processes governing both the use of land and buildings and their allocation to specific user groups. For example, available housing accommodation may not be accessible to families with children because of exclusionary zoning (Calvan, 1979) or restrictive rental practices (Marans & Colten, 1985). Children's environmental experiences are molded by such socio-political factors which help to create different, and often unequal, opportunities for social development.

## CONCLUSIONS

The conclusions of this chapter may be summarized as follows:

1. Research findings indicate interaction with peers and social adjustment as playing an important role in children's development.

2. Peer interaction may have both positive and negative implications; peers may reinforce desirable behaviors and they may model delinquent activities dependent on the prevailing norms, available opportunities, and other contextual factors.

3. In many studies, living in apartments has been confounded with living under high-density conditions; this has tended to obfuscate the effects which housing type and density may have independently of each other.

4. There is no evidence that apartment living per se has ill-effects on children's social adjustment. The lack of evidence is due to methodologically deficient research. The occurrence of effects and their nature seem to depend on contextual factors as, for example, building height and cultural values.

5. Studies show inconsistent effects of housing type on children's interactions with peers. Findings suggest that apartment living may be associated with having fewer friends as well as with having more friends. The relationship needs to be examined further within the context of additional variables such as children's age and parents' child-rearing values.

6. Research findings seem to offer some support for a relation between high household densities and the incidence of behavior problems and maladjustment in children. The anti-social nature of children's behavior has been determined principally by adult perceptions and legal definitions. The critical threshold beyond which adverse effects occur has not been identified. This threshold is likely to be culture-bound. Other factors found to affect the relationship include gender and household composition. Theories explaining the process(es) through which density effects occur have not been well articulated and tested. There are indications that also low household densities may have adverse effects.

7. Effects of household density on children's interactions with peers have been little examined. There are some indications that in high-density households parents tend to restrict their children's freedom to bring friends into the house.

8. Research findings do not demonstrate convincingly that high neighborhood densities contribute to maladjusted behavior. Some studies have found a relation between density levels and rates of juvenile delinquency; others have detected no such relation after removing effects of extraneous variables. Moreover, the existing evidence is based on aggregate correlations; an explanation involving "self-selection" may be equally plausible.

9. Some studies suggest that, in suburbs, children's interactions with peers are less frequent and less spontaneous and fewer times revolving around common interests than is the case in city environments. In these investigations neighborhood density has not been singled out for study as a variable which may, in part, be responsible for these differences.

10. Results from one study indicate that the density of children in the neighborhood is a potentially important factor in the friendship behavior of teenagers. As compared to their counterparts living in low-density neighborhoods, teenagers from high-density neighborhoods complained less frequently about a lack of friends, shared more activities with friends, and also had a larger number of friends.

11. Neighborhood density may be conceptualized as a factor contributing to the field of opportunities for interactions with peers. Such interactions may be either socially desirable or deviant. Except possibly for situations of extreme crowding or isolation, the acceptabilty of children's social relations does not appear to be related to the conditions of neighborhood density under which they come about.

12. Studies of density effects have tended to produce inconclusive findings because of a lack of methodological standardization and inadequate consideration of contextual factors which may aggravate or counterbalance any effects found to occur.

13. Neighborhood density patterns may be viewed as having a demographic, a functional, and a morphological dimension. Together, they constitute the environmental context for children's social development; this context, in turn, needs to be considered within a broader framework of personal, social, cultural, economic, political, and other factors.

## REFERENCES

Aiello, J. R., Nicosia, G., & Thompson, D. E. Physiological, social, and behavioral consequences of crowding on children and adolescents. *Child Development,* 1979, *50,* 195–202.

Alexander, C. The city as a mechanism for sustaining human contact. In W. Ewald (Ed.), *Environment for man: The next 50 years.* Bloomington: Indiana University Press, 1967.

Allen, V. L. (Ed.). *Children as tutors.* New York: Academic Press, 1976.

American Public Health Association. *Planning the home for occupancy.* Chicago: Public Administration Service, 1950.

Baldassare, M. *Residential crowding in urban America.* Berkeley: University of California Press, 1979.

Barker, R. G., & Gump, P. V. *Big school, small school.* Stanford University Press, 1964.

Baum, A., David, G. E., & Aiello, J. R. Crowding and neighborhood mediation of urban density. *Journal of Population,* 1978, *1*(3), 266–279.

Bell, W. Social choice, life styles and suburban residence. In W. M. Dobriner, (Ed.), *The suburban community.* Putman, 1958, pp. 225–247.

Berg, M., & Medrich, F. A. *Children in four neighborhoods: The physical environment and its effect on play and play patterns.* Paper Children's Time Study, School of Law, University of California, Berkeley, 1978.

Bloom, B. L. A census tract analysis of socially deviant behaviors. *Multivariate Behavior Research,* 1966, *1,* 307–320.

Booth, A., & Edwards, J. N. Crowding and family relations. *American Sociological Review,* 1976, *41*(2), 308–321.

Booth, A., & Johnson, D. The effect of crowding on child health development. *American Behavioral Scientist,* 1975, *18*(6), 736–749.

Borukhov, E. The trade-off between density and other objectives: A reexamination of planning norms. In D. Soen (Ed.), *New trends in urban planning, studies in housing, urban design, and planning.* New York: Pergamon Press, 1979, pp. 176–190.

Bossard, J. H. S. A spatial index for family interaction. *American Sociological Review,* 1951, *16,* 243–246.

Breton, R. Institutional completeness of ethnic communities and the personal relations of migrants. *American Journal of Sociology,* 1964, *70*(2), 193–205.

Burt, C. *The young delinquent.* London: University of London Press, 1925.

Calhoun, J. B. Population density and social pathology. *Scientific American,* 1962, *206,* 139–148.

Calvan, R. Children and families – the latest victims of exclusionary land-use practices. *Challenge,* 1979, *10*(11), 26–28.

Cappon, D. Mental health in the hi-rise. *Ekistics,* 1972, *196*(33), 192–195.

Carnahan, D., Gove, W., & Galle, O. R. Urbanization, population density, and overcrowding: Trends in the quality of life in urban America. *Social Forces,* 1974, *53,* 62–72.

Carr-Saunders, A. M., Mannheim, H., & Rhodes, E. C. *Young offenders: An inquiry into juvenile delinquency.* Cambridge: Cambridge University Press, 1942.

Chapin, F. S., Jr., & Kaiser, E. J. *Urban land-use planning.* 3rd ed. Urbana: University of Illinois Press, 1979.

Chilton, R. J. Continuity in delinquency area research: A comparison of studies for Baltimore, Detroit, and Indianapolis. *American Sociological Review,* 1964, *29,* 71–83.

Chombart de Lauwe, P-H. et al. *Famille et habitation.* Vol. 1, Sciences humaines et conceptions de l'habitation. Paris: Centre National de la Recherche Scientifique, 1959.

Christaller, W. *Die zentralen Orten in Süddeutschland.* Jena: Gustav Fischer, 1933.

Clarke, A. D. B., & Clarke, A. M. Formerly isolated children. In A. D. B. Clarke and A. M. Clarke (Eds.), *Early experience: Myth and evidence,* pp. 27–35. New York: The Free Press, 1976.

Coleman, J. C. Friendship and the peer group in adolescence. In J. Adelson, (Ed.), *Handbook of adolescent psychology.* New York: Wiley, 1980.

Cooney, E. W. High flats in local authority housing in England and Wales since 1945. In A. Sutcliffe, (Ed.), *Multi-storey living.* London: Croom Helm, 1974, pp. 151–180.

Cowen, E. L., Pederson, A., Babijian, H., Izzo, L. D., & Trost, M. A. Long-term follow-up of early detectable vulnerable children. *Journal of Consulting and Clinical Psychology,* 1973, *41*(3), 438–446.

Curran, J. P. Pandora's box reopened? The assessment of social skills. *Journal of Behavior Assessment,* 1979, *1*(1), 55–71.

Davis, D. L., Bergin, K., & Mazin, G. When the neighbors get noisy we bang on the walls: A critical exploration of density and crowding. Paper presented at the 69th Annual American Sociological Association meetings, Montreal, 1974.

Davis, K. Final note on a case of extreme isolation. *American Journal of Sociology,* 1947, *45,* 554–565.

Downing, G. L. A., & Calway, J. P. T. Living in high flats – problems of tenants and management. *Roy. Soc. Health Journal,* 1963, *5,* 237–243.

Durkheim, E. *De la division du travail social: étude sur l'organisation des sociétés supérieures.* Paris: Felix Alcan, 1893.

East, W. N., Stocks, P., & Young, H. T. P. *The adolescent criminal: A medico-sociological study of 4,000 male adolescents.* London: J. & A. Churchill, 1942.

Essen, J., Fogelman, K., & Head, J. Children's housing and their health and physical development. *Child: Care, Health and Development,* 1978, *4,* 357-369.

Farley, J. *Effects of residential settings, parental lifestyles and demographic characteristics on children's activity patterns.* Ph.D. dissertation, Department of Sociology, University of Michigan, 1977.

Feldman, M. J., & Gaier, E. J. Correlates of adolescent life satisfaction. *Youth and Society,* 1980, *12*(2), 131-144.

Ferguson, T. *The young delinquent in his social setting: A Glasgow study.* Oxford: Oxford University Press, 1952.

Filipovitch, A. J. *The relationship between the housing environment and the child's behavior: Strategies for adapting the multifamily housing.* Ph.D. dissertation, Portland State University, 1975.

Fischer, C. S. *The urban experience.* New York: Harcourt, Brace, Jovanovich, 1976.

Foster, S. L., & Ritchey, W. L. Issues in the assessment of social competence in children. *Journal of Applied Behavior Analysis,* 1979, *12,* 625-638.

Fox, B. J., Fox, J., & Marans, R. W. Residential density and neighbor interaction. *The Sociological Quarterly,* 1980, *21,* 349-359.

Freedman, B. J., Rosenthal, L., Donahoe, L. P., Schlundt, D. G., & McFall, R. M. A social-behavioral analysis of skill deficits in delinquent and non-delinquent adolescent boys. *Journal of Consulting and Clinical Psychology,* 1979, *46,* 1148-1163.

Freedman, J. L. Population density, juvenile delinquency and mental illness in New York City. In S. Mills Mazie, (Ed.), *Population, distribution and policy.* Washington, D.C.: U.S. Government Printing Office, 1972, pp. 511-523.

Galle, O. R., Gove, W. R., & McPherson, J. Miller. Population density and pathology: What are the relations for man? *Science,* 1972, *7,* 23-30.

Gans, H. J. *The Levittowners,* Vintage Press, 1967.

Geruson, R. T., & McGrath, D. *Cities and urbanization.* New York: Praeger, 1977.

Gillis, A. R. Population density and social pathology: The case of building type, social allowance and juvenile delinquency. *Social Forces,* 1974, *53*(2), 306-314.

Gillis, A. R. Household density and human crowding: Unravelling a non-linear relationship. *Journal of Population,* 1979, *2*(2), 104-117.

Gittus, E. *Flats, families and the under-fives.* London: Routledge & Kegan Paul, 1976.

Goldfarb, W. The effects of early institutional care on adolescent personality. *Journal of Experimental Education,* 1943, *12*(2), 106-129.

Gordon, R. A. Issues in the ecological study of delinquency. *American Sociological Review,* 1967, *23,* 927-944.

Gottman, J. M. Toward a definition of social isolation in children. *Child Development,* 1977, *48,* 513-517.

Gottman, J., Gonso, J., & Rasmussen, B. Social interaction, social competence, and friendship in children. *Child Development,* 1975, *46,* 709-718.

Gove, W. R., Hughes, M., & Galle, O. R. Overcrowding in the home: An empirical investigation of its possible pathological consequences. *American Sociological Review,* 1979, *44,* 59-80.

Green, K. D., & Forehand, R. Assessment of children's social skills: A review of methods. *Journal of Behavioral Assessment,* 1980, *2*(2), 143-159.

Grégoire, M. The child in the high rise. *Ekistics,* 1971, *186,* 331-333.

Gunn, A. D. G. The medical-social problems of multi-story living. *Nursing Times,* 1968, *64,* 468–469.

Hagan, J., Gillis, A. R., & Chan, J. Explaining official delinquency: A spatial study of class, conflict and control. *The Sociological Quarterly,* 1978, *19,* 386–398.

Hagarty, L. M. *The family at home: A comparison of the time-budgets of families in high-rise apartments and detached houses in suburban metropolitan Toronto.* Ph.D. dissertation, Faculty of Social Work, University of Toronto, 1975.

Harlow, H. F., & Harlow, M. K. The effect of rearing conditions on behavior. *Bull. Menninger Clinic,* 1962a, *26,* 213–224.

Harlow, H. F., & Harlow, M. K. Social deprivation in monkeys. *Scientific American,* 1962b, *207*(5), 136–146.

Hart, R. *Children's experience of place.* New York: Irvington Press, 1979.

Hartup, W. W. Peer interaction and the behavioral development of the individual child. In E. Schopler & R. J. Reichler, (Ed.), *Psychopathology and child development.* New York: Plenum Press, 1976.

Hartup, W. W., & Lougee, M. D. Peers as models. *School Psychology Digest,* 1975, *4*(1), 11–26.

Hassan, R. *Families in flats: A study of low income families in public housing.* Singapore University Press, 1977.

Herbert, D. T. An areal and ecological analysis of delinquency residence: Cardiff 1966 and 1971. *Tijdschrift voor Economische en Sociale Geografie,* 1977, *68,* 83–99.

Hewitt, J. P. *Self and society: A symbolic interactional social psychology.* Boston: Allyn & Bacon, 1976.

Huba, G. J., & Bentler, P. M. The role of peer and adult models for drug taking at different stages in adolescence. *Journal of Youth and Adolescence,* 1980, *9*(5), 449–465.

Jaco, E., Gartly. The social isolation hypothesis and schizophrenia. *American Journal of Sociology,* 1953, *19,* 567–577.

Jacobs, J. *The death and life of great American cities.* New York: Random House, 1960.

Jephcott, P. *Homes in high flats.* Oliver & Boyd, 1971.

Kara-Pesic, Z. et al. *Children's living and play areas in the local community.* Belgrade: Yugoslav Institute for Town Planning and Housing, 1975.

Keasey, C. B. Social participation as a factor in the moral development of preadolescents. *Developmental Psychology,* 1971, *5*(2), 216–220.

Kendall, M. G., & Hill, A. B. *The sources and the nature of the statistics of the United Kingdom.* London: Oliver & Boyd, 1952.

Kohn, M., & Clausen, J. Social isolation and schizophrenia. *American Journal of Sociology,* 1955, *20*(3), 265–273.

Lander, B. *Towards an understanding of juvenile delinquency.* New York: Columbia University Press, 1954.

Lantz, H. R. Number of childhood friends as reported in the life histories of a psychiatrically diagnosed group of 1000. *Journal of Marriage and Family Living,* 1956, *18,* 107–108.

Levy, L., & Herzog, A. N. Effects of population density and crowding on health and social adaptations in The Netherlands. *Journal of Health and Social Behavior,* 1974, *15,* 228–240.

Liska, A. E. Causal structures underlying the relationship between delinquent involvement and delinquent peers. *Sociology and Social Research,* 1973, *58*(1), 23–36.

Loo, C. M. The effects of spatial density on the social behavior of children. *Journal of Applied Social Psychology,* 1972, *4,* 372–381.

Maas, H. S. Preadolescent peer relations and adult intimacy. *Psychiatry,* 1968, *31,* 161–172.

Macey, J. P. Problems of flat life. *Royal Society of Health Journal,* 1959, *79,* 183–192.

Marans, R. W., & M. E. Colten. U.S. rental housing policies affecting families with children:

Hard times for youth. In: W. van Vliet —, E. Huttman, & S. Fava (Eds.), *Housing needs and policy approaches: Trends in 13 countries.* Durham, N.C.: Duke University Press, 1985.

McCandles, B. R. *Children: Behavior and development.* New York: Holt, Rhinehart, and Winston, 1967.

McGrew, P. L. Social and spatial density effects on spacing behavior in preschool children. *Journal of Child Psychology and Psychiatry,* 1970, *11,* 197–205.

Mead, G. H. *Mind, self and society,* C. W. Morris, (Ed.). Chicago: University Press, 1934.

Michael, C. M., Morris, D. P., & Sorsker, E. Follow up studies of shy, withdrawn children; II, Relative incidence of schizophrenia. *American Journal of Orthopsychiatry,* 1957, *27,* 331–337.

Michelson, W. *Man and his urban environment,* (rev. 1970 ed.). Reading, Mass.: Addison-Wesley, 1976.

Michelson, W. *Environmental choice, human behavior and residential saisfaction.* New York: Oxford University Press, 1977.

Michelson, W., & Roberts, E. Children and the urban physical environment. In W. Michelson, S. V. Levine, A. R. Spina et al. (Eds.), *The child in the city: Changes and challenges.* Toronto: University of Toronto Press, 1979, pp. 410–478.

Ministry of Housing. *Families living at high density.* London: Her Majesty's Office, 1970.

Mitchell, R. E. Some social implications of high density housing. *American Sociological Review,* 1971, *36*(1), 18–29.

Morris, T. *The criminal area: A study in social ecology.* London: Routledge & Kegan Paul, 1957.

Mumford, L. *The city in history.* New York: Harcourt, Brace, Jovanovich, 1961.

Murray, R. The influence of crowding on children's behavior. In D. Canter & T. Lee, (Eds.), *Psychology and the built environment,* 1974, 112–118.

Nelson, T. L. Residential satisfaction in the crowded urban neighborhood. *International Review of Modern Sociology,* 1979, *8*(2), 227–238.

Patterson, A. H. Housing density and various quality of life measures among elderly urban dwellers. *Journal of Population,* 1978, *2*(3), 203–215.

Pearse, J. Children in the sky. *Town & Country Planning,* 1968, Oct.-Nov., 479–481.

Piaget, J. *The moral judgment of the child.* New York: Free Press, 1932.

Plant, J. S. The personality and an urban area. In P. Hatt et al. (Eds.), *Cities and society,* 1937, pp. 647–665.

Popenoe, D. *The suburban environment.* Chicago: University of Chicago Press, 1977.

Pritchard, M., & Graham, P. An investigation of a group of patients who have attended both the child and the adult departments of the same psychiatric hospital. *British Journal of Psychiatry,* 1966, *112,* 603–612.

Roff, M. Childhood social interactions and young adult bad conduct. *Journal of Abnormal and Social Psychology,* 1961, *63*(2), 333–337.

Roff, M. Childhood social interaction and young adult psychosis. *Journal of Clinical Psychology,* 1963, *19*(2), 152–157.

Roff, M., Sells, B., & Golden, M. M. *Social adjustment and personality development in children.* Minneapolis: University of Minnesota Press, 1972.

Rosenberg, G. High population densities in relation to social behavior. *Ekistics. 25,* 425–427.

Rubin, Z. *Children's friendships.* Cambridge: Harvard University Press, 1980.

Saegert, S. The effect of residential density on low income children. Paper presented to the Annual Meeting of the American Psychological Association, Montreal, 1980.

Salmon, P. Differential conforming as a developmental process. *British Journal of Social and Clinical Psychology,* 1969, *8,* 22–31.

Schaefer, C. The impact of peer culture on residential treatment of youth. *Adolescence,* 1980, *15*(60), 831–845.

Schmitt, R. C. Density, delinquency and crime in Honolulu. *Sociology and Social Research,* 1957, *41,* 274–276.

Schmitt, R. C. Implications of density in Hong Kong. *Journal of the American Institute of Planners,* 1963, *24,* 210–217.

Schmitt, R. C. Density, health, and social organization. *Journal of the American Institute of Planners,* 1966, *32,* 38–40.

Sengel, R. H. A graph analysis of the relationship between population density and social pathology. *Behavioral Science,* 1978, *23*(4), 213–224.

Sennett, R. *The uses of disorder: Personal identity and city life.* New York: Knopf, 1970.

Shaw, C., & McKay, H. D. *Juvenile delinquency and urban areas.* Chicago: University of Chicago Press, 1942.

Shichor, D., Becker, D. L., & O'Brien, R. M. Population density and criminal victimization: Some unexpected findings in central cities. *Criminology,* 1979, *12*(2), 184–193.

Simmel, G. Die quantitative Bestimmtheit der Gruppe. In G. Simmel *Soziologie; Untersuchungen über die Formen der Vergesellschaftung.* Leipzig: Von Duncker & Humblot, 1908, pp. 47–133.

Sobal, J. Social participation, household density, and experienced crowding. Paper presented at the 75th Annual Meeting of the American Sociological Association, New York, August 1980.

Sommer, R. *Personal space: The behavioral basis of design.* Englewood Cliffs, NJ: Prentice-Hall, 1969.

Statistics Canada. *Population and housing characteristics: Census 1976.* Ottawa, 1978.

Stevenson, A., Martin, E., & O'Neill, J. *High living: A study of family life in flats.* Melbourne: Melbourne University Press, 1967.

Stokols, D. On the distinction between density and crowding: Some implications for future research. *Psychological Review,* 1972, *79*(3), 275–277.

Stone, P. J. Child care in 12 countries. In A. Szalai et al., *The use of time.* The Hague: Mouton, 1972, pp. 249–264.

Ullman, C. A. Teachers, peers, and tests as predictors of adjustment. *Journal of Educational Psychology,* 1957, *48,* 257–267.

United Nations Statistical Office. *Statistical Yearbook 1978.* New York: United Nations, 1979.

Usher, R. D., & Hunnybun, N. K. Overcrowding as a factor in personality maladjustment. *Mother and Child,* 1933, *4,* 415–417.

U.S. Department of Housing and Urban Development. *Annual Housing Survey.* Washington, D.C.: U.S. Government Printing Office, 1978.

van Vliet--, W. Neighborhood evaluations of city and suburban children. *Journal of the American Planning Association,* 1981, *47*(4), 458–467.

van Vliet--, W. Families in apartments: Sad storeys for children? *Environment and Behavior,* 1983a, *15*(2), 211–234.

van Vliet--, W. Exploring the fourth environment: an examination of the home range of city and suburban teenagers. *Environment and Behavior,* 1983b, *15*(5), 567–588.

Verbrugge, L. M. Consequences of population density and size. *Urban Affairs Quarterly,* 1980, *16*(2), 135–160.

Wallis, C. P., & Maliphant, R. Delinquent areas in the county of London: Ecological factors. *British Journal of Criminology,* 1967, *7,* 250–284.

Watt, N. F., Storulow, R. D., Lubinsky, A. W., & McClelland, D. C. School adjustment and behavior of children hospitalized for schizophrenia as adults. *American Journal of Orthopsychiatry,* 1967, *37,* 725–731.

Webb, S. D., & Collette, J. Urban ecological and household correlates of stress-alleviating drug use. *American Behavioral Scientist,* 1975, *18,* 750–769.

Wicker, A. W. Undermanning, performances, and students' subjective experiences in behavior settings of large and small high schools. *Journal of Personality and Social Psychology,* 1968, *10,* 255–261.

Williamson, R. C. Socialization in the high-rise: A cross-national comparison. *Ekistics,* 1978, *45*(268), 122–130.

Winsborough, H. H. The consequences of high population density. *Law and Contemporary Problems,* 1965, *31,* 120–126.

Wirth, L. Urbanism as a way of life. *American Journal of Sociology,* 1938, *44*(1), 1–24.

Young, S. Social and psychological effects of living in high-rise buildings. Ian Buchan Fell Research Project on Housing, University of Sydney, Dept. of Architecture, 1976.

Zehner, R. B., & Marans, R. W. Residential density, planning objectives and life in planned communities. *Journal of American Institute of Planners,* 1973, September, 337–345.

# 9 Habitats for Children: The State of the Evidence

Willem van Vliet--
Joachim F. Wohlwill
*The Pennsylvania State University*

## INTRODUCTION

At the outset, it should be noted that this concluding chapter is quite different in scope and focus from the preceding chapters. The latter were prepared following a first meeting of the SRCD Study Group on the Role of Residential Density in the Development of Children in which an agenda of issues meriting attention was determined. Papers prepared by Study Group members addressing these issues were precirculated for a second meeting during which they formed the basis for a discussion of their implications for further research and policy. This discussion generated a set of nine questions around which this chapter is structured. These questions serve as an organizing framework adopted by the editors in the hope of pulling together the diverse perspectives and findings presented in the preceding chapters in a synthesizing review.

The first three questions concern overall impacts of high density on children's psychological functioning and health, the impacts of conditions of low density (i.e., isolation), and the role played by a specific factor ecologically correlated with density, viz. noise. The next set of questions concerns the role of adaptation to long-term exposure to particular conditions of density, as well as the role of factors that may mediate or modulate those effects, such as resource availability and institutional size. The role of particular residential characteristics is the subject of a further question, leading to the specific question of the relevance of existing zoning codes and housing standards for needs and requirements of children. Finally, current demographic trends are examined in terms of their significance for our topic. In a concluding section of the chapter, major policy issues arising from the preceding review are pointed out, and directions for research required to provide answers to issues that remain unresolved are indicated.

## Question 1

What are the impacts of high-density conditions in the home on the development of children?

As a very partial answer to this question, one that needs to be qualified in several important respects, the generalization appears to be warranted that high-density conditions in the home *can* negatively affect a young child's general development, although those effects may be less marked in older children. They may be mitigated as well, even for younger children, by counteractive forces operating within the psychosocial environment.

A more adequate answer to this question must take into account, first of all, the ways in which high-density conditions in the home affect a child. Among the most significant, particularly with regard to infants and young children, is the effect of crowding in the home in raising general activity-level and noise level. That is, the members of the young child's social environment, under conditions of crowding, function in a manner quite different from the responsive, interactive character that we commonly associate with it, notably in the case of the mother-child dyad. Because of the propensity of people (of any age) to move around and to make noise, verbal and of other kinds, the aggregation of persons in larger numbers within a small or moderately-sized home is apt to result in a considerable heightening of the level of activity surrounding the child, as well as in ambient noise levels. As a consequence we may expect the child's arousal level to increase, possibly leading to an impairment in the ability to attend selectively to relevant stimuli, along with other effects, both cognitive and motivational. (See chapter 3 for a fuller treatment of these questions.)

Unfortunately it is difficult to specify at what point positive social stimulation changes into negative background stimulation. Not only does this represent a continuum, rather than a threshold function, but the manifestation of the "significant others" around the child and the role they play in the child's environment are obviously dependent on a host of factors: the amount and kind of interaction they engage in with the child (itself based in part on age and sex, e.g., in the case of the child's siblings), the amount and kind of space available in the home, in relation to the number of persons occupying it, the permeability of the space in the home to visual and auditory stimuli, and to noise in particular, etc.

There is indeed research to support the proposition that infants and young children growing up under conditions of crowding appear to be impaired in their early cognitive development (see chapter 3). Yet the same body of research (notably the work of Wachs and his associates, reviewed by Heft in chapter 3) also points to a particular influence that may act to mitigate effects of crowding, i.e., the availability to the child of a "stimulus shelter," typically a room of its own, into which it can retreat to reduce the amount and intensity of the physical and/or social stimuli impinging on it.

Evidence in this regard comes primarily from research on the first few years of life (up to the age of three). The situation is rather more uncertain once we move to the older age levels. While children of various ages have been shown to be susceptible to the effects of crowding under restricted laboratory conditions, or in nursery school settings—particularly with respect to aggressive behavior—both the epidemiological and the behavioral evidence suggests that crowding in the home exerts less consistent effects for older children and adults (see chapters 5 and 7; also Mitchell, 1971). These findings might be attributed in part to adaptation effects, but more likely represent the progressively lessening role that the home plays in the life of the child, as the latter's life-space expands to include an ever expanding range of loci and areas outside the home: playgrounds, streets, schools, stores, clubs, etc.

It might thus be argued that the "stimulus shelter" that plays such a major role in infancy becomes generalized for older children to the world outside the home, to the extent that a given child has access to it. Obviously this is a gross oversimplification, since the outside world—e.g., schools, buses and subways, playgrounds—may well be characterized by higher levels of density, as well as of activity level, noise, etc., than the home; in fact, typically it is. Nevertheless, the opportunity for a child living in a crowded, congested home to escape from it for periods of time undoubtedly plays an important part in permitting the child to cope with possibly stressful conditions within the home environment.

A further closely related factor, which probably increases in importance as the child approaches adolescence or adulthood, is that of the perception of control over its environment (see chapter 5). That is, a child who is able to temporarily escape from home may experience conditions of stress within the home as less severe because of the sense of control that it perceives having over the environment. Knowing that one can escape a disagreeable or stressful environment acts to make those very conditions more tolerable, even in the absence of action directed at implementing that sense of control—though one suspects that occasional exercise of it is necessary for the individual to retain the sense of perceived control.

The evidence thus suggests that providing children who are subjected to severe crowding in their home with a feeling of control may help to mitigate the untoward effects of such crowding to some degree. Clearly the most effective source of that feeling is the provision of relatively free and unimpeded access to less crowded settings outside the home, for children old enough to venture into the outside environment on their own. This is in part of course a matter of providing the necessary conditions of access (e.g., through adequate transportation, reasonably safe streets, satisfactory playgrounds and other meeting places for children, etc.). At the same time promoting adults' awareness of children's needs in this regard, and the benefits to them from obtaining periodic relief from overly crowded conditions in the home is clearly important. By the same token such awareness may also be of help for much younger children, by enhancing the parents' sensitivity to the need for "stimulus shelters" in whatever form, and of periodic exposure to less congested settings outside of the home, e.g., through walks, excursions, etc.

While the preceding material has emphasized the child's behavioral and social development, the question of relationships between density and the physical health of the child needs to be considered as well. Here the bi-polar nature of the density continuum becomes particularly apparent. In principle one might suppose that high-density living conditions would foster the spread of contagious diseases. At least indirect support for this view comes from an investigation by Fanning (1967), comparing the incidence of various physical and psychological health problems in families living in apartments, as opposed to detached houses. In every age group, from infancy and early childhood through maturity, the incidence of persons consulting a general practitioner was substantially greater among the apartment dwellers. (Since all families included in this survey came from a homogenous population of families of Armed Forces personnel, they were presumably equated at least approximately in terms of socioeconomic status).

In regard to density as such, however, a number of studies (e.g., Booth and Johnson, 1975; Essen, Fogelman, & Head, 1978) show little if any evidence of a relationship between residential density and general health, or incidence of illness.[1] But Worth (1963), while confirming this result with respect to a density measure of number of persons per area, did find that the incidence of contagious diseases in children (particularly tuberculosis and mumps) reflected inside crowding, i.e., varied with the ratio of people to a room. (This study was carried out in various settlements in Hong Kong, and thus under comparatively severe conditions of crowding.)

Under *low* density-conditions, on the other hand, health-care delivery tends to become unreliable and access to it difficult, so that children's health should be expected to be impaired on the average. Information on this point is not, however, readily available, and would in any event be contaminated by the obvious effects of correlated socio-economic conditions differentiating low-density rural from higher-density (small town or urban) settings.

---

[1]A partial exception in this regard is represented in the finding by Booth and Johnson (1975) of an adverse effect of household crowding on physical growth (i.e., weight and height) showing up primarily in children beyond the age of nine years.

Question 2

What are the effects of low-density environments and of relative geographic isolation on children?

This question might seem to be of more theoretical than practical interest, as isolation is undoubtedly a far rarer condition for children today than is the other end of the density dimension — crowding. Yet, if we consider some of the diverse settings in which children do in fact grow up — farms and home-steads that are miles away from the nearest town; small, inaccessible islands, parklands and wilderness-like areas, tiny fishing villages cut off from the outside except for occasional coastal vessels; remote outposts in desert and mountain areas being developed through mining or the like — the situation taken world-wide is by no means negligible. In the United States, further-more, demographic patterns may be operating to bring families increasingly to relatively low-density areas beyond metropolitan regions, as indicated in the data from the 1980 census (cf. Long & DeAre, 1982). Thus the number of persons residing in counties containing no communities of population greater than 2,500 increased by about 565,000 (or 14.6%) over 1970, while counties whose largest settlement is between 2,500 and 10,000 increased by about 1,300,000 or 13.1%.

The available evidence of effects of low-density conditions on children re-mains quite limited and relates to problems of isolation only in a relative sense, since few if any children live under the more extreme forms of isolation studied in adults under special conditions, e.g., Antarctica, underwater labo-ratories, etc. (cf. Rasmussen, 1973). Furthermore, there has been a reversal in the nature of the effects that have been shown. In the 1930s, studies of children growing up in remote pockets of rural Appalachia (the so-called "hollows") disclosed a rather grim picture of across-the-board deficit which became increasingly pronounced with age. But more recent studies of chil-dren growing up on isolated farms (carried out in Norway and Hungary) as well as on canal-boats in Germany, indicate that whatever negative impact such isolation may exert is much more selective in nature, confined primarily to verbal, and social-role aspects of cognitive development, and possibly also more easily reversible.[2] The discrepancy between these two sets of findings may well reflect the much more widespread access of contemporary isolated children to school (as well as to television), although concrete evidence in this regard is not available.

Our information concerning the development of children living in low-density areas with regard to aspects of their development other than cognitive

---

[2]For a review of findings from earlier studies of the intelligence of children growing up under conditions of social, cultural, and geographic isolation, see Anastasi (1958). For more recent evi-dence, see Hollos and Cowan (1973) and Hollos (1975), as well as Hoehn (1974).

and intellectual growth is even less adequate. Yet it is quite posible that it is in areas such as exploration and curiosity, personality traits, and interpersonal behavior that more pronounced effects may be revealed.[3] Thus we are very far from being able to provide a good indication of the probable effects on children of the incipient movement of segments of the population to more rural areas, but the matter clearly deserves much additional study.

It is important to remind ourselves that, as argued in chapter 2, one cannot identify isolation with some arbitrarily chosen index of population density, but must take into consideration the "connectedness" of children to their peers, and to the broader social and cultural environment surrounding them. Thus, in a functional sense, a farm child may be less isolated than a child in a ghetto area, whose parents may confine him or her to the home or to a very restricted area surrounding it, out of fear of harm coming to the child from free contact with others on the outside. Furthermore, as Schoggen and Schoggen argue effectively in chapter 4, opportunity for exploration, and for participation in social activities, is more a matter of the number of behavior settings potentially available to a child than of geographic isolation or population density per se.

Assuming that isolation does exert some residual effects on children, the ways to mitigate them are fairly obvious, i.e., by providing for intermittent opportunities for increased levels of social interaction, both directly (through trips, visits, etc.) and vicariously (through telecommunications—telephone, tapes, mail). The latter may be of particular importance in the case of families that may be denied opportunities for trips and other temporary escapes from their residential quarters, whether for economic reasons, or for reasons of geographical inaccessibility and difficulty in traveling. In addition, there are cultural factors to be taken into account, which in some cases (e.g., the Amish) may lead families to actively preserve the conditions of isolation in which they find themselves. Note that television in and of itself is not likely to be very effective in this regard, because of its unidirectional, non-interactive nature, though it has probably contributed to reducing the overall impact of isolation in the cultural sense.

Finally, it should be pointed out that it would be a mistake to regard low-density conditions, such as are to be found in environmental settings in which children grow up today, as constituting necessarily a negative influence on the child's overall development. While there may be certain aspects of development that are adversely affected, such effects appear to be highly selective, as noted above. It is in fact quite possible that there are other aspects, e.g., in

---

[3]A considerable impact of cultural and geographic isolation on the development of farm children in Norway has, in fact, been documented by Haggard (1973) in the areas of personality, affect and interpersonal behavior. See also Haggard (1964) for a general review and theoretical analysis of the effects of isolation on personality.

the realms of exploratory behavior, personality, etc., where the reduction in amounts and intensities of stimulation from both the physical and the social environment may have a beneficial impact on the child, or perhaps more plausibly result merely in a difference in behavior patterns that cannot be termed as either positive or negative. Similarly, differences in the social structure and family interaction patterns characteristic of rural as compared to urban areas may be associated with different patterns of role performance (such as participation in household chores) on the part of the children. Again, with the notable exception of Haggard's work (see footnote 3), concrete data on these questions at the psychological level are hard to find.

## Question 3

What is the impact of environmental noise on children, and how is such impact related to density? How is it alleviated?

Among the variables that are more likely to be implicated as mediators of density effects on psychological development that of noise deserves particular consideration for several reasons. First, noise is likely to be correlated with density both directly and indirectly. That is, the greater the number of persons in a given space, the higher the noise level that one may expect them to generate through their speech (consider the background noise at a cocktail party). In addition, the activities engaged in by individuals residing in a child's home (or within earshot of the child) are important sources of further noise, from machinery (large and small appliances; typewriters, tools, etc.), entertainment instruments (hi-fi and TV sets, musical instruments), and indoor sports and games (e.g., video-games). There is thus reason to believe that ambient noise level increases monotonically with density and quite probably in a non-linear and perhaps even exponential fashion, though good data on this question are not readily available.

At the same time, because of small children's relative lack of control over their environment and limited ability to self-select environments, as well as their lesser ability to tune out irrelevant stimuli, they appear to be particularly prone to detrimental effects of background noise, so that density-related noise becomes of particular concern.

We have seen that there is in fact some evidence of negative effects of noise levels in the home on the very young child, though this literature does not specifically establish a tie to density. While conclusive information on this point would obviously be valuable, there are sufficient grounds, as just noted, for assuming such a tie to exist to justify a prima facie concern over problems of noise under any conditions of relatively high residential density. More positively, we may suggest that such conditions call for particular attention to ways of mitigating the associated increase in noise level — notably by providing means for the child to escape from or insulate itself from such noise. Proper insulation, as well as the provision of the "stimulus shelters" referred to in the first section, are clearly important in this regard.

Additionally, the sources of noise external to the home require attention. Effects of environmental noise similar to those emanating from airports in the vicinity of the school, as discussed by Aiello, Thompson, and Baum in chapter 5, may be expected from traffic, industrial noise, and the like. Ecologically, such sources are apt to be most marked in neighborhoods of relatively high density (e.g., in inner-city areas). They are thus likely to combine with relatively high interior noise levels, enhancing the potential for negative impacts. A combination of measures for noise abatement through the design of housing and of planning to reduce major noise sources from residential areas is called for to deal with this problem.

Finally, it should be noted that there exists an entirely different type of noise-related stressor, namely constraints imposed by the parents on children's activities to keep their noise levels low enough so as not to annoy neighbors. Raven (1967) has suggested that such behavioral restrictions promote more sedentary hobbies and passive leisure activities such as television watching.

## Question 4

To what extent do children adapt to environmental conditions of either high or low density through prolonged exposure to them, and how does such adaptation change with age? What are the long-term costs of such adaptation, if any?

It has been suggested (e.g., Booth, 1976) that one possible explanation for the relatively weak evidence of effects on behavior and social functioning related to density in adults may be the phenomenon of adaptation, that is, the tendency for the individual to come to terms with any set of environmental conditions compatible with life, given sufficient time. The pattern for density effects to be more pronounced the younger the child might seem to bear out this view, whether one interprets it as based simply on the lesser amount of time that the individual has had to adapt the younger his or her age, or assumes a lesser ability of the immature organism to adapt.

Despite the patent importance of this question, in both a practical and a theoretical sense, our lack of conclusive evidence concerning it is abysmal. The most plausible reason for this glaring void in our knowledge is undoubtedly the need for longitudinal information — or, more specifically, for data on children who experience a major change in their environmental conditions and are followed up for an extended period of time, subsequent to that change. While there is a scattering of studies dealing with children who have moved from a rural to an urban environment or from an underdeveloped to a developed area or country,[4] this research is limited by its restriction to measures of cognitive development (generally IQ). Moreover, it does not provide specific information on the nature of the environmental change, so that the results obtained are difficult to interpret; adequate control groups from both the host and the receiving communities to provide a basis of comparison are generally lacking as well. In any event, none of this work gives any indication of effects of change in residential density conditions, much less of the child's mode of adaptation to these over the course of extended exposure to them.

It may be useful, in connection with this issue, to differentiate between two different ways in which adaptation may take place, all the more since that distinction is relevant to the possible role of age as a mediator of adaptation. On the one hand, adaptation may occur in an essentially passive manner, that is, the individual's response to his or her conditions or circumstances becomes attenuated, or more neutral—essentially a "getting used to it" kind of adaptation. This is to be contrasted to a different process, adjustment of the environment (Wohlwill, 1974), by which an individual may act to alter the conditions to which he or she is being exposed. In the case of density this might entail seeking a temporary change in the actual conditions of crowding, by escaping to less crowded quarters; it might be based on physical or psychological shielding from the impinging social stimulation (by turning off or avoiding such stimulation); finally, it might entail a direct intervention in the environment to create a change, e.g., by prevailing on certain members of a household to move elsewhere.

Young children's ability to adjust their environment in this active sense is rather limited—with the exception of the retreat to a stimulus shelter, where available, as discussed earlier. For the most part, one suspects that the young child is reduced to the more passive mode of adapting to its environmental circumstances. While there is abundant evidence that such adaptation can and does indeed occur over prolonged periods of time (cf. Wohlwill, 1974, for relevant evidence), again there is no specific evidence on adaptation to crowding. Furthermore, the possibility must be considered that such adaptation, even where it may occur, results in untoward side effects—e.g., a heightened tendency to disregard social stimuli; a lowered threshold of irritability or frustration-tolerance—at least in the light of laboratory evidence of such effects (Glass & Singer, 1972). On the other hand, reliance on such passive adaptation might be reduced by providing temporary respite from

---

[4]Lee (1951) has reported data on the intelligence of black children who had moved from the (predominantly rural) South to the Philadelphia area, while a similar study of rural-urban migration in Italy, employing Piagetian measures of cognitive development, has been contributed by Peluffo (1962). Rather more limited evidence comes from a study by Watson (1973) on changes in IQ of children who emigrated from the West Indies to England.

conditions of stress such as crowding may entail, either by taking the young child out of the home, on walks, car rides, short trips of various kinds, or, where feasible, encouraging the child to create desirable changes in the level of incoming stimulation on its own — a recommendation obviously more applicable to older children.

Aiello, Thompson, and Baum (chapter 5) argue convincingly — backed up by some relevant evidence — for just this type of change in children's mode of coping with conditions of crowding, with older children resorting increasingly to avoidance and temporary escape. In fact, this strategy results in problems of its own, in leading to an increasing sense of lack of control by parents over their children under high-density conditions (see also Mitchell, 1971). At the same time it is apparent that to the extent that high-density conditions in the home and associated factors (e.g., noisiness) serve to encourage children to seek out alternative settings for their play, interaction with peers, etc., they act in a centripetal direction, weakening the child's sense of satisfaction in and identification with its home. The other side of the coin is that such escape and avoidance strategies presumably lead to the development of a sense of control over their environment on the part of children, and thus serve to mitigate whatever sources of stress that environment contains. This, rather than adaptation per se, may well be the explanation for the much weakened role played by density in the behavioral functioning and experienced well-being of adults.

## Question 5

How is resource availability related to density, with particular regard to the needs of children?

A likely mediator of density impacts of a very different kind from that considered under the previous question is that of resource availability. It appears reasonable to assume that, as density increases — particularly within the home — material resources become relatively less available to its residents, and to children in particular. This is true by definition as regards the amount of space available to the child for play and other activities — certainly a resource itself of considerable importance for the child's development. But it undoubtedly extends to material resources, in the form of facilities and environmental supports (basic furniture, bathrooms), and above all in the form of resources that may be shared by all children of a household, or all of its members altogether — such as toys, games, television sets.

The assumption that these resources are inversely related to density might be questioned: numbers of TV sets in a household, and possibly even sheer numbers of bathrooms, do reflect to some extent the number of persons in the household. But economic factors necessarily operate to keep both amount of space and amount of material resources from increasing linearly with the number of persons occupying a household, considering the population at large — especially given the fact that there is an inverse relationship between number of children in a family and family income. The net result is that one may confidently expect a negative relationship between density and resource availability.

Given this ecological correlation, the question arises to what extent density effects may be mediated by resource availability. Common sense suggests that competition for material resources can breed frustration and goal-blocking, and thus lead to aggression and other modes of response to frustration, e.g., withdrawal. Some evidence in support of this notion is provided by studies of children in nursery-school settings in which density and resource availability have been independently varied, which have shown that the latter variable is indeed correlated with aggressiveness. But more revealing is the suggestion that these two variables *interact*. That is, rather than resource availability accounting for effects of density, or the two variables operating additively, it is the combination of high density with low resource availability that tends to produce most consistent negative effects on child behavior, and on aggressiveness in particular. The significance of this finding is apparent, considering the prevalence of precisely this combination in inner-city and other economically disadvantaged areas.

It should be noted that the resource-availability factor, thus far considered only in regard to material resources, can profitably be extended to the social environment. Thus the question arises whether children in high-density homes or crowded playgrounds are the beneficiaries of equivalent amounts and — more important — kinds of stimulation and response from their elders and peers as children in less crowded areas. We don't have good evidence on this question as yet, but for diverse reasons it seems reasonable to assume that high levels of density impair the more intense, interactive kinds of social relationships that children enjoy with both their parents and teachers and their siblings and peers. Such an impairment may be deduced from the infringement on privacy—i.e., opportunity for interaction in dyads or small groups—that is a presumed consequence of high density levels, as well as from the fractionation of the individual's resources of time, energy, etc., in the service of interpersonal interaction, that results from the need to interact with a considerable number of others at close quarters. Number, rather than density, might seem to be the controlling variable here, and in the case of parent-child relations that may in fact be the case, though ecologically, as already noted, family size is apt to be correlated with density. On the other hand, density per se probably enters as a prime factor for children interacting with their peers, e.g., on the playground, since it is likely to affect children's ability to interact effectively in small groups. Increase in group size as such, on the other hand, need not create such problems, as long as sufficient space for the children to spread themselves out properly is available—as many playgrounds attest. Note, finally, that we are undoubtedly dealing with a U-shaped relationship here. That is, groups that are too small, or too low in density may likewise inhibit the formation of optimal social-interaction patterns. This effect would be expected due to the lower opportunity for a child to select individual children as playmates, and the concomitant increase in competition for such playmates, which is apt to lead to an enhancement of isolate patterns of behavior. Although systematic data on this issue remain to be obtained, available research on children's friendships (Rubin, 1980; van Vliet--, 1981; see also chapter 2) and on children's outdoor play does bear out the potential disadvantage of residing in low-density suburban developments. (Admittedly, one would not generally consider these as representing conditions of isolation, but in an ecological sense they may, in fact, approximate some of the aspects of even more dispersed life in certain low-density rural areas, for instance.)

## Question 6

How adequate and appropriate to the special needs of children are standards for housing density and land use that have been specified for residential buildings and developments, and for public and institutional facilities? What evidence is available bearing on the effects of violation of those standards?

The United Nations periodically collects information on the housing situation of people in a great number of countries. Their most recent housing survey shows that people in different countries live under widely different density conditions (U.N. Department of International Economic and Social Affairs, 1976). In part, these differences are accounted for by differences in economic and industrial development which have an impact on the housing construction process. However, even in comparisons within Europe, between countries of approximately equal prosperity, appreciable differences in density conditions are found. For example, in 1979, floor space in dwellings varied from a high of 101 m² (square meters) in Belgium to a low of 81.8 m² in Ireland (in Eastern Europe, much lower levels are common, e.g., Hungary: 46.3 m², and Poland: 41.8 m²) (Economic Commission for Europe, 1980). Likewise, the number of rooms per dwellings ranged from 5.7 in Ireland to 4.2 in Austria (ibid.) and the number of dwellings per 1000 of the population was 420 in Switzerland and only 337 in The Netherlands (ibid.). In spite of common national legislation, considerable differences in density conditions may also prevail between communities in the same country, and such differences even occur between subareas of communities governed by the same local building codes and zoning ordinances. For example, in 1980, the average occupancy rate of dwellings in Amsterdam ranged from a low of 1.77 in one neighborhood to a high of 6.05 in another (Bestuursinformatie, 1981, pp. 236–237).

In addition to the variability in density conditions across space, density conditions also vary over time. Changes over time result from a number of factors, including demographic ones (e.g., growth and redistribution of population, declining household size), economic and technological ones (e.g., scale and means of housing construction), and normative ones (e.g., rising expectations). The point is obvious, and there is no need to belabor it — density conditions are not the same everywhere, and they change over time.

The question which now arises is: to what extent are variations across space in actual density conditions accompanied by corresponding variations in density standards, and to what extent are changes over time in actual density conditions preceded by corresponding changes in density standards? There has been very little research on this question. However, it is clear that different countries apply quite different criteria to define density conditions. Some illustration of this point may be enlightening. Consider the following different definitions of what constitutes a room. In West Germany and Norway, rooms with a floor space of less than 6 m² are not counted as rooms; in Ireland kitchens with a floor space of less than 10 m² do not qualify as rooms, whereas in Canada only bedrooms are counted, and kitchen and living rooms are excluded; in the Netherlands, kitchens are not included, regardless of size; and the Swedes disregard all rooms with a floor space of less than 7 m² and not receiving daylight (U.N. Department of International Economic and Social Affairs, 1980). Similarly, outdoor play space requirements are determined by the number of square meters per bedroom (Brazil), the number of square meters per bedroom excluding the master bedroom (Canada), and the number of square meters per dwelling unit (Denmark), and the number of square meters per child (Yugoslavia). Obviously, discrepant definitions and criteria such as these hinder accurate interpretation of comparative data. In an international inventory and comparative study of legislation and guidelines for children's play spaces in the residential environment, Esbensen (1979) circumvented these definitional problems by developing a conversion model in order to create a common unit of measurement so as to permit comparisons of standards for different countries. National and municipal standards and guidelines in 25 different countries were found to range from 35 m² per dwelling unit in Denmark (for projects consisting of 40 more units) to 18 m² per dwelling in Spain to 9 m² per dwelling in England to 4 m² per dwelling in the U.S.S.R. (Esbensen, 1979, pp. 14–15).

Although the conversion model employed by Esbensen clearly improves the possibilities for international comparisons, the difficulties go beyond differences in standards. For example, in Canada local play space requirements may be traded for cash which is applied toward large recreational facilities serving a regional area (located beyond distances recommended for children). Also, standards do not necessarily apply to all housing developments; low-density environments are generally excluded. And there are further differences. For example, Sweden supplements the purely quantitative standards with guidelines concerning the preservation of the national environment in residential areas; The Netherlands and Sweden are increasingly concerned with "infill" play spaces in older quarters; Hong Kong and Finland provide financial aid, and in Israel the government itself often takes full responsibility, whereas in many other countries the cost is shifted to the residents; standards in countries like West Germany and Yugoslavia designate play spaces for different age groups (Esbensen, 1979). Unfortunately, Esbensen's report remains very descriptive, offering very little insight into the processes and conditions which may be responsible for differences in play space requirements. However, the list of countries suggests that those with the more generous standards are characterized by a well-developed economy and a pro-child ideology as well as public acceptance of government interference in planning.

Equally sparse is research on changes in actual conditions as they relate to changes in standards. In Israel, the average square floor area per dwelling has increased from 44.6 m² in 1955 to 66 m² in 1968 to 80.7 m² in 1980 (Israel Ministry of Housing, 1982). During the same period, the average number of rooms per dwelling increased from 2 to 3.25. Rising standards for floor space in public housing paralleled those increases. However, it is unclear to what extent the former mirror the latter, and to what extent the standards were really instrumental in bringing about changes in actual conditions.

One rather comprehensive investigation reviewed research conducted over the past 20 years in the Netherlands in order to compare standards for play spaces, recreational facilities, shopping, and transportation with the actual usage of these environments by residents (Van Eijkeren, 1979). One of the report's findings with respect to play space was that the numerous studies had rarely concerned themselves with the appropriateness of standards and had rarely adopted a combination of environmental, behavioral, and personal variables of sufficient specificity to permit the testing of standards through secondary analysis. An examination of the evolution of standards showed the emphasis on functional segregation and large scale open spaces in low-density environments, typical of the 1960s, changing to a more holistic approach in the 1970s, stressing enclosure of multifunctional spaces and preservation of natural elements, integrated in more compact "total" residential environments.

Summing up the scant literature, the plain truth is that we know very little about the antecedents and implications of differences in child-related planning standards and how they are related to actual living conditions, or about the consequences of living in "substandard" conditions. Some studies have shown that improvement in rather extreme housing conditions may have favorable effects on children's school performance and health (Wilner et al., 1962; Wegelin, 1978). Additional data come from the British National Child Development Study, a unique longitudinal investigation monitoring the development of 16,000 children at age 7 (1965), 11 (1969) and 16 (1974). Results from this research show that 7% of all 16-year olds lived in households which exceeded the crowding criterion of 1.5 persons per room and, further, that one in five of all children at school-leaving age had experienced an overcrowded home, these figures being considerably higher in the private rental sector, in lower social classes, and in some geographical regions (Essen & Parrinder, 1975; National Children's Bureau, 1977). At the age of seven, children in overcrowded homes were, on the average, three months behind in reading, and at age 16 the truancy rate was higher among them. Also other studies have sometimes found adverse affects of high residential densities on children (e.g., Schmitt, 1966; Galle et al., 1972; see chapters 5 and 8 for reviews), but have failed to specify the exact threshold(s) involved. In this regard, it is somewhat disconcerting to note that little advance has been made beyond painstaking research conducted some 25 years ago in France in which minimum (and maximum!) space requirements for family living were empirically established (Chombart de Lauwe et al., 1959). Since such critical ranges are space- and time-bound, replication of this research would certainly be in order.

At a more general level, the question of the appropriateness of standards for housing density and land use raises both normative and practical issues. First, the question has to be resolved whether the benefits of inserting minimum environmental requirements into residential planning outweigh the externalities associated with such interference. This is essentially a political decision based on the perceived need to structure a planning process which would otherwise be propelled by a free market mechanism. Once standards have been accepted as an integral component of the planning process, the normative issues narrow down to the specific nature and implications of given standards. These issues were discussed earlier. Next to the normative issues, there are practical ones concerning the implementation of standards, often constrained by economic factors. In this connection, developing countries with relatively few resources allocated to residential planning have frequently developed criteria which are used as guidelines, rather more than enforceable standards.

Objections to the use of standards need not exclusively stem from an ideology of permissive planning.[5] It may be argued that standards of physical

---

[5]Webber (1969) and Heywood (1969) provide a polemical discussion of permissive planning, explicating the pros and cons of planning with minimum standards versus non-interference in the free market mechanism.

space are meaningless because children's use and experience of *physical* space are modulated by their positions in *social* space. Thus Ashcraft and Scheflen (1976: 171-5) excoriate building codes in New York City which prescribe that each child in a household shall have 60 square feet of living space, arguing that the amount of space needed by children depends on the activities they engage in, the times of day, the layout of the dwelling, and provisions in the neighborhood supporting the interior living space. In much the same way, it has been suggested that a factor shown to carry developmental significance, at least among Western children, namely privacy (Wolfe, 1978), is related rather less to the amount of available space than to the functionality of that space, that is, the range of activities which it can accommodate, either successively or concurrently (Priemus, 1969). And there are further studies providing ample evidence of how environmental experiences in general, and those of density conditions in particular, are modified by features of social space such as family structure, ethnic background, social class, and so forth.

However, few people will doubt the intervening and interacting effects of social factors; the question of the appropriateness of standards really goes beyond this obvious fact to another obvious fact: children do not exist in a vacuum but need, *mirabile dictu,* a space to live. In other words, there *are* minima; and this returns us full cycle to the original question — what are these minimal requirements? The answer is that we simply do not know much beyond the distances which children will walk to schools and playgrounds (Levin & Bruce, 1968; Dee & Liebman, 1970). It is quite obvious, however, that the functional value of a patch of space reserved for children very much depends on qualities other than its quantitative dimensions; the objects in that space, the use of it made by other persons with whom it is shared, and its integration into the surrounding environment are just some of the variables having an influence in this regard. Cognizant of factors such as these, Hill and Alterman (1979) examined the implementation of public land use norms in 36 Israeli development towns. The extent to which space was over- or underallocated according to those norms was found to be dependent on the particular type of land use and on socioeconomic, demographic, institutional, and environmental properties of the communities involved. Hill and Alterman propose to use information of this kind as a basis for establishing norms which recognize the behavioral needs of specific user groups. In view of the pervasive variability of standards and actual conditions observed in the previous pages, further development of such flexible allocation schemes is warranted.

## Question 7

Which density-related characteristics of housing are either conducive or inimical to the optimal development of children? What processes mediate such effects, whether positive or negative? How may adverse effects be mitigated by social and environmental factors?

The implications of residential density for children are best understood not as a factor *sui generis,* but rather as variables intervening in and interacting with other environmental conditions and social processes to produce positive as well as negative effects on children. Foremost among the relevant residential conditions are housing interior and type and location of residence. Regarding the first, the number of rooms is of obvious significance in light of the needs for privacy and a stimulus shelter, discussed elsewhere in this volume. Thus, for a family of four, a dwelling of 120 m² with three rooms will be less suitable than a same sized dwelling having four rooms. Beyond the number of rooms the type of room is important, as is relative size. It is desirable, for example, that a four bedroom house have a kitchen adequate in size and furnishings to the needs of the individuals occupying the four bedrooms. The layout of the house and other aspects of its design are similarly of importance. In this connection mention was made already of the multifunctionality of dwelling space, allowing it to be used for various different activities, if not simultaneously, at least successively. Also modular design may modulate density effects by enabling a family to adjust design features to its needs as these change over time, although there are indications that when this flexibility exists the design solutions chosen tend not to be innovative and restricted by experiences with conventional designs (Priemus, 1969). Furthermore, Heft's analysis of the incidence of sounds as a correlate of density conditions (chapter 3) implies that adequate soundproofing is a sine qua non in residential settings which bring people in close proximity to each other.

Chapter 8 has discussed in some detail the role of housing type as a special density-related variable potentially affecting children's peer interactions and social adjustment. There appears to be little evidence for consistent effects, either positive, or negative. However, one unanimous finding, reported by research conducted world-wide, is the importance of easy access to the immediate outdoor environment (van Vliet--, 1983a). Such easy access permits spontaneous play by children and supervision by their parents and other adults. More pertinent to a concern with density, easy access facilitates the staggering of the activity schedules of individual household members in such a manner that the number of people at home during given periods of the day may be regulated so as to have the least disruptive effects.

The staggering of activity schedule points to two further factors of importance. First is the local environment. Easy access to what? To a busy traffic artery, a playground, or a wooded field? To a strictly residential area or to one where there are shops, a community center, a library, and public transportation stops within walking distance? Clearly, the amount and type of resources available in the local environment *and* accessible to families play an important role in alleviating possible adverse effects of household density. Therefore, in addition to aspects of housing interior and housing type, location of housing relative to community facilities is a third major environmental condition that needs to be taken into account when considering effects of residential density.

The staggering of activity schedules also calls attention to more generic processes whereby the behaviors of family members become or do not become synchronized in time and synchronized in space with respect to each other as well as to institutional structures supporting the family's functioning (e.g., schools, daycare centers, places of employment, stores). These processes have been extensively studied, most notably by time-geographers,[6] and represent an as yet little exploited focus for interventions directed at alleviating congestion levels and orchestrating optimal participation patterns in public and private activity junctions in space and time.

Further factors interacting with density are household structure and culture. The ages of the children, their gender, and the presence of a grandparent or boarder are all factors which have an impact not captured by household size. Also, the parents' child-rearing values and their preferred lifestyles may aggravate or alleviate density effects.

Finally, an important factor that directly affects density conditions of families with children is the functioning of the household market. The availability of appropriate dwellings not only depends on the responsiveness of private and public housing policies to demographic trends and changing family lifestyles and needs, but also on the openness of the market. A study, conducted recently in the U.S. (Marans & Colten, 1985), surveyed a national sample of renters and the owners of their units. The aims of the study were to assess the attitudes of the owners or managers renting to families with children, as well as the attitudes of renters toward living near children and, further, to document the effects which exclusionary policies have had on families with children. The results show that restrictive practices have increased (in 1975, one in six units was not available to families with children; in 1980, it was one in four) and place a real burden on families with children by reducing the available options, resulting, among other things, in a greater incidence of crowding and substandard housing conditions (Greene & Blake, 1980, pp. 15–19, 20–21). A data base compiled by the Children's Environment Advisory Service (1979) on the housing situation of Canadian children also indicates problems experienced by households with children living in rental housing, and for the U.S. it has been established that such problems are much worse still among female headed households (Yezer, 1978).

---

[6]See e.g., Carlstein et al. (1978); Parkes and Thrift (1980); and Mårtensen (1977) for an application to children specifically.

Question 8

What is known concerning the effects of institutional and community size on children? To what extent do these effects occur independently of density?

There exists a very extensive and diverse literature on the implications of group size. One of the first theoretical discussions was Simmel's treatment of dyadic and triadic relationships. His analysis preceded numerous psychological and sociological studies which have empirically examined the significance of size in institutional settings such as factories, hospitals, churches, correctional centers, schools, political organizations, and housing developments. Another strand of psychologically oriented research has concerned itself with the variation in individual behaviors and attitudes as a function of community size or its correlates; research along this line is paralleled by anthropological work which has explored differential patterns of cultural organization along a folk/rural-urban continuum and by studies in political science regarding effects of community size on participation and voting behavior. Economists have been interested in the relationship between income, cost of living and urban size, and geographers have examined the market functions of communities of different size and patterns of diffusion along settlement hierarchies. Still others have studied how community size may be linked to structural differentiation, status attainment, residential satisfaction, and housing preferences.

Thus, size has implications along a number of dimensions and on multiple levels. It is beyond the scope of this discussion to review what the specific implications are for the development of children. However, using some selected findings, it is possible to make some general observations concerning the mechanisms which transmit effects of size as they manifest themselves in two contexts of children's daily experiences: the school and the community.

Ecological psychologists have conducted various studies bearing on the effects of school and community size (see chapter 4). With respect to schools, it has been found that, compared to students in large schools, those in small schools reported more satisfactions related, among others, to the development of competence, to being challenged, to engaging in important actions, and to being valued. Furthermore, in small schools the participation of academically marginal students in voluntary behavior settings was more strongly encouraged than in a large school where only the involvement of more qualified students was sought and accepted. These findings, suggesting that smaller schools are more supportive of enhanced development, seem to be corroborated by the results of a secondary analysis, based on a nationally representative sample of 21,371 U.S. college applicants, which indicated higher accomplishment in several activity spheres (e.g., writing, leadership, dramatic art) by students from smaller schools (Baird, 1969). Several other studies have obtained results in regard to the role of community size similar to those just cited. It thus appears that small-scale communities may represent more protective and nurturing developmental environments, providing more challenging opportunities for close involvement.

The neighborhood unit formula, advanced by Perry (1939), has been an attempt to specify guidelines that would create small-scale communities in large cities by applying principles of physical planning. Before long the neighborhood unit idea became closely intertwined with the notion of a socially balanced neighborhood population, displaying all the virtues of (romanticized) small-town life. Sociologists have not been remiss in criticizing proponents of this strand of planning, accusing them of nostalgia, a-historicism, faith in physical determinism, and a wish to foster inward-looking communities, focused on local issues, in order to prevent conflict over societal inequalities (e.g., Mann, 1958; Dennis, 1958).

Returning to the effects of larger size, at least in regard to communities, an argument could also be made for a beneficial role, counteracting the kinds of negative effects just cited and emphasized by the ecological psychologists on the basis of behavior-setting considerations, as detailed by Schoggen and Schoggen in chapter 4. Increases in size generally go hand in hand with a greater differentiation of the community's structure, thus offering a greater diversity of resources and opportunities for the development of specific competencies. For example, in a small town it will be harder to become an apprentice in a symphony orchestra or to learn Finnish wood carving.[7] Of course, the greater opportunities for the acquisition of specialized skills found in large cities may also act in a less benign direction, i.e., in diverting youth into forms of delinquent or otherwise socially disapproved behavior (e.g., vandalism, theft, gambling).

The issue of the effects of community size on the individual, and on behavioral development, is thus far from simple. The problem is further complicated by the generally imprecise nature of standard measures of size based on population (in the case of cities or towns), or on membership (in the case of institutions such as a school); such measures may be more meaningful when applied to homogeneous subsystems (e.g., a neighborhood, or a class) than to the heterogeneous system of a large institution or a major city.[8]

Effects of size, moreover, do not operate in isolation but in conjunction with influences from other contextual variables. In this regard, there is a

---

[7]Also relevant to this point are data indicating that Nobel Prize winners originate in disproportionate numbers in metropolitan centers (Berry, 1981, p. 384); the same is true of patents on inventions (Ogburn and Duncan, 1964, p. 143).

[8]This is not to say that environmental dimensions are irrelevant with respect to institutional size. A case in point would be the positive relationship found between size of student dormitories and occupancy density (e.g., number of students per room) (see chapter 5). Here environmental adjustment is as pertinent as socio-behavioral adaptation.

noteworthy difference between schools and communities. Negative effects of large school size may be mitigated by the *social* organization of activities, for example, the introduction of another schedule or the development of a greater number or diversity of behavior settings and roles commensurate with developmental needs. In comparison, on a community scale the *spatial* organization of activities is more important with respect to overcoming negative effects of size. One crucial factor in this regard is density, to the extent and in the ways that land uses generally require a certain minimum level of population density. In practice, size tends to be positively correlated with density (see chapter 1), at least in modern western cities. Nevertheless, there are cities of similar size with widely different population densities. In this connection, density is relevant in providing the critical mass of people needed to support particular land uses and, thus, in influencing the accessibility of opportunities in the environment. The response to the next question more fully addresses the issue of population distribution.

## Question 9

What are the implications and consequences for children of the current patterns of movement of the population (a) from the center of metropolitan areas to the periphery, and (b) from metropolitan to non-metropolitan areas? What directions for a national population-distribution policy are suggested by these considerations? How congruent are these with actual population policies presently under discussion?

Chapter 1 identified the movement of population away from metropolitan cities to fringe areas, and away from metropolitan areas to small towns and rural areas as two major trends in the redistribution of the U.S. population. During the 1970s, the population growth in rural areas and small towns for the first time surpassed that of metropolitan areas (Herbers, 1981). This reversal of the historically contrary pattern has been well documented for the U.S.A., for Canada, and for a number of West European countries.[9]

In an economic view, these population shifts might be explained as a function of the relocation of jobs due to employers' cost-benefit considerations (e.g., the price of land, wages, taxes) and changes in the structure of productive activity (e.g., the growth of the electronics industry which is less dependent on historically developed transportation nodes). Critics of this traditional view might attribute the population deconcentration to corporate expansion

---

[9]Data for the USA are reported by Beale (1977); Berry and Silverman, (1980); Brown and Wardwell (1980); Heaton and Fuguitt (1980) and Long and DeAre (1982); while a similar trend in Canada has been shown by Bourne and Simons (1979). European evidence comes from research reported by Klaassen (1978); see also Hall and Metcalf (1978).

(Sewell, 1977) or to spatial expressions of the functional requirements of the capitalist mode of production (Gordon, 1978). In both the traditional and radical view, residential location of families is very much seen as a function of economic factors; volition and choice are highly subordinate factors.

An opposite view acknowledges preferences on the part of the population for a bucolic lifestyle and processes of self-selection (Bell, 1958) as important instigating forces behind patterns of population redistribution. The American aspiration for detached houses in low-density environments has been well established in the literature (Fischer, 1976; Michelson, 1967, 1977). According to a public opinion poll conducted in the fall of 1973, about 75% of all Americans — regardless of race, community size, or region — preferred single-family dwellings spread more or less evenly across the whole region over clustered multifamily housing with open spaces in between (Gallup, 1978, pp. 300–301). This preference has two components: deconcentration and low density. It is likewise manifested in a marked preference for living in exurban and even rural areas (DeJong, 1977; Fuguitt & Zuiches, 1975), a preference which seems to have been increasing in recent years (Zuiches & Rieger, 1978). These preferences are, of course, reflected in the movement of people from metropolitan to rural areas and also accord with the space usage by Americans, which has increased from .2 acres of urban land per average resident in 1950, to .35 acres in 1960, to .4 acres in 1970 (Regional Plan Association, 1975, pp. 32–3).

However, low densities are not necessarily concomitant with deconcentration. Possible future energy shortfalls have generated a polemical discussion regarding the savings purportedly associated with different settlement patterns. In 1974, the Real Estate Research Corporation published "The Costs of Sprawl," a three-volume report on a study commissioned by the Department of Housing and Urban Development, the Environmental Protection Agency, and the Council on Environmental Quality. In a comparison of different settlement patterns it concluded that high-density developments would cost about 40% less than low-density developments (RERC, 1974). The study has been severely criticized on methodological grounds (Windsor, 1979), but there are others who have maintained that more compact and integrated urban forms will result in energy savings, however modest relative to other conservative strategies (Van Til, 1979; Keyes, 1982). In a thoughtful analysis, Rickaby (1981) has identified six alternative configurations of energy-efficient settlement, indicating that low-density patterns may be an acceptable option when they provide for small-scale integration of land uses in an array of quasi-self-sufficient settlements. In other words, concentration and density are not necessarily interdependent (cf. Figure 8.1, in chapter 8). For example, in The Netherlands planning policy has promoted "bundled deconcentration," the development of well-defined settlements outside urban areas.

The preceding discussion leads to several questions bearing more directly on children: to what extent can we devise settlement patterns which are most congruent with children's needs? In which ways do these settlement patterns diverge from the deconcentration trend which, as the 1980 census figures indicate, shows no signs of abating (Long & DeAre, 1982)? The response has to be informed by some sobering realities. To begin with, to put it mildly, children's developmental needs have never formed a high priority in the formulation of policies of population redistribution, and the previous pages suggest that more structural factors will continue to be the major determinants. The improbability of effective policy recommendations is increased by the lack of clearcut conclusions as to what the implications of different settlement patterns are for children. Weisner (1981) recently reviewed the literature to determine whether a relation existed between type of habitat and the incidence of stress in children. His intra- and intercultural assessment offered no support for the existence of systematic differences. Of course, this finding may be explained either by the actual absence of such differences or by deficiencies of the research on this topic. In the latter case, advice concerning desired population patterns based on children's needs suffers in credibility, while in the former there is little point in formulating such advice.

The above observations should be seen in the context of the overall practicability of influencing population patterns by public policy. Attempts in this direction have been only moderately successful, even in countries such as Great Britain and The Netherlands where the central government has traditionally played an important role in spatial planning (DeJong, 1981). Some have even suggested that patterns of population growth follow a dynamics of their own, and that the best policy would be one of "benign neglect" (Banfield, 1974) or one which fosters the effective performance of the economic processes underlying spontaneous developments as they historically evolve (Oosterbaan, 1980; cf. Kasarda, 1980).

Elsewhere in this volume the concept of spatial separation was chosen as a tool to analyze the relation between children and their environment (chapter 8). Adopting this notion, it becomes possible to rephrase the questions stated earlier to inquire about ways which maximize children's access to and involvement with people and settings needed for their optimal development. This new approach would appear to be a more fruitful one, since it goes beyond broad variables such as size and density. These, to be sure, delineate population distributions in the aggregate, but also leave room for widely different habitats for children; both small towns *and* large cities have in principle the potential of supplying children with enriching as well as impoverishing developmental experiences, the particular outcome being dependent on the configuration of specific features making up the child's environment. At this level of analysis, there are empirical findings indicating that, for example, city and suburban types of habitats may be distinctly different contexts for growing up (van Vliet--, 1981, 1983b; Medrich et al., 1982). At a conceptual level, attempts to derive guidelines for environmental design from children's developmental needs hold promise (e.g., Pollowy, 1977; Alexander, 1977). Inductive and deductive work along these lines may converge to identify environmental types possessing manipulable characteristics and differing in developmental implications. Such a habitat typology might then become an integral component in policy making regarding human settlement patterns.

## CONCLUDING COMMENTS[10]

The material reviewed under the foregoing nine questions has distilled some of the major findings presented in the main part of this volume, while pointing to significant gaps in our knowledge. We believe that it provides the outlines for a comprehensive picture of the role of the residential environment in the development of children, and of the diverse ways in which given conditions of density may affect development. In a broader vein we see this material as a contribution to the emergence of a true ecology of child development, in a sense similar to that intended by Bronfenbrenner (1979), but transcending it in terms of a view of the environment which encompasses both the social and the physical realms.

But the Study Group's objective was not defined exclusively in terms of theoretical concerns. An implicit assumption underlying its formation was that, both directly and indirectly, particular conditions of density do make a difference in interfering with or enhancing the optimal development of children's potential. The Group was clearly concerned with possible adverse effects of high- and low-density situations on the child and with ways of alleviating such adverse effects. Thus its work should be seen as having relevance for child-oriented public policies. Indeed, we would have liked to include a separate section in this final chapter which would have drawn together the various domains studied by our group in a coherent set of statements, outlining implications for the formulation of public policy, comparable to those that sociologists and planners (e.g., Doxiades et al., 1979; Michelson et al., 1979; Jordan, 1982) have recently enunciated. We decided, however, that such a section was not warranted, for three reasons. First, research to date has simply not demonstrated unequivocally any direct, adverse effects of density on children, except under atypical and extreme conditions. Thus, generally, there is no firm basis for enjoining particular courses of action. Secondly, some manifestations of residential density (e.g., national

---

[10]The editors are pleased to acknowledge James Garbarino's contribution to this final section of the chapter.

population redistribution) refer to a high level of aggregation (e.g., that of an urban area, or of a region). Policies in this realm tend to lose their significance for the real-life world of children, which is primarily defined by home and community contexts. Thirdly, at the other end of the spectrum, there are applications of knowledge gathered in this volume that are of greater specificity, concerning aspects of children's environments such as the need for adequate sound-proofing of dwellings and the provision of suitable opportunities for interactions with adults and peers. These points are not enumerated here, since they are already discussed in the constituent chapters and reviewed in this chapter.

A broader question confronting the work of the Study Group concerned the appropriate role of researchers in the formulation of public policy. Just what is this role? We believe that the primary responsibility in this regard is one of raising the quality of public debate. Rather than presenting answers, the researchers' task is to help formulate and articulate the questions, to comment on the logical and empirical character of those questions, and to help evaluate existing answers (cf. Habermas, 1968). Accordingly, this volume has attempted to explicate alternative and conflicting assumptions about the role of residential density in the development of children, and, more generally, to promote rational argumentation among and between the producers and consumers of relevant policies in the public arena. To the extent that this book succeeds in achieving that aim, the Study Group will have fulfilled its mission.

## REFERENCES

Alexander, C. et al. *A pattern language.* New York: Oxford University Press, 1977.

Anastasi, A. *Differential psychology.* (3d ed.). New York: Macmillan, 1958.

Ashcraft, N., & Scheflen, A. E. *People space: The making and breaking of human boundaries.* New York: Anchor Books, 1976.

Baird, L. L. Big school, small school: A critical examination of the hypothesis. *Journal of Educational Psychology,* 1969, *60,* 253–260.

Banfield, E. C. *The unheavenly city revisited.* Boston: Little, Brown, 1974.

Beale, C. L. The recent shift of United States population to nonmetropolitan areas, 1970–1975. *International Regional Science Review,* 1977, *2,* 113–122.

Bell, W. Social choice, life styles and suburban residence. In W. M. Dobriner (Ed.), *The suburban community.* New York: Putnam, 1958. Pp. 225–247.

Berry, C. The Nobel scientists and the origins of scientific achievement. *British Journal of Sociology,* 1981, *32,* 381–391.

Berry, B. J. L., & Silverman, L. P. (Eds.). *Population redistribution and public policy.* Washington, D.C.: National Academy of Sciences, 1980.

Bestuursinformatie. *Yearbook 1980.* Amsterdam: Gemeente Afdeling Statistiek, 1981.

Booth, A. *Urban crowding and its consequences.* New York: Holt, Rinehart & Winston, 1976.

Booth, A., & Johnson, A. D. The effect of crowding on child health and development. *American Behavioral Scientist,* 1975, *18,* 736–749.

Bourne, L. S., & Simmons, A. J. W. *Canadian settlement trends: An examination of the spatial pattern of growth, 1971-1976.* Report to the Ministry of State for Urban Affairs, Ottawa, 1979.

Bronfenbrenner, U. *The ecology of human development: Experiments by nature and design.* Cambridge: Harvard University Press, 1979.

Brown, D. L., & Wardwell, J. M. (Eds.). *New directions in urban-rural migration.* New York: Academic Press, 1980.

Carlstein, T., Thrift, N., & Parkes, D. (Eds.). *Timing space and spacing time.* 3 Volumes. London: Eden Arnold, 1978.

Children's Environments Advisory Service. *Housing Canada's children: A data base.* Ottawa: Canada Mortgage and Housing Corporation, 1979.

Chombart de Lauwe, P. H. et al. *Famille et habitation, Vol. 1.* Sciences humaines et conceptions de l'habitation. Paris: Centre National de la Recherche Scientifique, 1959.

Dee, N., & Liebman, J. C. A statistical study of attendance at urban playgrounds. *Journal of Leisure Research,* 1970, *2,* 145-160.

DeJong, G. Residential preferences and migration. *Demography,* 1977, *14,* 169-678.

DeJong, G. F. The impact of regional population redistribution policies on internal migration: What we can learn from The Netherlands and Great Britain. *Social Science Quarterly,* 1981, *62,* 313-323.

Dennis, N. The popularity of the neighborhood unit idea. *Sociological Review,* 1958, *6,* 191-206.

Doxiades, S. et al. *The child in the world of tomorrow.* New York: Pergamon Press, 1979.

Economic Commission for Europe. *Major trends in housing policy in ECE countries.* New York: United Nations, 1980.

Esbensen, S. B. *An international inventory and comparative study of legislation and guidelines for children's play spaces in the residential environment.* Research Project 1, Children's Environments Advisory Service. Ottawa: Canadian Mortgage and Housing Corporation, 1979.

Essen, J., Fogelman, K., & Head, J. Children's housing and their health and physical development. *Child: Care, health and development,* 1978, *4,* 357-369.

Essen, J., & Parrinder, D. Housing for children: Further findings from the National Child Development Study. *Housing Review,* 1975, (July/August) 112-114.

Fanning, D. M. Families in flats. *British Medical Journal,* 1967, *18,* 382-386.

Fischer, C. S. *The urban experience.* New York: Harcourt, Brace, Jovanovich, 1976.

Fuguitt, G. V., & Zuiches, J. J. Residential preferences and population distribution. *Demography,* 1975, *12,* 491-504.

Galle, O. R., Gove, W. R., & Miller McPherson, J. Population density and pathology: What are the conditions for man? *Science,* 1972, *176,* 23-30.

Gallup, G. H. *The Gallup poll, 1970-1975.* New York: Random House, 1978.

Glass, D. C., & Singer, J. E. *Urban stress: Experiments on noise and social stressors.* New York: Academic Press, 1972.

Gordon, D. M. Capitalist development and the history of American cities. In W. K. Tabb & L. Sawers (Eds.), *Marxism and the metropolis.* New York: Oxford University Press, 1978. Pp. 25-64.

Greene, J. G., & Blake, G. P. *How restrictive rental practices affect families with children.* Washington, D.C.: U.S. Department of Housing and Urban Development, Office of Policy Development and Research, 1980.

Habermas, J. Wissenschäftliche Politik and öffentliche Meinung. In J. Habermas (Ed.), *Technik and Wissenschaft als "Ideologie."* Frankfurt: Suhrkamp, 1968. Ppp. 120-146.

Haggard, E. A. Isolation and personality. In P. Worchel & D. Byrne (Eds.), *Personality change.* New York: Wiley, 1964. Pp. 433-469.

Haggard, E. A. Some effects of geographic and social isolation in natural settings. In J. E. Rasmussen (Ed.), *Man in isolation and confinement.* Chicago: Aldine, 1973. Pp. 99-144.

Hall, P., & Metcalf, D.  The declining metropolis: Patterns, problems, and policies in Britain and Mainland Europe. In C. L. Leven (Ed.), *The mature metropolis.* Lexington: D. C. Heath, 1978. Pp. 65–90.

Heaton, T. B., & Fuguitt, G. V.  Dimensions of population redistribution in the United States since 1950. *Social Science Quarterly,* 1980, *61,* 508–523.

Herbers, J.  Rural areas end trend, surpass cities in growth. *The New York Times,* March 3, 1981, 14.

Heywood, P. R.  Plangloss: A critique of permissive planning. *Town Planning Review,* 1969, 251–262.

Hill, M., & Alterman, R.  The problem of setting flexible norms for land allocation for public facilities. In D. Soen (Ed.), *New trends in urban planning: Studies in housing, urban design and planning.* New York: Pergamon, 1979. Pp. 94–103.

Hoehn, E.  Schifferkinder: Eingeschrenkte Umwelterfahrungen in früher Kindheit. *Psychologische Beiträge,* 1974, *16,* 254–276.

Hollos, M.  Logical operations and role-taking abilities in two cultures: Norway and Hungary. *Child Development,* 1975, *46,* 638–349.

Hollos, M., & Cowan, F. A.  Social isolation and cognitive development: Logical operations and role-taking abilities in three Norwegian social settings. *Child Development,* 1973, *44,* 630–641.

Israel Ministry of Housing. *Hatsa-at Taktsiv Le-Shanat Ha-Kaspim 1982.* (Budget for the fiscal year, 1982). Jerusalem: National Accounting Office, 1982.

Jordan, T. E. (Ed.).  *Child development, information, and the formulation of public policy.* Springfield, Ill.: C. C. Thomas, 1982.

Kasarda, J. D.  The implications of contemporary redistribution trends for national urban policy. *Social Science Quarterly,* 1980, *61,* 373–400.

Keyes, D. L.  Energy for travel: The influence of urban development patterns. *Transportation Research,* 1982, *16,* 65–71.

Klaassen, L. H.  Het desurbanisatie proces in de grote steden. *Economisch Statistische Berichten,* 1978, 4–1, 8–10.

Lee, E. S.  Negro intelligence and selective migration: A Philadelphia test of the Klineberg hypothesis. *American Sociological Review,* 1951, *16,* 227–233.

Levin, P. H., & Bruce, A. J.  Primary schools and where to site them. *Town & Country Planning,* 1968, *36,* 460–463.

Long, L., & DeAre, D.  Repopulating the countryside: A 1980 census trend. *Science,* 1982, *217,* 1111–1116.

Mann, P. H.  The socially balanced neighborhood unit. *Town Planning Review,* 1958, *29,* 91–97.

Marans, R. W., & Colten, M. E.  U.S. Rental housing policies affecting families with children: Hard times for youth. In W. van Vliet –, E. Huttman, and S. Faua (Eds.), *Housing needs and policy approaches: trends in 13 countries.* Durham, N.C.: Duke University Press, 1985.

Mårtensson, S.  Children interaction and temporal organization. *Economic Georgraphy,* 1977, *53,* 99–125.

Medrich, E. A., Roizen, J., Rubin, V., & Buckley, S.  *The serious business of growing up: A study of children's lives outside school.* Berkeley: University of California Press, 1982.

Michelson, W.  Potential candidates for the designers' paradise: A social analysis from a nationwide survey. *Social Forces,* 1967, *46,* 190–196.

Michelson, W.  *Environmental choice, human behavior and residential satisfaction.* New York: Oxford University Press, 1977.

Michelson, W., Levine, S. V., & Michelson, E. (Eds.).  *The child in the city: Today and tomorrow.* Toronto: University of Toronto Press, 1979.

Mitchell, R. E.  Some social implications of high density housing. *American Sociological Review,* 1971, *36,* 18–29.

National Children's Bureau. *Children's housing: A research review.* London: National Children's Bureau, 1977.

Ogburn, W. F., & Duncan O. D. City size as a sociological variable. In G. W. Burgess & D. J. Bogue (Eds.), *Urban sociology.* Chicago: University of Chicago Press, 1964. Pp. 58–76.

Oosterbaan, J. *Population dispersal.* Lexington, Mass.: Lexington Books, 1980.

Parkes, D. N., & Thrift, N. J. *Times, spaces and places: A chronogeographic perspective.* New York: Wiley, 1980.

Peluffo, N. Les notions de conservation et de causalité chez les enfants provenant de different milieux physiques et socio-culturels. *Archives de Psychologie, (Genève),* 1962, *38,* 275–291.

Perry, C. A. The neighborhood formula. In W. L. C. Wheaton et al. (Eds.), *Urban Housing.* New York: Free Press, 1939. Pp. 94–100.

Pollowy, A. M. *The urban nest.* Stroudsburg, Pa.: Dowden, Hutchinson & Ross, 1977.

Priemus, H. *Wonen: Aanpassing en kreativiteit.* The Hague: Mouton, 1969.

Rasmussen, J. E. (Ed.). *Man in isolation and confinement.* Chicago: Aldine, 1973.

Raven, J. Sociological evidence on housing. *The Architectural Review,* 1967, *142,* 236–240.

Real Estate Research Corporation. *The costs of sprawl.* Washington, D.C.: U.S. Government Printing Office, 1974.

Regional Plan Association, *Growth and settlement in the U.S.: Past trends and future issues.* RPA Bulletin #124. New York: RPA, 1975.

Rickaby, P. A. Six regional settlement patterns: Alternative configurations for energy-efficient settlement. *Environment and Planning B,* 1981, *8,* 191–212.

Rubin, Z. *Children's friendships.* Cambridge: Harvard University Press, 1980.

Schmitt, R. C. Density, health and social organizations. *Journal of American Institute of Planners,* 1966, *32,* 38–40.

Sewell, J. Where the suburbs came from. In J. Lorimer et al. (Eds.), *The second city book.* Toronto: James Lorimer, 1977. Pp. 10–17.

U.N. Department of International Economic and Social Affairs. *World Housing Survey 1974.* New York: United Nations, 1976.

U.N. Department of International Economic and Social Affairs. *Compendium of social statistics: 1977.* Statistical Papers, Series K No. 4. New York: United Nations, 1980.

Van Eijkeren, R. *Voorzieningen in de directe woonomgeving.* Tilburg (The Netherlands): IVA, Institute for Social Science Research, 1979.

Van Til, J. Spatial form and structure in a possible future: Some implications of energy shortfall for urban planning. *Journal of the American Planning Association,* 1979, *45,* 318–329.

van Vliet--, W. Neighborhood evaluations by city and suburban children. *Journal of the American Planning Association,* 1981, *47,* 458–467.

van Vliet--, W. Families in apartment building: Sad storeys for children? *Environment and Behavior,* 1983a, *15,* 567–588.

van Vliet--, W. Exploring the fourth environment: an examination of the home range of city and suburban teenagers. *Environment and Behavior,* 1983b, *15,* 567–588.

Watson, P. Stability of IQ of immigrant and non-immigrant slow-learning pupils. *British Journal of Educational Psychology,* 1973, *43,* 80–82.

Webber, M. M. Planning in an environment of change: II. *Town Planning Review,* 1969, *39,* 277–295.

Wegelin, E. A. *Urban low-income housing and development.* Leiden: Nijhoff, 1978.

Weisner, T. S. Cities, stress, and children: A review of some cross-cultural questions. In R. H. Munroe, R. L. Munroe, & B. B. Whiting (Eds.), *Handbook of cross-cultural human development.* New York: Gurland Press, 1981. Pp. 755–783.

Wilner, D. M., Wallaley, R. P., Pinkerton, T., & Tayback, M. *The housing environment and family life: A longitudinal study of the effects of housing on morbidity and mental health.* Baltimore: Johns Hopkins Press, 1962.

Windsor, D. A critique of the costs of sprawl. *Journal of the American Planning Association,* 1979, *45,* 279-292.

Wohlwill, J. F. Human adaptation to levels of environmental stimulation. *Human Ecology,* 1974, *2,* 127-147.

Wolfe, W. Childhood and privacy. In I. Altman & J. Wohlwill (Eds.), *Children and the environment. (Human behavior and the environment: Advances in theory and research, Vol. III.)* New York: Plenum Press, 1978. Pp. 175-222.

Worth, R. M. Urbanization and squatter resettlement as related to child health in Hong Kong. *American Journal of Hygiene,* 1963, *78,* 338-348.

Yezer, A. *How well are we housed?* Washington, D. C.: U.S. Department of Housing and Urban Development, Office of Policy Development and Research, 1978.

Zuiches, J. J., & Rieger, J. H. Size of place preferences and life cycle migration: A cohort comparison. *Rural Sociology,* 1978, *43,* 618-633.

# Author Index

# Subject Index